Penguin Handbooks

The Penguin Book of Basic Gardening

Alan Gemmell, the well-known broadcaster from the BBC
Radio programme, 'Gardeners' Question Time', was Professor
of Biology at the University of Keele until his retirement in
1977. He has been a lecturer at the Universities of Glasgow and
Manchester and Visiting Professor at the University of Shiraz,
Iran. He is a fellow of the Royal Society of Edinburgh and of
the Institute of Biology, is Biological Adviser to the Universities
of Malawi, Lesotho, Botswana, Sierra Leone and Swaziland,
and has been a scientific member of the BBC Gardening
Brains Trust since 1950. He is the author of *Science in the
Garden, Developmental Plant Anatomy* and *The Sunday Gardener,*
and has published a number of articles on plant pathology
and ecology in scientific and gardening journals. His latest
book is *The Practical Gardener's Encyclopaedia.*

by *Alan Gemmell*

The Penguin
Book of
Basic Gardening

Penguin Books

Penguin Books Ltd, Harmondsworth,
Middlesex, England
Penguin Books, 625 Madison Avenue,
New York, New York 10022, U.S.A.
Penguin Books Australia Ltd, Ringwood,
Victoria, Australia
Penguin Books Canada Ltd,
2801 John Street, Markham,
Ontario, Canada L3R 1B4
Penguin Books (N.Z.) Ltd,
182–190 Wairau Road, Auckland 10,
New Zealand

First published 1975
Reprinted 1976, 1977, 1979

Made and printed in Great Britain by
Richard Clay (The Chaucer Press) Ltd,
Bungay, Suffolk
Set in Monotype Plantin

Contents

1 Essential Preliminaries

To own a garden for the first time is an exciting experience. At last you can grow your own food, and have flowers to decorate the house and a place for children to play. You will have a hobby which is not only healthy and rewarding, but which opens a new world to you and may even provide arguments for the rest of your life.

A garden can be very demanding if you let it. It all depends on who is the master, you or it. If you are a perfectionist and want to grow everything in the most difficult way you can easily make a great deal of work for yourself (which you may enjoy). Most people, however, want a garden which looks all right and is interesting, where they will work regularly but which won't take a lot of their spare time and which can be left during holidays without irreparable damage. This book is for this kind of person. It starts at the beginning and describes, I hope clearly, simple things to do and simple ways of doing them: if there are a number of paths to a particular goal I have tried to give the easiest; the lists of plants are not meant to be exhaustive but simply to indicate those which are easy to grow in most circumstances. I have also assumed that the reader knows little or nothing about gardening and wants to be informed about it in simple language.

Gardening does involve technical terms which cannot be avoided but they are all fully explained at least once; if you come across a word such as 'humus' or 'crown bud' which you don't understand, look it up in the index at the back of the book which marks in bold the page number on which that particular term is defined.

You should treat this book as an introduction and then, as your interest grows, go to your local library and get more specialized books on the technicalities of specific subjects. For example . there are many ways of pruning apple trees and all have their virtues, but for the sake of simplicity and clarity I have given only the one which I consider to be the most straightforward and the most foolproof.

So, to start at the beginning, here are the tools you need in order to do any sort of job at all (Fig. 1); although good tools do not make a good gardener, bad tools certainly make gardening difficult. There is an enormous range of tools, gadgets and devices to help gardeners, but I have given only those which are necessary, drawing attention to the points you should look out for.

GARDEN TOOLS

Before deciding on any tool you should take a good look around and test the feel and balance, bearing in mind different factors such as weight, length of handle, size and cost, and always buying the best you can afford. Many tools are now made in stainless steel and although these are more expensive they are good to handle and will last for many years. They also make the job easier – the effort required to push a stainless steel spade into soil is much less than with the normal iron type.

There are a number of tools essential for gardening and I will deal with these first.

Spades (Fig. 1a)

A growing number of gardeners are beginning to doubt the wisdom of digging with a spade – some say it is unnecessary to disturb the soil surface and so digging should be abolished, while others say digging with a fork is much easier and the spade is an outmoded tool. However, if you are starting a garden from scratch a spade is essential for getting the surface cleared and in good order, for making drains where necessary, for planting trees etc., and so the first buy should be a good spade.

How do you recognize a good spade? Here you should go for stainless steel at all costs. It will lighten labour, be easy to clean and last for ever. Many beginners rush out and buy a big heavy spade which looks as if it will dig deeply and well. This is a mistake; you should buy a spade which is light to handle – in fact many of the best gardeners I know use a medium (or even a lady's) spade – and the maximum size of blade should be $11\frac{1}{2} \times 7\frac{1}{2}$ inches though $10 \times 6\frac{1}{2}$ inches is easier. When you rap the blade with your knuckle it should give the ringing sound of well-tempered steel which will not bend even under the greatest strain, and the handle should be straight-grained. Handles are of different shapes, usually in the form of a D or a T. I prefer the T shape, but that is a personal

1. *Essential gardening tools: (a) spade (b) rake (c) secateurs (d) trowel (e) fork (f) dutch hoe (g) wheelbarrow.*

preference. Before you buy your spade, take a good look at where the steel and the wood meet and at the handle in order to satisfy yourself that they are smooth and well finished. A good stainless steel spade should cost about £8 and an ordinary steel one about £3.50. It is a false economy to buy cheaper models.

Forks (Fig. 1e)

The simplest and most satisfactory fork has four flat prongs and can be used instead of a spade as it is very much lighter and easier to push into the ground when digging. A fork is also useful for weeding, spreading manure, lightly turning the surface and breaking up clods of earth. Again make sure it has a good smooth grip, preferably

9

strapped with iron as this will reduce the chance of the handle splitting if it is dropped on a hard surface. Forks do come in stainless steel, but this is not so important unless you are going to use your fork for digging. A stainless steel fork costs about £8 and an ordinary medium one about £3.50.

Hoe (Fig. 1f)

Hoes have been out of favour lately, largely because of the use of chemical weed-killers and the destruction of the myth that hoeing conserves moisture in the soil. Nevertheless, a good hoe is a joy to use and it is still the best weeding tool in areas where it would be dangerous to use chemicals. Hoes can be used for different purposes and have different names. The *Dutch Hoe* is probably the most useful as it is designed to slice weeds below soil level, is light and easy to use and is really efficient. The standard pattern is shown in the illustration (Fig. 1f) but there are many variants, each with their own advantages – I get great satisfaction and pleasant use from a stainless steel hoe made by Wilkinsons which is of the 'scuffle hoe' type. Then there is a 'draw hoe' which is very useful for making drills in a seed bed, but which is not essential and can be purchased in later years. An alternative is the triangular hoe, but again this is not a necessity. Hoes cost about £2 in ordinary steel and approximately £6 in stainless steel.

Rake (Fig. 1b)

A rake is probably an essential piece of equipment. It is certainly vital in a new garden where you have to prepare seed beds for a lawn or vegetables or to level a gravel path, although in a well-established garden it may be largely unnecessary and could be dispensed with (but it does give flower beds a neat, well-finished look). In most towns you can buy a second-hand rake for a few pence and this is perfectly adequate when one considers the small amount of use it gets.

Wheelbarrow (Fig. 1g)

Except in very small gardens a wheelbarrow is an absolute essential for moving all sorts of material around the garden. Wooden wheelbarrows were once the only type but nowadays the all-metal barrow has enormous advantages: it doesn't rot if left out in the rain, it is relatively light and is fitted with grips which are comfortable to hold. Wheelbarrows with hard, solid or pneumatic tyres should be avoided. The best type of tyre is the large balloon type filled with soft rubber which absorbs shocks, does not leave deep tracks on the lawn, and cannot deflate. There are also a number of two-wheeled cart-type barrows with detachable containers for easy emptying. They are easier to wheel and are usually rather more manoeuvrable than the standard model. Some, however, are difficult to empty with a shovel or spade; so before you finally decide on any particular wheelbarrow, consider size (not too big), weight, type of tyre and ease of filling and emptying. A good wheelbarrow is not very expensive – about £6.50 – and second-hand or old ones are usually available.

Small Hand-tools (Figs. 1c and 1d)

There is a very wide variety of these for many purposes, but only two are essential at the beginning. The first is a *hand trowel* (Fig. 1d). This is used for planting out small plants and for digging up troublesome and deep-rooted weeds, where it takes the place of a hand fork. Again, if you can afford it, buy stainless steel. The second essential is a good pair of *secateurs* (Fig. 1c). If you are going to grow any shrubs, fruit or trees a certain amount of pruning or cutting back will have to be done and a sharp pair of secateurs makes the job easy and safe. I say 'safe' advisedly, for bad secateurs which crush rather than cut and which split or tear the wood are responsible for the death of many newly planted trees and shrubs.

The only other two things which come to mind can easily be made. One, a *garden line*, consists simply of two small but strong stakes connected by a long piece of string, and is very useful for planting in straight lines – you just put one stake at the end of the drill and unreel the string, stretching it tight by putting the other stake at the other end of the drill. You then plant following the line closely. Two, a *dibber*, is simply a piece of wood with a handle and with one end brought to a rounded point; the handle of a broken spade or shovel will do very well after you have sharpened the broken end. This is used for making the holes in the soil into which you drop plants such as cabbage or brussels sprout. The hole is then closed by pushing the dibber in beside it, levering sideways and so closing the soil around the roots of the plant.

Other Equipment

A *mower* is of course an essential, and they are considered in Chapter 5, p. 90. A *sharp knife* can be very handy for taking cuttings, and a sieve is useful on occasions but can easily be dispensed with, as can edging shears, though the latter do help to keep the edge of lawns neat if it is impossible to cut right to the edge with the mower. A *watering can* is essential, both to use in the normal way to soak plants in dry periods, and to apply chemical weed-killers. Many gardeners have two watering cans and keep one exclusively for the weed-killer in order to make sure that no chemicals left in the can get on valuable shrubs or vegetables. If you cannot afford two, always be very careful to wash the can out very thoroughly after using weed-killer. A watering can may also be used to apply fungicides or insecticides to, say, rose bushes. This is not a very efficient way of doing the job as there is not enough pressure to drive the liquid into all the small crevices on the plant. It is far better to use a syringe or some form of sprayer. A suburban gardener with a small area will find a syringe perfectly adequate but, if you have a bigger area and tall trees or shrubs, then as prayer is preferable.

The above list is formidable and if you bought them all at once those tools would mean considerable capital outlay. Fortunately most beginners can borrow old tools from parents and friends and these do perfectly well while new and more efficient ones are slowly bought. If, however, I can make one plea, it is for a good spade or fork; this is so useful that the expense is well worth while, and will make the heaviest work easier when you are not used to it.

Gardening is a wide-spread and engrossing hobby and many old and partially disabled people derive a great deal of pleasure from 'pottering about' in the garden. Some find the standard tools difficult or even impossible to manage, say, with one hand or if crippled with arthritis, and there are now a number of firms who manufacture special tools for physically handicapped people. The firm producing probably the widest range of such tools is R.H. Garden Supply, Hannazone, Burnt Mills Road, Basildon, Essex. Write for their catalogue which contains many ingenious devices. The Disabled Living Foundation have also given much thought to techniques and suitable garden tools and can be contacted at 346 Kensington High Street, London, W.14.

CARE AND STORAGE OF EQUIPMENT AND CHEMICALS

If you clean your tools before putting them away they will not only last longer, but will be easier to handle and much more efficient at their job. Spades, trowels, etc., should be washed after using, and if you are too lazy to do it every time, be sure to do it before you put them away for any long period. If you are using stainless tools regular cleaning is not so important, but if you only have ordinary metal tools the blades should be rubbed with an oily rag to prevent rust. Tools put away for the winter (and the summer for that matter) benefit by having the wooden shaft lightly rubbed with linseed oil – this lengthens the life and improves the elasticity of the wood.

Cutting tools such as shears, secateurs and mowers are most vulnerable to rust so you should make a special point of wiping the cutting surfaces with an oiled cloth immediately after use; you should also get these cutting tools sharpened each winter, either by yourself with a steel file or even a small grindstone, or by any expert.

Storage conditions are important in keeping tools in good order – a dry cool shed is ideal. Not everyone has this but no matter what kind of storage accommodation you have there are a few points to watch out for. For example, try to hang as many tools as possible from cup-hooks or nails in the garage or tool shed; this reduces clutter on the floor, the tools are less likely to be damaged by chemicals and they are easily seen when you want them. Make a small wooden platform to raise bags of fertilizer or compost off the floor to reduce the amount of damp seeping in from below; you can also increase the water-proofing by covering the platform with old polythene bags.

My last advice concerns safety. Many garden chemicals are poisonous and must be handled with care. After using them you should wash your hands thoroughly, having placed the chemicals on a high shelf to keep them out of the reach of children. Every year there are a small number of tragedies due to children eating, drinking, or even getting splashed by poisonous substances. Follow these safety rules very rigorously from the beginning and the habit will grow.

(1) Keep dangerous chemicals on a high shelf or preferably in a locked cupboard away from toddlers and ten- to twelve-year-olds.
(2) Label each substance clearly and, if it is poisonous, write 'POISON' clearly on it in very large letters.
(3) Never put liquids in bottles which have once contained lemonade or Coke or anything like that. Most accidents are due to *children* drinking a liquid from what were lemonade bottles, so store liquids in the container in which they came.
(4) Never mix chemicals except under advice and, if you lose a label, don't make a guess at the contents; throw them away after diluting them with volumes of water.

PLANTS
Seeds

A garden is a place in which you grow plants. These may be trees or vegetables, shrubs or flowers, but no matter what kind of gardening interests you, you have to get plants from somewhere and to the beginner this can be a difficult first step. The commonest thing is to buy a few packets of seed from a local shop, follow the instructions on the packet and hope for the best. Most plants are very tough, so usually you get some kind of result from this very simple procedure. However, the range of seeds in any shop is generally limited to those lines which the shop knows will sell well. Thus your choice is very restricted and you cannot of course expect these to include shrubs or trees.

It is only fair to give seed packets their full measure of praise – they are well-nigh foolproof and the instructions are concise and clearly written. If you follow them carefully you will get good results but you do need to use a little common sense in the interpretation of the instructions, for they are purposely worded in a slightly vague way. (This book is also a little vague in places because although Britain is not a very big country it contains a surprising range of climates and soils.) To put boldly on a seed packet 'Sow outside in March' might be absolutely correct for Torquay, but three weeks too early for Sheffield and may be six weeks too early for Aviemore. Therefore when it says on the packet 'Sow outside in March or April (March/April)' it means that in mild areas March sowing is correct, but that in colder, wetter, later districts April is the best time. So use your judgement *and* your eyes, for you can get very good advice by watching hedges or even weeds – when they start to grow you know that the weather is all right for some plants.

You also have to use your judgement in relation to depth of planting. The packet may say 'Sow three to four inches deep'. This you interpret according to your soil, choosing the deeper figure if the soil is light and sandy and the shallower if you are on a heavy clay. This is easy to remember if you think of the seedlings trying to force their way through the soil – this is very difficult in clay and so you should sow shallowly.

There is now 'pelleted seed' on the market. These are ordinary good seeds enclosed in a pellet of material which dissolves away in the soil and feeds the seedling as soon as it emerges. This seed is more expensive and in a poor sandy soil produces better results, but I am not at all convinced of the need for pelleted seed in all circumstances.

Another type of seed is often described as 'dressed' or 'treated', which means that the seed has been shaken up with a chemical dust which reduces the chance of its going mouldy in a cold wet soil or if the weather doesn't allow quick germination. Treated seed is most useful for early sowings of a crop such as peas, though instead of buying treated seed you can buy little cartons of the chemical and simply puff some on your seed before sowing. This is cheaper, since the chemical will last for two years if properly stored.

Finally, you can store or collect your own seed. It is very common to end the season with a number of half-used packets of seed, and be tempted to use the remainder the following season. Under good, dry, damp-free conditions this is possible, but most gardeners just cannot provide these conditions, so it is always safer to get fresh seed each year and put the old seed in the dust bin. Collecting your own seed is a very tricky business, for if you collect too early the seed will be damp and go mouldy. So until you have a great deal of experience, do not try to collect and save your own seed. It leads to too many disappointments.

Buying plants

The next source of plants is the *garden centre*. These have grown up all over the country and are a rich and very good source of material for all gardeners with cars. They have two great virtues. Firstly you can walk around, see a wide range of shrubs and trees of all kinds and choose what you think will do best in your garden. Secondly, most of their plants are container-grown and so can be easily planted at almost any time of year (see p. 168). Remember, however, that there are plants and plants: some like clay, some sand; some like limestone and some die on limestone; so before you buy any of the more expensive trees or shrubs have a word with the owner of the centre and describe your kind of soil to him. Most gardeners will be very keen to help, especially if you go to the centre in mid-week when they are not run off their feet.

Rather similar to the garden centre is the *local market*. There are two plant stalls in my local market and they sell many good things, but I do find that you have to be careful and take a good look at the plants, for occasionally the roots may have dried out a bit, or been exposed to frost. Rapid changes of temperature can harm plants, especially house plants, and it is wiser to buy only tough things in an open-air market and get your more tender plants from a garden centre, a good florist or a local nursery.

Lastly, there is always less variety in shops and market sand people who want to be a little different from their neighbours should go for the specialist *catalogues*. Catalogues are the last word in plant buying – if you have the right catalogue you can buy almost any plant on earth. Most big growers or dealers issue them and the best contain very full descriptions of plants with notes on their peculiar likes and dislikes and their cost. Others simply contain lists of species and variety names and the price. The large glossy coloured informative catalogues are expensive to produce and dealers often charge for them; lists of species and prices, however, are often supplied free except for the postage.

Many catalogues are designed for growers who want to specialize in one particular form of plant, e.g. bulbs, orchids, or water plants. Most beginners are quite right to be a bit shy of specializing from the start, but if you live in a district which is good for roses a specialist catalogue on roses will give you some idea of the vast range of colour, form, etc. You will see many varieties at the garden centres, but even the best garden centre never grows all the varieties of all types of rose, and you will certainly not find much to help you in the vegetable line.

It would be impossible for me to list all the catalogues for every kind of plant, but here are the names and addresses of a few – unfortunately leaving out many absolutely first-class growers.

Name	Address	Speciality
Baker's Nurseries	Codsall, Wolver-hampton	Perennials
Blackmoor Nurseries	Liss, Hampshire	Hardy fruits
Blackmore and Langdon	Bath, Somerset	Delphinium, begonia, phlox
de Jager	Marden, Kent	Bulbs
Hillier and Sons	Winchester, Hants	Trees and shrubs
McGredy's Nurseries	Portadown, N. Ireland	Roses
Thompson and Morgan	Ipswich, Suffolk	Seeds of all kinds
Webbs	Redditch, Worcs.	Flower and vege-table seeds
Woolman's Nurseries	Shirley, Birmingham	Chrysanthemums

Most of the above will send a catalogue on request, although the very full illustrated catalogues, e.g. Hillier's 'Trees and Shrubs' Catalogue, may cost £3·25. This is quite expensive but they can be used for a few years although inevitably the price of the plants or seed goes up every year.

Reading and understanding a catalogue is simple when you know how, but there are a number of abbreviations to get used to at the start. Thus an entry on the first page of Thompson and Morgan's delightful catalogue for 1971 reads: 2029v Petunia (F1) Grandiflora Starship mixed HHA 9–12 ins. June/October. An explanation of this is as follows:

(1)   *2029v* is simply the number given by T. and M. to that entry or seed sample.

(2)   *Petunia (F1) Grandiflora Starship* shows that it is the species *Petunia grandiflora* and the variety is Starship. If two pure strains or species are crossed the plants which result are known as F1 hybrids – F1 stands for the filial (i.e. the son) first generation. Such plants often have increased vigour, size and even earliness of ripening. Unfortunately they do not breed true, you cannot grow F1 hybrids from seeds obtained from an F1, and the two pure strains have to be re-crossed each year.

(3)   *Mixed* – not all the plants will have flowers of the same colour, i.e. the colours will be mixed.

(4)   *HHA* is an abbreviation standing for half-hardy annual, meaning that it cannot stand frost. You will also meet *HA* – hardy annual, *P* – perennial, *HP* – hardy perennial, *GP* – greenhouse perennial, *B* – biennial, etc.

(5)   *9–12 ins.* is the normal maximum height of the plant.

(6)   *June/October* are the months in which it will be in flower. Other catalogues simply give numbers from January as No. 1 to December, No. 12. Thus instead of June/October you may see 6/10.

Most catalogues have their own peculiarities and abbreviations but nearly all provide a key to the abbreviations either at the beginning of the catalogue or at the introduction to each section.

One of the best and most popular ideas is to buy a selection of plants or seeds. These are sold as 'package deals' – you can get, for example, a collection of six named varieties of delphinium or Michaelmas daisy at specially reduced prices. This is a useful way of trying out a number of varieties rather cheaply to see which particular species and varieties do well in your soil and weather conditions.

While on the subject of what to grow, I must remind you that many towns have local parks where you can see a wide range of the plants that will grow in your area. Park superintendents or gardeners employed by local authorities have a vast store of local knowledge from their work in the parks and open spaces in many parts of town, and polite requests for advice and help can produce excellent advice. If possible, a visit to any large garden open to the public will lead to new ideas on plants.

Finally, when thinking about what to grow, be prepared to be a bit adventurous. Don't simply settle for the usual plants laid out in the garden in the usual way. Try to buy new varieties and species. This is not to say that you should abandon the old tried and trusted favourites – however, to restrict yourself to well-tested plants removes the element of excitement and pleasure when you find that you can grow plants which no one else around you has tried. You will have your failures – every gardener must expect these – but as you learn and your fingers become greener they will decrease and you will get to the stage when almost by instinct you will know what you can and cannot grow.

HOW TO WORK IN THE GARDEN

Keeping a garden trim and flourishing takes time and energy, no matter how small the patch you have to care for. A large part of the idea behind this book is to cut work to a minimum where possible, for many people have neither the time nor the inclination to spend a lot of their leisure in the garden. You can be sure, however, that if you are willing to spend an hour or two per week, and especially if you do a few construction jobs and plant some trees or shrubs at the beginning, you will begin to get a lot of pleasure and – without stretching the point too far – you will add a new dimension to your life. I can hear a lot of people snorting and saying 'Not for me. I've enough to occupy my time without being bothered with gardening.' If this is the case, gardening is not for them. But to those willing to give it a try it will be a source of pleasure, pride and exercise which can be continued into retirement and old age.

As with so many other things there are good and bad ways of doing a job and a few simple obvious hints often make it easier. The basic fact is that you are dealing with the soil on which you walk which obviously means that it is under your feet and so *below* you. A lot of gardening work therefore involves bending and stooping which can be very hard on the back, especially if you are out of condition. In fact a common picture of a gardener is of a man who has just straightened up and is standing with one hand holding the small of his back while the other rests on a spade.

This is a true picture – I've done it myself – and this reinforces my first point, namely to work slowly and steadily *a little at a time*. Most old gardeners seem to spend half their time leaning on their spade or hoe and yet the jobs get done. This is because they time themselves and don't rush headlong in a first fine frenzy of enthusiasm. They take it easily and steadily and in the end cover much more ground than someone who tries the 'bull-at-a-gate' approach.

For the householder whose gardening is essentially part-time, it is wise to have a few jobs in hand, so that when you are weary of digging you can go and do something else for a change. This does not mean that you have to hop from one job to another all the time, but simply that variety brings fresh interest and interest eases tired bones and muscles.

It will take a little while to find out which way of working suits you best. As in many other things people who are normally right-handed may find that they dig better left-handed, so do not be afraid to switch around as most tools, except for scythes and hooks, can be used equally well in right or left hand.

Again, since the soil is below you, many operations involve bending, stooping or kneeling. I find all of these are equally tiring and so tend to switch from one to the other. Many gardeners prefer to carry a piece of sacking around with them to lay on the ground and kneel on, for on the whole kneeling is less hard on the back than stooping. As with everything, practice brings improvement and gradually muscles which creaked and groaned at the beginning of the season ease out and most of the aches vanish.

I have already advised you to have a few jobs in hand at any time. Start with the heaviest when you are fresh and then turn to the lighter ones when you begin to tire. One of the things which irks me most is to do a spell of digging or weeding, to get tired of that and decide to do some pruning or tidying up among the trees and shrubs, and then to have to walk back to the house in order to get the secateurs. The moral of this is to take a selection of tools in the barrow when you go out so that if you decide to do something else the appropriate tool is handy. And carry a knife and a long piece of string or twine in your pocket. It is amazing how often you find that a piece of string would be very handy and you haven't got it with you.

DRAINAGE AND DRAINS

Although Britain does not in fact have an excessive rainfall there are a large number of wet days at all times of year and the rate of water loss from the soil back into the air is fairly low, resulting in an accumulation of water, especially in heavy soil. Such wet soils can usually be diagnosed by the type of weed which they grow; for example, rushes are obvious indicators of damp conditions, as are mosses and silver-weed. If you move into a new garden dig a few test holes about 1 foot in diameter and 2 feet deep in various places and observe the depth of water in them after a rainy spell. If the holes fill and then stay full for two or three days, the soil drainage is undoubtedly bad. Bad drainage can arise from a number of causes, each with a different remedy:

(1) There may be a hard impervious layer below the topsoil. This can be produced by continuous use of a cultivator to one depth only and is called 'panning'; it can be cured by the simple

expedient of double digging (see p. 100), especially if you incorporate strawy material into the lower spit as you go along.

(2) The soil may be a heavy clay which by its structure (see p. 28-29) is impervious to water. If this is the case dressings of lime or gypsum and peat will dramatically improve the situation (see p. 29).

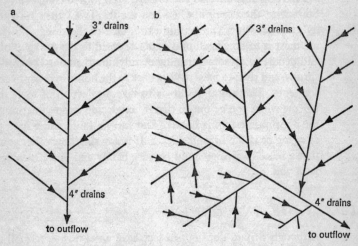

2. (a) A very simple pipe drainage system with only one slope. (b) A much more complex drainage system for a larger contoured area.

(3) There may be deep layers which hold water, in which case the surface water can only be removed by making drains. This is a task which should be done before the garden is made, for it involves a considerable upset. If you have to drain, remember the cardinal point that water runs downhill and arrange the drains accordingly, by first of all digging out the main channel from the highest to the lowest point in the garden. This channel should be about 2 feet deep and one foot wide. Side trenches should then be dug about 18 inches deep to run into the main drain in a herring-bone fashion, making sure that each 'bone' has a downhill tilt. Depending on the heaviness of the soil these side 'feeder' drains should be 15–20 feet apart and the trenches on one side should not meet the main drain

opposite each other but should be staggered as in the diagram (Fig. 2). The actual draining materials can be earthenware pipes, 3–4 inches in diameter in the main drain and 2–3 inches in diameter in the feeders. These should be laid with a gap of about ½ inch between adjoining pipes to allow water to get into the pipes. The pipes should then be covered with a layer of stones or clinker about 3 inches deep, above which should be a layer of inverted turf to stop soil being washed in. The top soil should then be replaced (Fig. 3a).

If there is a plentiful supply of brickbats or stones a layer of these will act as effective draining agents provided they are not packed

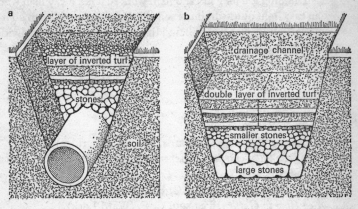

3a. *A pipe drain – note the stones becoming larger over the drain pipe, and the layer of inverted turf.*

3b. *A rubble drain – the water is carried downhill in the crevices between the large stones at the foot of the drain. A soakaway is a deeper and larger pit built on the same principle.*

tightly and will not consolidate. These stones can be covered with turves upside down and the soil replaced. The turves help to prevent the stones being choked up with soil (Fig. 3b).

An old method of draining was to use willow branches at the foot of the trench and these brushwood drains have been found to be quite effective after even a century or two.

In any case water will collect in the drains and be led downhill to an outflow. If possible this should be a ditch and then your troubles will be over, but if as in most towns there are no ditches a 'soakaway' will have to be made at the lowest point of the garden. This is a big pit, at least 3 feet deeper than the deepest drain and about 4–6 feet square. It is a very sizeable hole and should initially be left open so you can see how your drains are working – after a heavy rain you will get an idea of the volume of water you need to accommodate. If the hole is too small, enlarge it and, once you have the right size, fill it loosely with old broken brick or large stones, cover with a layer of turf and replace the topsoil.

Draining is a long job and hard work so it is a lucky man who has an easy light quick-draining soil; if you have to do it, then do it well and carefully and you will find that it will pay handsome dividends in future years.

BOOK LIST

Gardening Explained: Edwards, D. J. (Collingridge)

Be Your Own Gardening Expert: Hessayon, D. G. (Pan Brittanica Industries)

Basic Gardening: Pearson, C. E. (Ward Lock)

See How to Garden: Pearson, C. E. (Ward Lock)

Basic Gardening: Whitehead, S. B. (Dent)

Gardening the Modern Way: Hay, R. (Penguin Handbook)

Small Gardens: Lucas, C. E. (Pan Books)

Easy Plants for Difficult Places: Smith, G. (Collingridge)

Planters' Guide: Hellyer, A. G. L. (Collingridge)

Gardens for Small Spaces: Brookes, J. (Pan Books)

Weekend Gardening: Shewell-Cooper, W. E. (English Universities Press)

2 *The Basic Material – Soil*

The first question any gardener will ask you is 'What kind of soil have you got?' This is because the soil is the basic material in which plants grow and from which they derive their food. In making a garden, or in keeping a garden in good condition, one must always pay slavish and loving attention to the soil.

The fact that the soil is very important need not frighten those who know nothing about it, for much of its treatment is common sense. There is also the great comfort that the soil is like a cushion or a buffer which will often protect you against yourself and act as a reservoir of food for some years even if you do little or nothing for it. Thus the complete beginner is safeguarded against total disaster or his own mistakes for a few years while he is learning the ropes and gaining the feel of gardening.

Nevertheless, if every gardener understood the soil and its workings a little better, many disappointments would be avoided and much useless expenditure saved. Here is a simple, brief account of the common types of soil, fertilizers, and soil cultivation.

Soils can be classified in many ways, but British gardens have a limited range of types. Once you classify your soil then the basic treatment becomes easy to carry out. Your garden may not fit exactly into any of the categories given below but if so, there is no need to worry – if you select the type most like your own soil that will be perfectly adequate, for the simple reason that the categories themselves are not clear-cut but grade into each other. Maybe your garden is sufficiently large to show a range of soil types; if so it is wise to plan the garden taking the variation of soil into account and growing the right plants in the right places. Later in this book lists of plants suitable for certain conditions will be given (see p. 35-37).

SOIL TYPES AND THEIR TREATMENT

If you are a beginner moving into an established garden, you should proceed very slowly and for a growing season or a year just observe what is growing well and what badly. Do the necessary chores, weeding, pruning, grass cutting, etc., and gradually get the feel of the place and the soil type and the sort of problem it raises. You can then sit down with a few catalogues and books and embark on any re-planning you like.

If, however, you move into a new house which is surrounded by the usual sea of mud and waste, then the problem is more urgent. A few general pieces of advice may therefore be of value.

Firstly, do remember to make haste slowly. If you have any doubts about planting something in the first year, don't do it, especially if you are thinking in terms of trees or shrubs. There is always a great desire to tidy up the area around the house and to get things planted and growing. People should certainly work hard in the first flush of enthusiasm, but beware of doing anything permanent or costly until you've lived with the garden long enough to appreciate its subtleties. Sow annuals or vegetables which will be cleared in the autumn.

Secondly, you can learn a great deal from neighbours' gardens and from walks in the local park if any. In each of these places, you will see plants growing under conditions reasonably like those in your garden and so you can make a list of the plants you like, or maybe some plants or cuttings will be given to you by neighbours. However, don't slavishly copy the kinds of flowers etc., grown by neighbours, for this results in everyone growing the same things in the same way. Remember to use their advice as a helpful comment and not as a command.

There are many local myths too. For example, I was told that no one could grow wisteria in my area. I believed this until a friend brought one up from Surrey, planted it and had great success. Of course, it might have failed, but it was a modern variety and was presumably more able to withstand our conditions than the old-fashioned standard ones.

Thirdly, you will begin to get experience with the soil. As you work on it, handle it, maybe cultivate it, you will be able to see how quickly it drains or whether it stays sticky and wet. In summer you will see if it cakes hard or stays as an open loam.

Sandy Soil (*Also Gravel*)

Sandy soil has a number of properties, all of which arise from the fact that it is composed of fairly large mineral particles, namely grains of sand. Such soil holds very little water and so is liable to dry out during droughts. Further, as water drains through it very quickly, plant foods are rapidly washed out (or leached) by the rain, producing what is called a 'hungry soil'. Sandy soils are usually acid but one needs to bother about this only if it is extreme. Because of the very open texture there is not only quick drainage, but also a good air supply which allows very good, deep root development.

Though sandy soils are not very good in a garden, they have a number of virtues. For example, the fact that they are quick-draining may remove plant food, but it also makes the soil light and easy to work since there are no great quantities of water locked up in the soil as you dig. The lack of water also increases the rate at which sandy soils heat up in spring and early summer, so many of the early crops of potatoes, cauliflower, sugar beet, etc., are grown on these light soils and, if well treated, they will grow excellent shrubs and young trees, fruit and early vegetables.

How does one get the best from a light sandy soil? If the area is small the addition of quantities of organic manures such as farm-yard manure, compost, etc., will make the soil much more productive, and small doses of artificial fertilizers, such as Growmore, at about 2 oz. per square yard will be immediately beneficial to the crop. Such soils also need potash and if they get too acid, crushed limestone should be put on every three years at 3 oz. per square yard.

Loamy Soil

This is the dream of every gardener. Loams are usually dark in colour and have a nice crumbly structure. They drain well, yet still manage to retain a lot of moisture in the soil particles or crumbs so that plants are very rarely without adequate water even in the driest

27

weather. A good loam also holds its fertilizer value and there is little loss of plant foods through leaching or excessive drainage.

Loam actually lies in the middle of the range of soil types. Its particles are not so large as those of sand, but not so small as in clay. It usually contains a lot of decaying organic matter so that there is a big soil population of earthworms and soil insects. Although not so 'early' as a sandy soil, loam will still warm up quite quickly and therefore good crops of nearly anything can be grown on it. The only exceptions to this are those plants which demand special conditions, such as water plants, alpines and so on.

Since loams lie roughly in the middle of a continuous spectrum of soil types it is only natural that at one end of the range there should be sandy loams with some of the properties of a sandy soil, and at the other end 'heavy' or 'stiff' loam which shades easily into a real clay soil.

The treatment of loam is very simple and can be summed up in one phrase 'not too much of anything'; that applies especially to lime, which need not be used at all unless there are clear signs of acidity when the soil is tested for pH (see p. 50-51).

Feeding too is simple. You should always give as much compost or humus-containing materials as possible and supplement this with a top dressing of a good, general fertilizer twice per year, say in April/May and June/July. These should not be heavy dressings, simply 1 oz. per square yard. The actual rate may vary according to the fertilizer you buy, but no matter what rate is recommended it is usually easier to apply it in two separate doses, the first at seeding or planting time and the second when the plants are growing at their peak.

Clay Soil

New gardens on clay soil are getting more and more common, as most of the sand or gravelly soils have already been built upon. This applies especially to the South-East where the London clay or clay-with-flints form a large part of the soil pattern and on which new housing estates are mushrooming. Clay has a very bad reputation as a garden soil. However, treated well and planted with the right things it can be very productive both in quantity and quality.

Here are the qualities which give a clay soil such a bad reputation. Clays are cold and wet; when they are wet, they are heavy and difficult to cultivate and, when they dry out in the summer, they set rock-hard and it is difficult to get even a hoe below the surface. Clay soils swell when wet and shrink when dry. The shrinkage shows as surface cracks in dry weather and this expansion and contraction can tear the roots of plants. Because clay particles are very small they are remarkably retentive of water so that there is little movement of air in a clay soil. This limits root growth which in its turn can reduce the amount of top growth. Being wet, clay soils warm up very slowly in the spring and so are no good for early crops.

This is a black picture but with reasonable care and understanding much can be done. For example, since clay particles are small and so make for bad drainage, any technique which will encourage aggregation of these small particles into crumbs will improve things at once. Substances which do this job are classified as 'soil conditioners'. The best and cheapest is undoubtedly farmyard manure in any quantity which can be bought. Similarly, well-made compost (see p. 45), hop manure, spent mushroom compost, etc., if spread in the surface as a mulch in the summer and then dug in in the winter, will do a lot of good. (Here the amateur gardener is at a great advantage over the farmer, for in a small garden he can afford to be generous with this kind of material, whereas it would bankrupt the farmer.) One can generalize still further and say that any organic material, even weeds, can be dug in and will benefit the soil.

Another material which will help the structure and therefore the drainage of clay soils is lime. Lime is sold in many forms (see p. 50, 53), but the safest is probably crushed limestone and at 4 oz. per square yard it will sweeten and improve the drainage of even the heaviest clays. In such soils, it is advisable to apply lime every second year until the right soil texture is achieved.

Cultivation can help break down a clay soil, and many gardeners try to dig their garden in late autumn and leave the surface very roughly dug in ridges and furrows. This exposes a large surface of soil to the frost, and weathering of the heavy sticky lumps of clay breaks them down to a much finer texture or tilth. Recently, however, this approach has been called in question and some advanced growers are leaving the surface of a heavy soil covered with weeds, or the crop, throughout the winter, claiming that more harm is done by exposing bare soil to the constant beating of rain than benefit is derived from allowing frost to get at it.

On the credit side, fertilizers remain in clay soils as there is not the constant drainage which occurs in sand. It also takes a very prolonged severe drought to make plants in a clay soil wilt, for it does retain some water even in a hot summer.

A simple plan for the owner of a new house taking over an area of wet clay should then be, firstly, to try to get annual crops growing in it. Many people use potatoes as they give good ground cover, produce a good root system and in the end the gardener gets a crop. Any crop, however, will do just as well, although it is probably better to grow coarse subjects such as cabbages, turnips, beans, potatoes, tall peas and so on, rather than lettuce, cauliflower, etc. Put the waste material on a compost heap (see p. 46) and when ready dig it back in.

If it is autumn give a heavy dressing of lime (8 oz. per square yard) except in those areas where you can grow azaleas, rhododendrons or ericas. The following autumn lime again, and only then start thinking of permanent plantings.

If a lawn is part of your scheme, put extra effort into trying to arrange drainage (see p. 21-22), for grass does not grow too well on a clay soil. If you can get the lawn established and thick, the surface will be protected and your troubles minimized. Generally, however, lawns are never perfect on clay soils and most gardeners will have to be content with an average product unless they are willing to 'hollow-tine' it regularly and apply lots of very coarse sand.

Once the clay is broken down or the drainage improved, trees and flowering shrubs will do very well, particularly roses, viburnum and pyracantha. Perennials will also do well.

Chalk and Limestone Soils

The chalk and limestone areas of Britain are well marked and include the Downs, much of the Chilterns, Derbyshire, Yorkshire Wolds,

North Lancashire, etc. They thus encompass some of the very heavily populated areas around London, Sheffield and Bristol. The important point about chalk or limestone is that it is chemically active in the soil, since it not only supplies a lot of calcium to the plant and neutralizes soil acids, but also combines chemically with many elements in the soil which are essential for plant growth, making them unavailable to the plant. Plants in limestone areas are thus inclined to have deficiency diseases resulting from a lack of iron, manganese, boron or zinc.

Plants vary in their ability to tolerate the changes worked by calcium in the soil and so are divided into two categories, the *calcicoles* which grow well in chalk soil and the *calcifuges*, such as rhododendrons and azaleas, which cannot tolerate it. There are many lists of lime-hating and lime-tolerant plants, and I have given one on p. 35. The richest and most diverse flora in Britain is in fact found on chalk or limestone soils, so with care a chalk or a limestone garden can be made very beautiful indeed with a wide range of trees, shrubs and herbs.

In most areas the chalk is covered by a layer of soil, varying in thickness from a few inches to many feet. Chalk is a very porous rock, so the soils which form on it are light and quick-draining. They warm up quickly in the spring and grow excellent crops, provided they are well fed. The basis of feeding in chalk or limestone areas must be compost, farmyard manure or some other organic matter, for soils containing calcium are so chemically active that organic matter is used up very quickly and soil becomes thin and impoverished unless its humus content is continually topped up.

Even the most arrant amateur will realize that no lime should be added to chalk or limestone soils, although because of the rapid drainage the upper inches of soil may become acid. For a number of years enough lime will be brought to the surface by cultivation to keep the acidity at a reasonable level.

Very good lawns can be developed on a chalk or limestone garden – the quick drainage and thin soil are excellent for this. However, one must be sure to get the seed-bed down to a fine tilth as lumps of chalk may make the surface irregular and even reduce the strength of the grass.

Finally, a brief introduction to a serious problem likely to trouble gardeners on chalk or limestone: deficiency diseases. As we have seen this comes from the lime (really the calcium) in the soil reacting chemically with many soil minerals. The most common of these reactions takes place with iron so that iron is 'fixed' in the soil and is no longer available to plants. Plant leaves manufacture food materials using carbon dioxide from the air and combining it with water to produce sugars and starches. These are the basic materials of which the plant is made and which it uses as a source of energy. This very elaborate series of chemical changes (photosynthesis) is brought about by the action of sunlight and the green colouring matter (chlorophyll) in plant leaves. The manufacture of chlorophyll requires *iron* and so if the plant receives no iron, chlorophyll will not be made and the normally green parts of the plant, e.g. the leaves, will become yellow. This condition is known as *chlorosis*, and it has the obvious consequence of causing a reduction in the rate of photosynthesis. Affected plants therefore are weakly with yellowish leaves and in the case of fruit trees there is a very serious decrease in yield and fruit quality.

In the past affected trees were treated by adding iron to the soil, but this is of little value as the iron is simply locked up again by the lime. Sometimes trees were sprayed with salts of iron and enough of this compound would be absorbed through the leaves to remedy the condition. But very few gardeners have efficient spraying equipment and so it was a great step forward when iron chelates were put on the market. Iron chelates contain iron in a very special type of chemical combination. This combination prevents the calcium in the soil attacking the iron and making it non-available to the plant – the plant in fact absorbs the iron in the chelated form and uses it to manufacture the correct quantities of chlorophyll. Soil treatment with these compounds can speedily cure chlorosis.

Chelates are particularly useful for shrubs or trees but less so for annuals or bulbs or small herbaceous plants. These usually carry enough iron in the seed or get enough from surface layers of the soil (where the lime may be washed out) to suffice for their relatively short life.

Peaty Soils

There is not much really peaty soil used for gardening in Britain, but cottages in Wales and Scotland, Dartmoor or the Pennines may have gardens of this type. Peat is plant material which has not fully decomposed because of the waterlogging effect of excessive rain or bad drainage. Where there is a great deal of water in the soil, there is naturally a shortage of oxygen and the bacteria which normally would break plant material down to humus are unable to function.

As plants grow, die, and fall into this type of soil, they do not rot away but slowly accumulate for centuries. The semi-decayed plant remains is peat and in some parts of the country there are beds of peat twenty or thirty feet thick. Normally houses are not built on peat but at the edge of the moors and where rock crops out one sometimes finds houses with peaty gardens.

The problem with peaty soils is really twofold: there is the difficulty of drainage and such soils are very acid. The first thing therefore, is to improve the drainage by laying drains, by cultivation and by adding lime. Lime is very useful since as well as helping the drainage it counteracts the acidity. Put on crushed limestone at 8 oz. per square yard every three years. A warning here: many plants like azaleas, rhododendrons and ericas, which grow well in peaty soils, hate lime, so if you intend to grow them avoid the use of lime in that part of the garden.

Peaty soils are also very deficient in basic plant foods and vegetables need regular heavy dressings of complete fertilizers such as Growmore at, say, 2 oz. per square yard. Once this is done very good crops can be grown and a peaty garden can be made very productive.

It is not easy to grow large trees on peat as there is usually only a limited amount of soil in which the roots can anchor themselves, but bush fruit and small apple trees can do well. The chief difficulty is likely to be the weather, since the conditions which lead to peat formation usually include excessive rainfall, high altitude and cold. Choose crops and especially varieties very carefully therefore, and you will find that with a little experience all the ordinary

vegetables can be grown well – celery and cauliflowers revel in this
very humus-rich soil.

BOOK LIST

Student's Book of Soils and Manures: Russell, E. J. (Cambridge
University Press)
Horticultural Science and Soils: Coker, E. G. (Macdonald,
London)

SHRUBS AND CHALK OR LIMESTONE

LIME-HATING PLANTS	LIME-TOLERANT PLANTS	
Rhododendron	Clematis	Rhus
Azalea	Rose species	Ribes
Erica species except *E. carnea*	Cotoneaster	Syringa
Calluna species	Malus	Veronica
Vaccinium species	Pyrus	Viburnum
Camellia	Prunus	Vitis
Eucryphia glutinosa	Sorbus	Abutilon
Gaultheria	Spiraea	Ilex
Grevillea species	Berberis	
Kalmia species	Buddleia	
Pieris species		
Skimmia fortunei		
Some lupin species		

	Cistus	
	Cornus	
	Deutzia	
	Diervilla	
	Forsythia	
	Fuchsia	
	Hamamelis	
	Lonicera	
	Helianthemum	
	Philadelphus	

In addition most trees, e.g. beech, ash, walnut, cedar, poplar, juniper, laburnum, acacia, daphne, flowering cherry, elm, tamarisk, can tolerate lime although, unless their roots can penetrate deeply, very tall trees could be unstable.

Where the name of the genus is given, e.g. Prunus, it can be assumed that all species of that genus show the same degree of tolerance   The exception to this is the genus Erica where only *E. carnea* is lime-tolerant.

TABLE OF SOILS, SOIL TREATMENT AND SUITABLE PLANTS

SOIL TYPE	TREATMENT	PLANTS TO GROW
Sandy	Apply organic manures annually either dug in or as mulch. Artificials, especially nitrogen, and potash in frequent small doses. Lime every third year if needed 3 oz./yd². May need watering in drought periods.	*Trees and shrubs* – conifers, rhododendron, azalea, broom, heather, honeysuckle, gorse, roses, berberis, cistus, robinia, rowan, cydonia. *Flowers* – all bulbs, lilies, anemone, catmint, milkwort (polygala), viola, pulmonaria, potentilla, meconopsis, most rock plants. *Fruit* – strawberries, raspberries, currants, apples, pears. *Vegetables* – potatoes, peas, beans, lettuce, cauliflower, leeks and onions (not so well).
Loam	Needs little treatment other than regular dressings of artificials and compost. Rarely needs lime, but may benefit from mulching.	Will grow all plants well, save those with highly specialized demands. Because of its excellent growing powers, should be used for choice subjects of good quality, especially in vegetables and flowering shrubs.
Clay	As much organic material as possible. If necessary lime, 4 oz./yd² every second year. Artificials should be used regularly especially sulphate of ammonia, since it helps to change compost into humus.	*Trees and shrubs* – roses, pieris, kerria, philadelphus, forsythia, weigela, syringa. *Flowers* – carnations, sunflowers, astilbe, spiraea, andromeda, campanula, phlox, michaelmas daisy, delphinium. *Fruit* – apples, pears; if plenty of humus, all soft fruits. *Vegetables* – if given plenty of humus and drainage can grow all vegetables except carrots.

Chalk and Limestone Soils	Should be dressed each year with as much organic material as possible. Artificials as needed, especially potash and nitrogen. May require iron chelates to combat deficiency diseases.	*Trees and shrubs* – see Table p. 207. *Flowers* – see Table $$ p. 162. *Fruit* – all fruits especially plums, peaches, cherries and apples; if plenty of humus, all soft fruits. *Vegetables* – all cabbage, cauliflower, peas, beans, lettuce, NOT potatoes.
Peaty Soils	Generous liming is essential. Also give heavy feeding with compound fertilizer during the growing season.	*Trees and shrubs* – all ericas, rhododendron, azalea, calluna, camellia, pieris, hydrangea, veronica, yew, cedar, maple, birch. N.B. Many of the above are lime-haters so do not lime in spots where calcifuges such as rhododendrons will be grown (see p. 31). *Flowers* – primula, meconopsis, spiraea, astilbe, andromeda, all heath and bog plants. *Fruit* – currants, apples, gooseberries (none very well). *Vegetables* – potatoes, onion, leek, celery, cauliflowers, cabbage, lettuce.

3 *Fertilizers, Manures and Lime*

All you need to know about fertilizers and manures can be told with very little mention of chemistry, and the refinements of the subject can be left to the experts – the elementary principles governing the use of fertilizers are only common sense applied in a particular field and no one need be afraid of the subject.

The obvious beginning is the soil. As we have just seen, when any plant grows it takes some of its food from the soil, and if the plant dies where it grows and just rots on the spot, then anything it takes from the soil is returned in a continuous cycle. But in most gardens this does not happen since we cut flowers and trim hedges, dig crops and eat fruit; so every time we take something away from the spot in which it is grown, we are removing chemicals and plant food from the soil.

An obvious example will clarify this (Fig. 4). A row of cabbages remove food from the soil during their growth. We then cut the cabbages, take them away, cook and eat them. We use some of the food the cabbage has taken from the soil to maintain our body, and the rest is lost in the general sewage system of a town or city. Thus, if we grow a crop in the same spot the following year, there will be less plant food in the soil for the second crop. Over a period of years the food reserves (or fertility) of the soil will decrease until crops can scarcely be grown at all.

In order to maintain, and especially to increase, soil fertility plant food must be returned to the soil, and this is done by fertilizers and manures. This process has been carried out for centuries and in many primitive countries human excreta is used, but this is clearly difficult under our conditions and so alternatives have been devised to do the same job. These are firstly the so-called 'artificial' fertilizers and secondly natural organic products such as farmyard manure, which are sometimes thought superior to the former. There is, however, no evidence to show that one is better than the other in all circumstances, and experiments using artificials in the same field for over a century have produced *no* signs of deterioration in the crop or soil. There is a real and valuable place for many different kinds of soil additives, be they natural or synthetic, and I will attempt to give an unbiased account of the use and

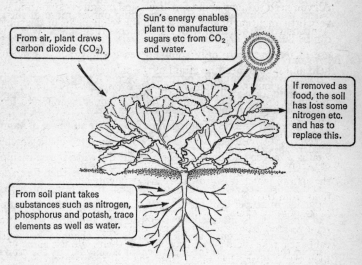

From air, plant draws carbon dioxide (CO_2).

Sun's energy enables plant to manufacture sugars etc from CO_2 and water.

If removed as food, the soil has lost some nitrogen etc. and has to replace this.

From soil plant takes substances such as nitrogen, phosphorus and potash, trace elements as well as water.

4. *A diagram illustrating the way in which food materials etc. circulate.*

results of different fertilizers. A table of fertilizers is given on p. 54.

The study of plant nutrition has shown that most plants obtain the same food materials from the soil. Some of these the plants use and need in large quantities – these are called the *major* elements. Other foods are required in only very small amounts and these have been called *minor* or *trace elements*. Most gardeners need only worry about the major elements for it is only on chalk or limestone or under intensive cultivation that trace elements become significant.

MAJOR PLANT FOOD ELEMENTS

All plants have been shown to require substantial quantities of three elements, nitrogen, phosphorus and potassium, and these three are

39

often called the 'golden tripod of plant growth'. In its pure form nitrogen is a gas, and phosphorus and potassium are solids which burn very easily and are extremely dangerous to handle. Thus, although a gardener talks about the elements nitrogen, phosphorus and potassium, he uses *salts* of these elements such as ammonium nitrate, calcium phosphate or potassium nitrate; this account will deal with compounds (salts) containing one or more of the three substances rather than with the elements themselves.

(a) *Nitrogen* (N)

The chemical symbol for nitrogen is N, but it may be combined with oxygen to form a nitrate with the formula NO_3, or with hydrogen to form ammonium salts with the formula NH_4.

The main sources of nitrogen in Britain are sulphate of ammonia $((NH_4)_2SO_4)$, nitrate of soda $(NaNO_3)$, and nitro-chalk which contains nitrogen and lime. Of these by far the widest used is sulphate of ammonia, which is made very cheaply and is therefore an easy and readily accessible source of nitrogen. It contains the high proportion of 20 per cent nitrogen. When applied to the soil, sulphate of ammonia is attacked by soil bacteria and after this process (nitrification) becomes usable by plants. The change takes anything up to three weeks, so the main benefit is only felt by the crop after this period of time.

A much quicker acting nitrogenous fertilizer is nitrate of soda $(NaNO_3)$ which is imported from Chile and so is called Chilean saltpetre and contains about 16 per cent of N_2 available *immediately* to the plant. It does, however, have some disadvantages. If it gets damp in storage it deteriorates very quickly; and if applied at too heavy a dosage it can scorch the crop. But for an immediate effect it is absolutely excellent.

When comparing fertilizers it is important to know (a) how much nitrogen they contain, (b) how much is available and can be used by the plant and (c) how quickly the nitrogen is washed out of the soil and so lost. When all these factors are taken into account, the 'best buy' for the amateur as a nitrogenous fertilizer is sulphate of ammonia; it can be used safely if it is always applied in damp, or not very dry, weather and is never mixed with lime.

There are other nitrogenous substances such as dried blood ($7-14\%$ N_2), in which the nitrogen is very quick-acting and has none of the disadvantages of potassium nitrate. It is relatively expensive, however, and is used mainly for house plants since it also contains a little phosphate and potash. Another valuable source is hoof and horn meal, which is very slow to break down but yields its nitrogen over a long period of time and thus ensures a steady supply of the element.

Extensive testing has shown that heavy dressing (2–3 oz. per square yard) of nitrogenous fertilizers substantially increases the yield of leaf and green material produced by a plant. Thus it is excellent for cabbages or Brussels sprouts, but is not needed in such quantities for peas or potatoes which are seed and root crops.

(b) *Potassium* (K)

This substance is usually represented by potash, a compound formed by potassium and oxygen (K_2O). It is generally applied to plants in the form of potassium sulphate (K_2SO_4), which is very pure indeed, containing up to 50 per cent of potash. It can be given as a top dressing and gradually worked into the soil at about 1 oz. per square yard. It dissolves easily in water and so is readily washed in; but soil holds it quite strongly and there is little loss of potash through drainage water. Consequently, provided your soil is not too acid, the potash is readily available to plants.

A shortage of potash leads to definite disease symptoms. Growth is stunted and often, for example in apples and gooseberries, the margins and tips of the leaves go brown and brittle. Brownish spots may appear between the veins of the leaves and the general condition known as 'scorch' occurs. Potash is also necessary for the best development of flower and fruit colours and flavours and has been called 'a substitute for sunshine'. Its other main function is to counterbalance the effect of excess nitrogen. Thus, if plants are growing too lush and soft because of an over-abundance of nitrogen, this can be counteracted with dressings of sulphate of potash. It is most needed in Britain in sandy light soils so it is a good plan to give a light dressing of sulphate of potash (1 oz. per square yard) as a routine measure in gardens of this type.

(c) *Phosphorus* (P)

The element phosphorus is always used in combination with other substances as a phosphate (PO_4) or phosphoric acid (P_2O_5). It is essential for plant growth and is especially important in the growth of roots and the development of seeds. Thus soils producing poor crops of carrots, swedes, potatoes, peas, etc., may show marked improvement after even a very light dressing of phosphatic fertilizers.

The main phosphorus fertilizer is called superphosphates. This contains about 20 per cent phosphoric acid and is very effective on ordinary soils where it acts quickly. It is often used as a spring dressing to get quick early growth. It is not so effective on acid soils; if a phosphatic dressing is required here, use basic slag, applied in the autumn.

Bone meal – an organic source – may contain up to 25 per cent phosphoric acid. The phosphate in bone meal is only very slowly absorbed by plants so it is often used in seed beds or potting compost for house plants, where it will give benefit over a period of months or even years.

COMPOUND FERTILIZERS

The more one explores the intricacies of chemical fertilizers, the more of a jungle it becomes. Different companies are constantly marketing feeds and fertilizers under all sorts of names, some displaying rather alarming analyses on the packet. For anyone just beginning to garden, the golden rule should be to avoid special mixtures for special plants and to concentrate on a good compound fertilizer for everything.

The best known compound fertilizer is Growmore. This contains nitrogen, phosphorus and potash in a specific proportion, and although the proportions are not ideal for all plants, they are safe and will benefit all types. The rate of application varies; 2 oz. per square yard is a safe dose, but it is always better and much more economical to give a number of light dressings throughout the year ($\frac{1}{2}$ oz. per square yard) rather than one big dressing at the beginning of the growing season.

Finally, when a dressing rate of, say, 2 oz. per square yard is given, this means what it says, and you will only do damage if you take the 2 oz. and sprinkle it on a small area around the base of a cabbage or a rose bush. Fertilizer dressings should be spread evenly over the surface, either using a spreader or scattering by hand. With a little practice a fairly even spread can be achieved, although this can be difficult at low concentrations. Roots are then encouraged to spread out and so anchor the plant more effectively and firmly in the soil.

ORGANIC MANURES

Organic manures are sometimes defined as 'manures which at one time have formed part of another living organism'. They include compost, leaf mould, dried blood, fish and bone meal, hops, farmyard manure and many others, and the important thing about them, from the gardener's point of view, is that they are *not* pure. Thus when farmyard manure is applied to a soil, not only are nitrogen, phosphorus and potash being added, but the manure contains small quantities of trace elements and very large quantities of undecomposed organic matter such as straw, leaves and so on. It is for the trace elements and the partly decomposed organic matter that the organic manures are most desirable and at this stage it is important to indicate very briefly the importance of organic material in the soil and its relation to soil structure.

Soil is not a simple aggregation of particles of weathered rock. It also contains many living things such as bacteria, fungi, insects, earthworms etc. These organisms feed largely on each other and ultimately on the debris of plants and animals which fall on the soil. In doing this, they gradually destroy the original chemical structure of the leaf or straw and convert it eventually into the ultimate simplification of carbon dioxide (CO_2) and water (H_2O). Such a change is the result of a long series of digestions, bacterial attack and other chemical reactions, and on the way to the end-products of CO_2 and H_2O the organic material added to the soil becomes black and finely divided and in this state is called humus.

Humus has many very important properties. For example it is

not only the food of many soil micro-organisms which carry out important changes such as nitrification, it also has the power of binding the tiny mineral particles in the soil together into larger aggregates called 'crumbs'. If a soil has a good crumb structure it allows water to drain through easily, at the same time holding large quantities of water in reserve. Thus a soil with lots of humus is not only well drained, but also does not dry out easily. For the same reasons, the crumbs will hold mineral salts such as nitrates and reduce leaching and wastage, and because such soils are well drained they are light and warm up easily in the spring.

For all these reasons humus is a major constituent of any fertile soil and organic manures are very valuable not so much for the food they add to the soil, but rather for the effect they have on soil structure. But in the end the organic materials become CO_2 and H_2O and are lost to the soil which again reverts to a collection of fine mineral particles. Therefore, organic manures must be supplied regularly.

The point is better made if we consider the Dust Bowl of America. During the First World War the fertile prairies were ploughed up and wheat planted. The land produced wheat for a number of years and each year the grain was cut and threshed and the straw either burned or used in other ways. Under this system little manure was added to the land each year and so the soil structure gradually decayed, lost its living inhabitants and its crumb structure. It has now become little more than a fine powder which is blown away in great dust storms when the winds come, or is washed off the hillsides in heavy rains. At the risk of repetition let it be said that really fertile soil must contain lots of humus and gardeners should think of this whole business in terms of nitrogen, phosphorus and potash feeding the *plants* while the organic manures also feed the *soil* (and both must be done).

(a) *Farmyard Manure* (FYM)

In the days of horse-drawn transport great quantities of horse manure were available. This is much less common now and the bulk of farmyard manure is the excretion of farm animals mixed with the straw or litter on which the animals were bedded down. Its chemical composition, therefore, varies with its source and age, but in general it contains about 0·2 per cent of nitrogen, 0·4 per cent phosphate and 0·5 per cent potash. Compared with the inorganic fertilizers it is therefore very low in its content of these essential elements, but it must be remembered that artificials are applied at 1 or 2 ounces per square yard, whereas FYM is applied in pounds per square yard; thus the difference is not as great as might appear at first sight. Besides, if you live in the right areas, you can buy a ton of FYM for the cost of a hundredweight of inorganic fertilizers.

FYM also contains many trace elements and eventually becomes humus to the continuing benefit of the soil. The change to humus is slow and may take years, so that FYM should be regarded as part of a long-term policy to build up soil fertility. One further complication needs explaining. The decomposition of FYM to humus is brought about by soil micro-organisms, which require other foods as well as manure, the most important of these being nitrogen. It has been calculated that in order to break down one part of FYM the soil bacteria need five parts of nitrogen, which they obtain from other soil sources. Now if fresh FYM is added to soil bacteria will be competing with the plants for the available nitrogen supplies. In this competition the bacteria usually win, and so heavy dressings of organic materials or FYM can temporarily worsen the growth of plants unless the grower remembers to add some sulphate of ammonia, say 1 oz. per square yard, after the manure has been dug in. It is wise therefore to stock FYM for a period before applying it to the soil, as it will start to rot in the heap and so make lighter demands on the soil nitrogen.

Well-rotted FYM can be applied at any time of year but is usually spread on top of the soil in the autumn and then dug in when the soil is turned over during the winter.

(b) *Compost*

This term is used to cover the humus-containing material which is formed when different kinds of waste vegetable matter are rotted down. Thus, a compost heap can be made from both garden and kitchen waste including, for example, lawn mowings, cabbage leaves and potato peelings. For the humus-forming process to proceed at a reasonable rate the heap has to be properly made, but if this is done the product is excellent and can be one of the best soil conditioners.

To make a compost heap, first delimit an area, either with wooden slats or wire-netting. A useful size is 3 × 4 ft; the netting can surround three sides of this rectangle or, if the material is being added from the top, a complete rectangle of wire can be made. The floor of the heap should consist of a nine-inch layer of vegetable and garden refuse, and on top of this it is helpful to sprinkle a handful

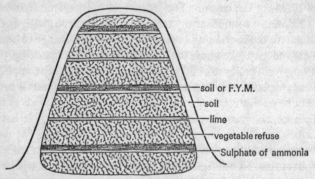

soil or F.Y.M.
soil
lime
vegetable refuse
Sulphate of ammonia

5. *Cross-section of a compost heap.*

of sulphate of ammonia – this additional nitrogen helps the bacteria to decompose the vegetable matter quickly. Many gardeners then sprinkle a thin (2 ins.) layer of soil or FYM on top to make sure the appropriate bacteria are present, then a further nine-inch layer of refuse, more sulphate of ammonia and so on until the heap is built up to a height of about 4 ft. 6 ins. (see Fig. 5). Every foot or so, sprinkle some lime over the surface of the heap, making sure it never comes directly into contact with the sulphate of ammonia. This helps to keep the decomposition going. When the heap is the right size and shape, cover the top with soil. Do not tread the heap down, as air is necessary for humification.

One can buy a number of aids to compost-making which speed up the process, but their main ingredients simply supply nitrogen, so it's cheaper, if a little slower, to use sulphate of ammonia.

It takes about six months for a compost heap to rot down sufficiently to be useful, and the longer it can be left the more complete will be the change to humus. In cities very good compost heaps can be made by building the heap as above, but a few layers of straw, preferably wheat straw, produce a greater bulk. If this is done the straw should be laid *across* the heap so that the ends of the straw protrude on two sides if possible. This technique allows air to get into the heap more freely and speeds up decomposition.

Compost can be used in the garden at any time, but is best either dug in in autumn or used as mulch in summer. It contains not only trace elements, but also the nitrogen added to the heap, and of course much humus. One word of caution: avoid using diseased refuse in compost heaps, e.g. cabbage roots with club root, and remember that heaps should be watched so that they do not become centres from which weeds can spread, or winter homes for slugs. To avoid the latter put a ring of slug pellets round the compost heap in autumn.

(c) *Peat*

Peat is sold for horticultural purposes in bales and is a rich source of soil humus. However, it is very slow to break down and may lie inert in the soil for years before it is completely humified. This resistance to breaking down is a distinct advantage on very light soils in which peat will act as a water-retaining substance even in very dry weather. Although it contains up to 2 per cent of nitrogen, it is best to look at peat not as a plant food, but as a soil improver. It is fairly good for clay soil but is best on sands and light loams. On chalky soils it decays much more rapidly and therefore FYM is preferable.

Peat is a very good mulch round shrubs such as roses – it protects the soil surface from drying out and also holds a supply of water. Any fertilizer dressings should be applied before the peat, otherwise the salts will get trapped by the peat and the plant will only benefit very slowly. Peat also plays a very important part in the manufacture of potting composts as it is often the moisture-holding ingredient in a compost which is otherwise mainly sand.

Peat can be applied at any rate since as it is very mild there is little (if any) risk of toxic effect. For the beginner with light sandy soil who finds it impossible to obtain farmyard manure and has no

room or time to make compost, liberal dressings of peat prove a
very useful soil conditioner.

(d) *Dried Blood*

This is a rich source of nitrogen – good samples of dried blood
contain up to 15 per cent as well as some phosphate and potash. It is
too expensive to use as a general fertilizer in the garden, but it
can give tired pot plants a quick lift. Just a little, say 1 oz., sprinkled
on top of a seven-inch pot and watered in will have the desired
effect. It can also be used on leaf crops such as lettuce – half a
teaspoonful around each plant will act as a growth stimulant.

MISCELLANEOUS ORGANIC MANURES

There are a large number of materials containing plant food which
are used as manures, and it would be nearly impossible to list them
all. However, since many are obtainable locally and may be very
cheap, it is useful to have a short comment on the most common.

(a) *Sewage Sludge*

This is often sold by local councils; its sale helps reduce the rates!
It is usually dried to a grey-black powder which is odourless and
has a reasonable plant food content. The actual percentages of
nitrogen, phosphorus and potash vary according to the degree of
dryness and the method of preparation, but you can expect about
2 per cent N_2, about 1·5 per cent P_2O and 50 per cent organic matter.
As you can see, there is very little potash. Some sewage sludge is
very alkaline. Check this before you use it and if it is alkaline avoid
using it around or near lime-hating plants.

Dried and powdered sewage is a very good lawn dressing and you
can give up to 8 oz. per square yard. (Grass does not need potassium
in any quantity, so the absence of this element doesn't matter.)
Dried sludge is also a very good activator for a compost heap as it
speeds up the rate of humification of all composted material. It
should be used in thin layers, say every foot of composting material.

Wet sludge is much less attractive and, although often supplied
free except for transport by local sewage works, is not very popular.

The reasons for this are obvious: it smells, you are paying for the transport of large volumes of water, and the material cannot be stored.

(b) *Spent Hops* (*Hop Manure*)

This is a cheap material with a high organic content sold in garden centres and stores. The only plant food it contains is a little nitrogen, so it should be used together with a general fertilizer. The chief advantage of spent hops is the rate at which it breaks down to humus; it is an excellent method of adding humus to light, thin soils. Its very low chemical content also makes it a good mulch. Many manufacturers add chemical fertilizers to spent hops and sell the combined product under the name of 'hop manure'. This makes a very good soil additive – not only is quick humus added, but the nitrogen in the hop manure helps speedy breakdown and so prevents the plants being temporarily deprived of food.

(c) *Seaweed*

Another locally plentiful, cheap material which, though low in phosphate, is otherwise very like farmyard manure. Most seaweeds contain quantities of trace elements such as iron and zinc, and other substances, generally grouped under the name of alginates, have a high reputation for improving soil structure. Seaweeds are best applied in autumn or winter; the rain will wash the salt away before it is dug in and it will have ceased to smell by spring and no longer attract flies. Any kind of seaweed can be collected from the seashore and used in the garden.

(d) *Wood Ash*

Good wood ash from a bonfire may contain up to 4 per cent phosphoric acid and up to 25 per cent of potash (K_2O). It lacks nitrogen and this must be added before ash can be used as a general fertilizer or even before it is added to the compost heap. The continued use of fine wood ash can lead to changes in the soil structure making it sticky and unworkable. Ash should therefore be used only occasionally. It should always be stored in a dry place or its most valuable ingredient, potash, will be washed out.

(e) *Leaf Mould*

This is the easiest of all composts to make for leaves naturally stack loosely and aeration is therefore good. Good leaf mould contains 2 per cent nitrogen and 0·1 per cent potash, but its chief value lies in its humus-forming properties. Further, fallen leaves are free for the collection and can be made into a heap which should be enclosed in wire netting, preferably in a site against a wall. The rate of decomposition is slow: it takes two years to turn into real leaf mould which looks like a good dark flake tobacco. If leaves are easily available make a fresh heap each year, simply replacing the two-year-old heap by a new one as the material is used in the garden.

Leaf mould is good as a surface mulch anywhere; it can be sifted and mixed with soil to form a potting compost, and it makes an ideal top dressing for lawns.

Different types of leaf make different qualities of mould, with oak and beech by common consent the best. Many a good gardener 'lays down' his leaf mould heaps like vintage port. Each heap is maturing while he sleeps and often he will say 'Seventy was a good year for leaf mould'.

LIME AND LIMING

Lime is one of the substances most frequently used in gardens and, although it is not strictly speaking a plant food, its rôle in the life of the plant and in the soil is so great that it deserves special mention.

Its first importance is its relationship with other soil chemicals. We have seen that in a chalky soil there may be deficiencies of such elements as iron or boron because they have been rendered unavailable by the excess lime in the soil. On the other hand, unless there is some lime in the soil much of the phosphate and potash will be unavailable. So you should always have some lime in the soil.

Secondly, lime is an antidote for soil acidity. Acidity can arise from two causes: (a) the continued leaching of the soil and (b) the normal processes of breakdown of organic materials to humus. Most plants prefer a slightly acid soil, about pH 6·5, but when the pH drops to 4 then many plants will not prosper.

Thirdly, lime affects the structure of clay soils. These soils are composed of very small particles and the numbers and size of the particles affect drainage. Lime causes these particles to stick together, or flocculate, and so form larger crumbs with improved drainage and aeration.

Fourthly, lime can be used to reduce certain diseases such as club root (see Chapter 6).

The beginner's first problem is therefore to know if his soil needs lime, for it should only be used when needed or the result may be chlorosis. To find out a very simple test should be performed. Make a little soil into a stiff paste with water and drop the resulting pellet into a small glass tube (test tube, small bottle). Buy some hydrochloric acid (HCl) from the chemist (costing a few pence) and put a few drops of HCl on the soil in the glass tube. The acid will react with the lime in the soil and a gas, carbon dioxide, will be released. The gas will appear as small bubbles and if there is lime in the soil you will see effervescence in the glass tube. If there are no bubbles put the tube to your ear and listen, for you can usually hear a bubbling and hissing, even if the gas cannot be seen. If you get this reaction you do not need to lime the soil; if there is no effervescence the soil requires liming.

A much more sophisticated form of this test uses a series of coloured liquids or papers, and a BDH soil indicator can give a fairly accurate estimate of the actual soil pH and an idea of how much lime to add. An advanced gardener may prefer these soil-testing outfits, but the simpler method is quite adequate for beginners. It is often possible to diagnose a shortage of lime by looking at the weeds in your garden. Corn spurrey, sheep sorrel, sour dock, woodrush are all indicators of an acid soil and so of a lime deficiency. Similarly if cabbages are attacked by club root there is certainly a shortage of lime.

If you find that your soil lacks lime, then the question is how, when, and in what form to apply it. There are a few general rules about liming soil and if these are followed most troubles will be avoided. Lime in any form should always be applied to the surface of the soil since it works downwards; as it is usually slow to produce its effect the ideal time to put it on is autumn or early spring. In fact lime applied in, say, November can be lightly forked in during February or March. Do not apply at the same time as any other artificial fertilizer – it is best to put the lime on first and then leave for six to eight weeks before putting on anything else. Lastly, only apply lime when tests show that it is needed and *never* put it on azalea, rhododendron, erica or potatoes.

For the non-chemist there are a bewildering variety of 'limes' on the market, but overleaf is a simple guide:

BOOK LIST

Fertilizers and Manures: Paisley, K. (Collingridge)
Fertilizers and Manures: Hall, A. D. (Murray)
Fertilizers and Manures: H.M.S.O. Bulletin 36
Manures and Fertilizers: Smith, A. M. (Nelson)
Soil Fertility and Fertilizers: Tisdale, S. L. and Nelson, W. L. (Macmillan, N.Y.)
Farming and Gardening for Health or Disease: Howard, A. (Faber)

GUIDE TO TYPES OF LIME

TYPE OF LIME	CHEMICAL CONSTITUTION	WHEN TO APPLY	REMARKS
Chalk Ground limestone Calcium carbonate	$CaCO_3$	Autumn	A slow acting, granular and safe form. It will continue to release lime over a number of years and its granular form makes it easy to apply.
Hydrated lime Calcium hydroxide	$Ca(OH)_2$	Autumn or spring	One of the safest and simplest forms of lime. A fine dry powder easily applied at any time. Fairly concentrated.
Quick lime Burnt lime Calcium oxide	CaO	Autumn	Caustic, dangerous to handle and can damage eyes, clothes and growing plants. Only advisable for the expert as it requires slaking.
Gypsum Calcium sulphate	$CaSO_4$		Excellent soil conditioner for heavy clays. Improves soil texture very quickly.

TABLE OF MAIN FERTILIZERS: CHEMICAL COMPOSITION AND USE

NAME	CONTENT %			RATE per sq. yd.	USE	WHEN TO APPLY
	N_2	P_2O	K_2O			
Basic slag	—	17	—	8 oz.	All green vegetables	Autumn/winter
Bone meal	4	20	—	7 oz.	All green vegetables	Autumn/winter
Dried blood	7–14	2·0	1	1 oz.	Pot plants, lettuce	Spring/summer
Farmyard manure	0·2	0·4	0·5	10 lb.	A general soil improver	Autumn
Garden compost	2·0	1·0	0·5	10 lb.	Apply to all, especially sandy, soils	Summer/autumn
Growmore	7·0	7·0	7·0	2 oz.	A very safe general fertilizer	Spring/summer
Leaf mould	2	0·1	—	5 lb.	An excellent soil conditioner	Autumn/summer
Nitrate of soda	16	—	—	1 oz.	All green vegetables	Spring/summer
Peat	1·5	0·1	0·1	5–10 lb.	Little food value, but good for light soils	Summer
Poultry manure	4·0	5·0	3	4 oz.	Best mixed in compost	Growing season
Seaweed	0·2	—	1·5		A soil conditioner and source of trace elements	Winter/spring
Sewage sludge (dried)	2·0	1·5	0·1	8 oz.	A good soil conditioner	Autumn/winter
Spent hops	3·5	1·0	trace	2 lb.	Should be mixed with 2 lb. Growmore per cwt of hops	Summer
Sulphate of ammonia	20	—	—	½ oz.	All green vegetables	Spring/summer
Sulphate of potash	—	—	50	1 oz.	All green vegetables	All year
Superphosphates	—	20	—	2 oz.	All green vegetables	Spring/summer
Wood ash	—	4·0	25		Use occasionally on fruit and flowers	Autumn

4 *Planning a Garden*

FIRST STEPS

Most people have a garden thrust upon them when it comes with the house they are buying or renting. You may think therefore that there is little use in reading a chapter entitled 'Planning a Garden', but an existing garden can quite easily be altered to improve the general effect and reduce work. But before you begin to do anything at all, sit down with your wife and family and *think*. Start with the question: 'Why do we want a garden?' The answer may be 'To be a beautiful setting for the house', or 'To make the area around the house tidy with the minimum amount of work' or 'To grow all the fruit and vegetables we need' or 'To be a safe area for the children to play in'. If the last, for example, you will need a cheap, hard-wearing lawn, possibly a large vegetable garden, space for games, trees without thorns, and shrubs and trees restricted to borders or sides of the garden; but every type of use will need a different garden.

The second important question on which you must decide is whether you want a labour-saving garden or one in which you hope to spend most of your spare time. Remember that no-one gets younger, and a garden which seems easy work in your thirties or forties can be a physical trial and mental worry in your fifties and sixties. In other words *think* a lot before you start and you will avoid many mistakes.

And now what about cost? Shrubs and trees, tools and equipment all cost money and you may simply not have the money to furnish your garden in one go. If so spread your planting programme (and so your costs) over a number of years, remembering that very little if anything is permanently lost by delaying a year in a garden which may last for fifty years. Hastening slowly also gives you a chance to change your plan as you learn more about local conditions. Even more important, most amateurs tend to overplant, trying to crowd too many plants into too small a space. As time passes you will see where you have done this and simply thinning these areas out by transferring plants from one place to another will save money without abandoning your general plan.

Make sure you allow adequate space in your garden for the things you plant to grow to their full size and shape. This is especially important with trees and tall shrubs often planted along the edge of a garden next to the road to give privacy. This is a good idea, but if the wrong species or varieties are chosen, ten or fifteen years later they may be shading and darkening rooms in the house, making them damp, and in some cases even threatening to destroy the house itself. They may also spread out and obstruct the footpath and you will be put to considerable trouble to keep them in check. You must have seen houses in Victorian suburbs whose front rooms are made dark and gloomy by the wrong trees planted by owners thirty years ago. So if you plan to use trees or shrubs remember the 'expansion factor' and site them where they will not block the view or shade the house when they are fully grown.

Most gardens basically consist of a lawn, trees, paths, kitchen garden and a work or 'dirty' area. The degree of variation possible within this framework is enormous. For the small-house gardener the plan must start at the wrong end. By this I mean that nearly every house has dustbins, a drying area with clothes poles, very often a tool-cum-bicycle shed, a compost heap and often a garage. Usually the garage sites itself, and for the sake of concentrating unsightly objects together the tool-shed, dustbin area and compost heap/bonfire area are best situated near the kitchen or the back door where, hidden by a hedge or screen, they will not spoil the general appearance of either the house or garden. In planning remember that the garage (if it is not an integral part of the house) should be at the end of as straight and convenient a drive-in as possible. If a turning-space can be contrived then the dangerous business of backing out can be avoided.

In a semi-detached house the garage often divides the area around the house into a front and back garden and so the chance of a fairly long vista is ruled out. In a detached house, however, where the drive-in and garage may block one side of the house, try to leave the other side open as this enhances the feeling of space around the house.

Another very important aspect of initial planning is simplicity. Many gardens are spoilt by being too fussy, with elaborately curved flower beds and much chopping and changing every few yards. The best type of small garden creates one or at the most two effects: a vista of some kind and an element of surprise. This may sound pretentious but I hope what I mean will soon become clear.

Finally, before we plunge into detail, if you have any natural features in your garden, a large rock, a tree, a change of level, anything that takes away the sense of uniformity and gives it variation in slope or surface, then preserve it and use it as best you can. In this way you will already have created what I mentioned above (an element of surprise) and you will have taken a decisive step away from the tendency to have uniform gardens in a uniform suburb.

Gardens in cities tend to be formally designed in straight lines because they are usually small and the best impression is given by a small neat tidy garden. In the country, on the other hand, where gardens may be bigger and be surrounded by or back on to fields, a pleasant informality is an advantage and, with the clean air and usually easy access to farmyard manure and plants, most gardeners will make a main feature of a kitchen and orchard area.

GRASS AND LAWNS (see Chapter 5)

Grass is often the basis of a garden and with few exceptions forms the largest proportion of the total area. Once established it is fairly easily cut, will always look good and is a place to sit or play on. If possible you should design the garden to have the lawn visible from the windows of the room you use most with a poorer area of grass (close to the back door) available as a drying green and the larger area as a decorative or play area depending on the kinds of grass you have sown.

If possible try to connect the front and back of the house with a lawn. This gives length to the garden and increases the number of aspects of the house. For example, if the back of the house faces north, the front will face south and unless you develop one or both sides of the house you will not get the benefits of east or west aspects.

Lawns with flower beds cut in them look very attractive, but remember that every extra foot of edge has to be trimmed, so unless you are a gardening fanatic keep the edge of the lawn straight and simple. If you feel you must have a rose bed in the garden and especially in the lawn, it is better to have one large bed cut in the lawn rather than a number of small ones, and the effect of massing the roses is much more striking. However do not make the bed in the middle of the lawn; put it to one side or make a rose border rather than a bed.

Because very few mowers will cut right up to a barrier such as a hedge, wall or trellis, most lawns have to end in a border. The border should be wide enough to grow small shrubs, roses, erica, hebe, etc. (see Chapter 8), but narrow enough to be hoed or weeded from the lawn edge. This avoids trampling on the shrubs and spoiling the grass at the edge of the lawn.

If you are keen, groups of herbaceous perennials can be planted among the shrubs or at the edge of the border. Polyanthus, campanula, Michaelmas daisy are all good for this, but remember that too great a variety in one bed can lead to weeding and cultivation difficulties, so *keep it simple*.

GROUND-COVER PLANTS

There is such a wide range of ground-cover plants that it is impossible to fit them neatly into a single category such as shrubs or annuals, so I will treat them mainly as a factor in garden planning. They are part of the lazy, or the ageing, gardener's way of life, for once ground-cover plants have been safely established they are capable of looking after themselves for many years.

As their name implies, the chief purpose of such plants is to provide a cover to the soil which will no longer need attention. But there is more to them than this, for they also act as a total weed-smother. They kill weeds by keeping out the light and in the early stages you may still need to do some weeding, but later this will be unnecessary. It is important however to remember the reason why ground-cover plants are effective: they are *stronger-growing* than the weeds. Such a strongly growing plant may of course be so effective in crowding out opposition that it begins to take over parts of the garden. Many a beginner has been told of the virtues of *Lamium galeobdolon* as good ground-cover with attractive yellow flowers, only to find that it can become so rampageous as to be a real threat to other plants.

Nevertheless, well-chosen and well-sited ground-cover plants allow the beginner to concentrate on certain areas of the garden and to leave the rest to look after itself.

The best ground-cover plant is actually grass but growing grass is so specialized a subject that it deserves a chapter of its own (Chapter 5). The other plants fall into four categories: shrubs which grow horizontally, are easily controlled and are very effective; climbers such as ivy which if it cannot climb will crawl along the ground giving a dense cover; perennials which either seed freely or have some means of rapid spread such as surface runners or underground rhizomes or stems; the tussock or clump plants which do not spread like the others, but which if planted fairly close together form clumps which eventually fuse to become a solid cover. Such a plant is heather, and from well-situated plants of, say, *Erica cornea* var. Springwood White, in a few years you will get a solid mass of beautifully flowering heather which will fill a bed or clothe a sharp slope.

Although tussock plants demand weeding until the tussocks meet, and so require work, they are often the most desirable form of cover plant since they are practically never invasive. They are expensive but most can be propagated, either by splitting (p. 134) or by cuttings (p. 182) and it is not too difficult to fill a large area over a few years.

Many cover plants with rather insignificant flowers have highly decorative leaves giving interest all the year round and not just during flowering time. You can have great subtlety of greens in different clumps, though remember that the yellow-leaved varieties of most plants are not so strong-growing as their dark green glossy relatives.

Cultivation of Ground-cover Plants

It is useless to dig a few holes, put a good cover plant in each, and go away and wait for the weeds to be smothered. Cover plants, like all other plants, require soil preparation and careful planting to give them a good start. The first job therefore is to clear the ground. You can dig this by hand or by machine and, if there are a lot of weeds, use paraquat (for any weed) or amitrole (aminotriazole) which is highly effective against ground elder or couch grass. Both these substances break up very quickly, so you need have no fear of building up high concentrations in the soil.

During digging put in some bone meal or other slow-acting fertilizer, for the cover plants will be there for many years and will need food to grow strongly. Most ground-cover plants should be planted in September after keeping the ground free of weeds for the whole summer. Large clumps should be divided into smaller pieces, for you get quicker cover from many small pieces set fairly close together than a few widely spaced large clumps. Ground-cover shrubs should be planted in the normal way as described in Chapter 8, p. 164.

Until the cover is safely established weeding will be necessary. Usually this is done by hand, though if you have lots of compost or peat this can be used as a weed-smother; apply thickly to the surface of the soil between the clumps. As time passes and the clumps fuse, the amount of weeding necessary will decrease and disappear. The plants will benefit from a light annual top dressing of good compost – if they lose their vigour a top dressing of bone meal or hoof and horn meal at 2 oz. per square yard applied in the winter should revive them.

A few remarks about special areas:

Steep slopes are difficult to cover for if the ground is dug there is a danger of soil being washed downhill with each shower of rain and the plants left in the poor sub-soil. Treat the bank with paraquat to kill everything and then clear away much of the dead vegetation by hand without loosening too much soil. The plants can then be set in specially prepared holes and fed liberally in the early years until the cover is complete.

Shady places demand careful selection of plants – some such as oxalis thrive in the shade, others such as helichrysum need full sun. The amount of shade tolerated is often apparent from the leaf colour – plants with silvery or yellow and purple leaves are best planted in full sunshine, while variegated or ordinary green leaves are able to thrive in partial shade.

Boggy areas should ideally be drained but often this is impractical, so you should make a feature of them by planting aruncus, astilbe, primula, trollius etc. In some gardens there is a brook or burn whose banks can be planted with dogwood or the smaller willows, e.g. *Salix x grahamii*, which not only look attractive but also help to prevent erosion of the banks. Do not cultivate before planting as too much working can harm the soil structure; kill weeds with paraquat, especially if it is a long-neglected area. But if the wet area has only low plants growing in it then tall-growing cover plants such as *Astilbe biternata* will be effective.

Finally, when buying ground-cover plants it is essential to check on the full name and variety of them. In every plant genus there is a wide range of form and size and only a few varieties are any good as ground-cover plants, so do not go to shop or garden centre and simply ask for a few phloxes. You must be much more specific than that and ask for *Phlox douglasii* May Snow or *Phlox stolonifera* – then you will get the type of plant you are looking for. You may often have to order seeds through a catalogue and if this is the case it is best to germinate the seed in a pot or tray in a cold frame or porch and to grow the seedlings on a little before planting out in the early autumn or spring.

PATHS

A word about paths may be useful. As a rule paths across a lawn are unnecessary and create work. Lawns are made for sitting, strolling, playing, sun-bathing, etc., none of which need a path. However, you may use a regular track, say, from the French window to a favourite seat, or from the garage to the door of the house, and in this case the lawn will be trodden down and the grass killed. So a path is called for.

TABLE OF GROUND-COVER PLANTS

NAME	HEIGHT OF PLANT	PLANTING DISTANCE	COLOUR OF FLOWER (F) OR LEAVES (L)
(a) SHRUBS			
Aucuba nana rotundifolia	2 ft	3 ft	Dark green L
Berberis darwinii prostrata	18 ins.	3 ft	Orange F
Berberis candidula	2 ft	1 ft	Dark green L Yellow F
Calluna vulgaris	2 ft	1 ft	White purple F
Chaenomeles Crimson and Gold	5 ft	6 ft	Orange F
Cistus lusitanicus decumbens	1 ft	2 ft	Dark L, white F
Cornus canadensis	6 ins.	2 ft	White F, berries
Cotoneaster *horizontalis*	2 ft	6 ft	Dark green L, berries
Cytisus scoparius prostratus	2 ft	4 ft	Yellow F
Empetrum nigrum	9 ins.	9 in.	Dark green L
Erica carnea var Springwood White	9 ins.	12 in.	White, various F
Genista pilosa	9 ins.	2 ft	Yellow F
Helianthemum hybrids	1 ft	2 ft	Various
Hypericum calycinum	1 ft	3 ft	Large yellow F
Lonicera pileata	2 ft	3 ft	Purple berries
Pernettya mucronata	3 ft	2 ft	White F, berries
Potentilla fruticosa Katherine Dykes	3 ft	3 ft	Yellow F
Rhododendron forrestii repens (but many varieties)	9 ins.	2 ft	Scarlet F
Ribes alpinum aureum	6 ft	7 ft	Cream F
Rosa nitida	18 ins.	2 ft	Pink F, red berries
Rosa wichuriana	18 ins.	2 ft	White
Salix x *grahamii*	1 ft	3 ft	Yellow catkins
Vinca minor (all varieties are good)	8 ins.	2 ft	Blue F

DECIDUOUS OR EVERGREEN	HABIT OF GROWTH	REMARKS
E	Hummock	Likes shade
E	Carpet	Easy esp. in sunshine
E	Hummock	Prickly and useful as a barrier
E	Hummock	Lime-free soil, require annual clipping
D	Thicket	Tall but flowers freely and can form a dense thicket
E	Hummock	Full sun, well-drained, mild
D	Spreader	Lime-hater, shade
D	Arching branches	Many varieties hardy, likes lime
D	Carpet	Full sun, well-drained
E	Hummock	Peaty wet soils
E	Carpet	Lime-free, full sun
D	Carpet	Lime-free, full sun
E	Hummock	Sunny, well-drained
E	Spreader	Any soil, sun
E	Hummock	Not particular
E	Spreader	Lime-free, humus-rich
D	Hummock	Full sun, humus soil
E	Carpet	Lime-free.
D	Hummock	Any soil, sun or shade
D	Thicket	Neutral soil, sun
D	Carpet	Any soil
D	Carpet	Moist, sunny
E	Carpet	Well-drained, part shade

NAME	HEIGHT OF PLANT	PLANTING DISTANCE	COLOUR OF FLOWER (F) OR LEAVES (L)
(b) HERBACEOUS			
Ajuga reptans	2 ins.	18 ins.	Blue F
Alyssum saxatile citrinum	10 ins.	18 ins.	Yellow F
Anemone x *hybrida*	18 ins.	2 ft	White/pink F
Armeria maritima	5 ins.	18 ins.	Pink F
Aruncus sylvester	5 ft	4 ft	Cream plumed F
Astilbe x *arendsii* Many varieties	12–18 ins.	2–3 ft	White/pink/red plumes
Bergenia cordifolia	1 ft	2 ft	Purple pink F
Campanula- poscharskyana	9 ins.	2 ft	Blue F
Campanula- poscharskyana	9 ins.	2 ft	Blue F
Convallaria Fortin's Giant	10 ins.	2 ft	White F
Dianthus fragans	4 ins.	1 ft	White F
Dicentra formosa alba	10 ins.	18 ins.	White F
Epimedium pubigerum	1 ft	1 ft	Cream F
Frankenia thymifolia	1 ft	9 ins.	Pink F
Geranium sanguineum	9 ins.	18 ins.	Crimson F
Hemerocallis fulva	3 ft	3 ft	Soft red F
Hosta Thomas Hogg	1 ft	2 ft	Lilac F
Iris graminea	18 ins.	2 ft	Purple F
Lamium maculatum aureum	6 ins.	18 ins.	Striped L, pink F
Lysimachia nummularia	1 ins.	3 ft	Yellow F
Nepeta gigantea	18 ins.	2 ft	Blue F
Phlox stolonifera	4 ins.	18 ins.	Lilac F
Physalis Franchetii (Chinese lantern)	1 ft	3 ft	Orange F
Polygonum campanulatum	3 ft	3 ft	Pink spike F
Potentilla alba	4 ins.	1 ft	White F
Saponaria officinalis	1 ft	3 ft	White/Pink F
Saxifraga stolonifera	6 ins.	18 ins.	Pink F
Sedum spurium	4 ins.	2 ft	Pink F
Stachys olympica	4 ins.	18 ins.	Woolly L
Thymus pseudolanuginosus	1 ins.	18 ins.	Lilac F

DECIDUOUS OR EVERGREEN	HABIT OF GROWTH	REMARKS
E	Carpet	Moist soil, sun or shade
E	Carpet	Sunny, well-drained
D	Spreader	Heavy soil, partial shade
E	Carpet	Light rocky soil, sun
D	Clump	Moist or boggy soil, sun or shade
D	Clump	Moist or waterside, wide range of colour and size
E	Clump	Any soil, sun or shade
E	Spreader	Well-drained, sun
D	Spreader	Well-drained, part shade
E	Carpet	Limy soil, well-drained
D	Spreader	Shade, moist soil
D	Spreader	Any fertile soil, sun or shade
E	Carpet	Sun, rock garden maritime
D	Spreader	Prefers slight shade
D	Spreader	Any soil, sun or shade
D	Clump	Humus rich, partial shade
D	Clump	Sunshine, well-drained
D	Carpet	Shade, under trees
E	Carpet	Moist soil, part shade
D	Clump	Well-drained, sunny
D	Carpet	Well-drained, sunny
D	Spreader	Sun, fertile soil
D	Clump	Damp soil, sunny
D	Carpet	Well-drained, sun
D	Spreader	Well-drained, sunny walls
E	Carpet	Heavy soil, mild shade
E	Carpet	Well-drained, rocky, sun
E	Carpet	Well-drained, sun
E	Carpet	Well-drained, sunny

If you are starting on a *new* garden it is a good idea to have all your paths sited and if possible made before you start on the garden proper. The cardinal rule is to keep them straight and short. A winding path may be attractive, but if you work on the principle that you only make a path where one is made necessary by regular traffic you will see that utility paths should be kept to a minimum and straight.

Most planners put a path directly from the garden gate to the front and back doors and maybe one other to give access to a tool shed and the working area. These paths should be as straight as possible and sufficiently wide to take the type of traffic likely to use them. Prams may have to be wheeled or barrows pushed along them and it is annoying to find your arms caught by shrubs, or to find that you cannot walk two abreast when you have visitors. Therefore, important service paths or drives should be made wide and straight and little utility paths kept narrow and simple. In a larger garden perfectly adequate paths can be made simply by cutting grass shorter. Mowing of course is an additional labour but if the garden is big enough to allow the grass in a shrubby area to grow fairly long then only the paths need to be mown frequently. If paths cut through longish grass are too narrow you will get your clothes wet as you brush against the long grass at the sides so be sure that this kind of path is wide enough for comfortable walking and not just a narrow little track.

How do you make a path? This is done by cutting out the size you want, lining the edges of the lawn with bricks or wood or concrete and covering the path with gravel, ash, tar macadam or concrete. All these make perfectly adequate paths, but notice that you have greatly increased the amount of edging you have to do and you have also given yourself the additional job of maintaining the path.

It is easier, cheaper and more effective to make a stepping-stone path by buying some concrete slabs (or making them, see p. 68), and sinking them in the lawn at appropriate distances. To do this, walk the necessary distance counting your steps and dropping a stone on the grass where your feet land. You then count the stones and mark the footprint areas. Depending on the

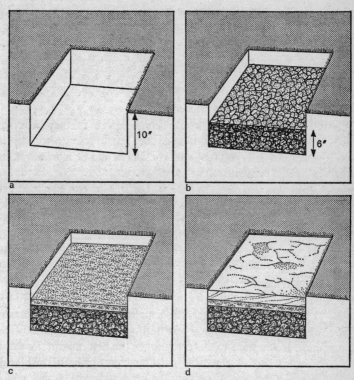

6. *Laying a slab path: (a) Dig a hole for the concrete flag or slab.
(b) Put in a rubble foundation. (c) Cover with a 2 in. layer of sand and pack
it all well down with a rammer. (d) Lay the flag with its surface just
below the surrounding grass.*

size of concrete paving slabs needed you can then get the right
number.

At the location of each step (or two if the slabs are large) cut out
the area of a paving stone. The hole should be about six or eight
inches deep and the bottom covered with ashes or rubble and
simazin to kill weeds. This in turn should be covered with a layer
of fine soil or sand and packed well down with a rammer. Lay the
flag carefully on top so that its surface is just below the surrounding grass. This serves two purposes – you will be able to mow over

67

the top without damaging the mower and the grass will creep over the edges of the paving stones and take away the hard concrete outline. If the slab wobbles at all when you stand on the corner, lift it up and adjust the sand surface.

MAKING CONCRETE SLABS

Not everyone will want to make concrete slabs for they are relatively easy to buy and not too expensive, but if you are willing to try your hand at it, you may gain confidence and be more adventurous in garden construction.

Firstly, concrete slabs must be 'cast'. I have to give the warning that concrete is very heavy and it may be simpler to cast a lot of smaller slabs than a few large ones, and be very sure that each slab can be lifted and moved without too much strain. Slabs $1\frac{1}{2}$ ins. thick are perfectly satisfactory for most jobs, although if the area of each slab is more than 4 sq. ft a thickness of 2 ins. is better (here again remember the weight factor and be sure you have a strong friend!).

The actual concrete can be bought ready mixed as a powder to which you add water and mix until you have the required consistency. If you want to make your own, the best mixture for this purpose is 1 part of cement : 6 parts aggregate or ballast. This aggregate is a mixture of very coarse sand and small stones which in coarse ballast may be $1\frac{1}{2}$ in. in diameter and in finer ballast not more than $\frac{3}{4}$ in. Coarse ballast is perfectly satisfactory for garden work. To simplify the actual quantities, 1 cwt of cement mixed with 6 cwt of aggregate or 1 stone of cement with 6 stones of aggregate will give the correct proportions.

If you are making slabs 2 ft × 2 ft × 2 ins. ($\frac{1}{6}$ ft) then the volume of each slab is $2 \times 2 \times \frac{1}{6}$ cu. ft $= \frac{4}{6} = \frac{2}{3}$ cu. ft. But aggregate loses $\frac{1}{4}$ of its volume when mixed with water so that for your slab you will need $\frac{2}{3} + \frac{1}{6}$ to make up the loss; that is, about 1 cu. ft of aggregate. To make the calculation easy let's say you require 12 slabs. You will therefore need 12×1 cu. ft of aggregate $= 12$ cu. ft. The amount of cement is one sixth of this, i.e. 2 cu. ft of cement. But 1 cwt of cement is $1\frac{1}{4}$ cu. ft so you will have a little to spare. In all cases you work out the amount of aggregate and then calculate the cement in relation to that. The order should therefore be 12 cu. ft ($\frac{1}{2}$ cu. yd in round figures) of mixed aggregate and 2 cwt of cement; you now have your prime material to hand.

A less accurate but suitable mixture could be equal parts of cement and sand and 4 parts of small chippings. This will be strong enough for most purposes, but even here the calculation of quantities can be tricky. If you are a complete beginner it is best to work in 'bucketfuls' or 'shovelfuls' for parts and see how far you get with the material you have bought before you order for the complete job.

Making the Concrete

Concrete must be made on a hard solid surface and never on the bare earth. Usually a board called a banker board is used for mixing or it is done on a concrete floor. Irrespective of which you use, it must be washed off and cleaned immediately after use. The aggregate, say 6 shovelfuls, should be placed on the board first, then the correct amount of cement dusted with the shovel over the top. The heap should then be thoroughly mixed by repeated turning over. To do this systematically, start at one side of the heap, push your shovel in along the banker board and turn over the cement and aggregate it contains. Gradually progress round the heap doing this and you will find that after the third or fourth circuit the heap has become a dull grey. If it is still patchy in colour, more mixing is necessary.

Once mixing is complete it is time to add the water. You give 1 gallon of water per cubic foot of aggregate, i.e. about 10 shovelfuls. The water should be added a little at a time all over the heap and mixed in between additions. When the correct quantity has been added the concrete will be not too 'runny' and a handful will 'ball' up and keep its shape when pressed. You must rinse your hands immediately after this.

Now you have a heap of correctly made concrete on the banker board or the garage floor and all that remains is to pour it.

Making a Form

A 'form' is simply a mould into which you will pour the concrete and leave it to set. The beginner can make a series of forms at the spots where he wants the slabs and simply pour the concrete *in situ*, or he can make one form and use it to make a series of slabs. This latter method is slow as you have to wait until each slab sets before you can lift it out of the form in order to pour the concrete for the next slab.

If we assume that you are making a series of slabs to form a stepping-stone-type of path, then it is simplest to dig out the areas where the slabs will be poured. Wooden boards of the same depth as the required slab are held in position, with wooden pegs driven into the ground, to contain the concrete. Each area is then bottomed to a depth of 2–3 ins. with broken brick, clinker ash or some other hard-core material and thoroughly consolidated with a rammer. It must be well beaten down, or the spaces will swallow up the concrete and the path will be costly. Many amateurs put a layer of sharp sand on top of the hard-core to seal off or 'blind' it. It does not matter a great deal in a stepping-stone path if all the steps are not exactly the same size or shape, so you have a certain amount of latitude. The wooden form can be given a coating of old engine oil to stop the concrete sticking to the wood.

Pouring the Concrete

The order of manufacture is to make the forms, bottom the area(s) with hard-core, mix the concrete and then pour the concrete. The last is the really satisfying job. Barrow the concrete to the area where it has to be used and put a heap at one end of the form. Then use a straight piece of wood 2 in. by 4 in. (the tamper) to level off the concrete with the top of the form. In doing this start at the heap and gradually smooth the concrete down, adding more if necessary until the form is completely filled. The tamper should be banged on the surface of the concrete to get rid of air bubbles and give a nice level surface. Leave the surface a little rough as it may be slippery in wet weather if it is too smooth.

To make a continuous path, do as above, except cut out and bottom the whole path. Then concrete alternate blocks or do the whole path as one slab.

Some words of advice may be useful. Firstly, never keep concrete wet as it 'goes bad' in a matter of an hour or so – too solid, and does not set well if disturbed again. Secondly, bottoming is tedious but essential to a good solid job. Thirdly, always add the water a little at a time, for overwet concrete will be weak; you can always add more water but cannot take it away.

GREENHOUSE

By now you should have finished most of the preliminary thinking. The garage is sited, so are the tool shed, dustbin area, drying green and paths, and you can think of the garden proper. If you want a greenhouse remember that its function is to provide not only heat and protection to plants but also light which would not be available in a heated room. The ideal situation, therefore, is an unshaded open part of the garden with the greenhouse running east/west so that light from the south falls along it and not on one end. A small greenhouse is usually put near the house where it can be reached without too much exposure to the elements. It is also an advantage to site the greenhouse near the tool shed which may be used for storing compost, seed boxes, tools, etc.

VEGETABLE GARDEN

Where you put the vegetable garden is a matter of taste. Many like it conveniently near the house; others, because it often looks untidy with rows of vegetables ripening off or some still uncut or collected, prefer to locate it further away where it will not spoil the general effect or appearance of the property. There is a good argument on each side, but in general one can say that if the total garden area is small there is no point in trying to hide a vegetable garden and it might as well be located where it is most convenient and where soil, drainage and light conditions are best. If you have a lot of space it is much easier to develop the kitchen garden further away from the house in a suitable area, screened by trees, a hedge or fruit bushes.

The purpose of a vegetable garden is to produce food and it would be silly to have the kitchen garden in a poor infertile part of the garden. Drainage is also important. A kitchen garden on a south-facing gentle slope is ideal, but very few gardens have this and if you have a badly drained clay soil then it is probably better and easier to scrap the idea of having a vegetable garden at all and use the area for fruit bushes or trees after dressings of compost. Most people have 'poorish' soils which makes the decision more difficult. If drainage is the problem, liming and artificially improving the drainage will help, but if the problem is shade with no hope of removing the cause of the shade, you will regretfully have to dismiss the idea of a vegetable garden.

The best vegetable gardens are rectangular. This allows you to have straight drills of known length so that you can judge the amount of each crop. It makes the application of manures, etc., easy to calculate. The drills should not be too short or there may be a lot more work than is necessary in staking; if they are too long, however, one row of cauliflowers may be more than you can use and you will be forced to change the crop half-way along a drill. Two differing crops in the same drill can create problems of weeding, disease control and harvesting. Maximum light is necessary for good vegetables, and drills running east/west get the most benefit from our southern sunshine.

FRUIT TREES

In a large garden it is relatively easy to find a fertile area not too close to the house, but sufficiently visible to enable you to ward off the attacks of small boys and to appreciate the beauty of blossom time. In a small garden, however, there are many problems in growing fruit and particular attention must be paid to pollination in choosing varieties. Details of cultivation are given in Chapter 9, and if space is at a premium it is quite possible to have dual-purpose hedges made up of blackcurrants, gooseberries or even dwarf apple trees. Many fruit trees can be grown against a wall, trellis or other framework as an espalier or cordon-type tree (see Chapter 9), so that the tree is made to grow as a single layer of branches (rather like a climber on a house) and can cover ugly walls or act as a dividing screen between the lawn and, say, the vegetable garden.

Alternatively a 'family' tree can be bought and simply used as a feature in a circular bed cut in the middle or at the far end of the lawn or even in a flower bed, though this creates shade problems. A family tree consists of a root stock of one apple variety on to which a number of different scions, or shoots of other varieties, are grafted. For example, the stock may be a dwarfing stock such as Malling IX and on to it may be grafted an early and a late eating apple and an early and a late cooking apple. This tree would have four main branches each bearing a different kind of apple, and is thus ideal for very small gardens.

Remember too that fruit trees can be bought on different root stocks to guarantee trees of different sizes. A large garden can easily accommodate apples on a vigorous stock with the tree reaching 20–25 ft, but this would dominate and destroy a small garden, whereas dwarfing stock or a bush tree may only reach 10 ft high and so be suitable.

GARDEN ORNAMENTS

There is considerable scope for the use of materials other than plants in a garden and I shall call all these things garden ornaments. In larger gardens seats, trellis-work, pagodas, fountains, sun-dials, statues and so on can all be interesting. For example, a circular area of concrete is very dull indeed and means very little, but a stone trough or a sun-dial in the centre looks very attractive.

Containers of many kinds, from barrels to painted oil drums, with appropriate plants can be used to break up dull areas. Many attractive and long-lasting pieces of stone or metal work can be bought cheaply.

Let it be said straight away, however, that lots of little gnomes or toadstools or boys fishing simply give the impression of a play corner for the kiddies and should be avoided by serious gardeners. They are all right in their place and can be made the focus of a fun corner in a garden, but as the main feature they defeat their own purpose and give a source of uneasy restlessness rather than quiet serenity. If you decide that you need some kind of focus in your garden, wait until you find the thing you want rather than clutter the place up with lesser things. One or, at the most, two objects are enough in any garden.

Many gardens provide some privacy and so an area of terrace or even a simple flagged path can be installed near the house. Here you can sun-bathe, have tea in good weather and, if there is room, put up deckchairs. You may ask, 'Why not sit on the grass?' and the answer is because of our very changeable weather. It may rain all morning and clear into a fine afternoon or evening ideal for sitting on the lawn, but the grass may be wet and soft and damaged by too much traffic.

Garden pools are now cheap and can be very nice. They are plastic, usually with an irregular outline, and are sunk in the lawn. I have seen three small pools connected on a slope and used to create a series of little waterfalls. A motor pumps the water back up from the bottom to the top. Few gardeners will go to this trouble, but for a few pounds a shallow pond can be made and used to grow marsh or water plants.

Finally, a lot of hard work as well as thought is involved in planning a garden. Many beginners shy away from anything that involves construction work of any kind because they have never done it and are afraid to start. I felt very much like this until a grass bank became so slippery that I was forced to build a flight of steps about four feet high. A friend advised me (and did most of the work) but in one short week I learned a lot about concrete and building and although I am not an expert I am no longer afraid of paths, steps, terraces or walls. So if you have something you want to build find someone with the necessary experience to help you and you'll certainly enjoy it.

FINAL PLANS

All the components of the garden have now been described and the plan you draw up should take into account most of the points I have tried to make. But each garden is a different thing and each house owner has a mind of his own and maybe different problems of size, shape and form which he will solve in his own way. Therefore, although I cannot tie the whole thing up in a nice formalized package, two specific examples may be useful.

Detached Bungalow

The first is a completely detached bungalow surrounded by a little flat ground. In the usual fashion this area is unequally divided by the house into a front and a rear area. Here is the rough plan of such a garden.

(1) First we place the garage and the driveway to it. Note that the drive has been widened to allow a turning space.

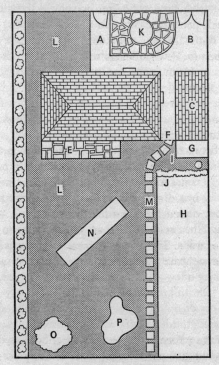

A   path
B   drive – in
C   garage
D   shrub border
E   patio
F   trellis with gate
G   tool shed
H   kitchen garden
I   dust bin
J   low hedge of fruit bushes if house faces South
K   standard rose or other shrub in crazy paving
L   lawn
M   sunken concrete slab path
N   flower or rose bed
O   small tree or other feature
P   pool or prostrate shrub

7. *Plan of a detached bungalow with long narrow garden.*

The Penguin Book of Basic Gardening

(2)   Then we decide to have a kitchen garden. This could be behind the garage where it would not be visible from the road – a trellis with a gate (or hedge) could close the gap between garage and house and act also as a screen for dustbins, tool shed, etc.

(3)   The rest of the garden will be for leisure, so we think of grass. But grass alone can be monotonous and the very regularity of the area demands some changes of pattern. This can be achieved in many ways, e.g. some concrete slabs from the Roads Department of the local council (or make your own, see p. 68) could be laid to form a patio outside the back of the house; a single rosebed of fair size could be placed across the lawn at an angle; or, if the area is too small to stand such a bed, a single tree (apple or flowering cherry) can serve to break up the area.

(4)   The garden is now in at least four parts, each of which could be different; for example, the front: the path should come straight from the gate to the front door, but the area can be either grassed or paved leaving spaces for a few dwarf shrubs. The grass should continue round the side of the house so that anyone standing on the road and looking in would see to the end of the back garden. Here I would suggest you have some particular feature, say a seat, a standard rose, a colourful shrub. Notice that any of those would also be visible from the house along the slanting rosebed.

(5)   The main lawn between the patio and the kitchen garden, untouched so far save for the rosebed, could be left as another piece of grass. Alternatively it could contain a small plastic pool set in the grass, or another small bed of annuals, or a prostrate juniper or berberis growing above the grass as a further feature.

(6)   The last thing will then be to decide how you are going to define the edges of your garden. This is usually done with hedges (see p. 170) – however, they do make work and require clipping, so many people are now planting a few small shrubs in a relatively narrow border and filling it in with ground-cover plants if necessary (see p. 58). This will be a personal decision affected by your neighbourhood, the animals around, the degree of privacy required, and so on. So I would advise you to keep hedges for essential borders, and then to limit them as much as possible.

Additional details

(7) Once you have a basic plan you can gradually add to it, say with a few good trees or even one. These can provide privacy or hide any particularly ugly view. One point: if you choose to plant trees, do so well away from the house and remember that you have neighbours who in some years' time may be affected by them; consider also how they will affect other people, their light, view, etc.

(8) You can get a great deal of pleasure from construction work. With cheap building blocks and ready-made concrete almost anyone can do a passable job. There are a number of books on construction work with details on how to make steps, paths, patios, terraces, retaining walls and so on, all for amateurs without any technical training (see list, p. 79).

Small Semi-detached House

The second house I want to consider is small and semi-detached with a long thin garden set in a row of near-identical houses. Here the problem is difficult for the house is not central in the garden and the opportunity for variation and surprise may be limited. The site could be represented as shown overleaf (Fig. 8):

(1) Again place garage and driveway. The garage could be lined up with the house and a trellis put in with a gate to close the gap. Behind the trellis are the tool shed, dustbins, etc.

(2) If the site is narrow it is often better to have the path to the front door leading off the driveway – a path of sunken slabs will do for this. Where the garden faces the road there could be a low wall and a shrub border along the common boundary with your neighbour.

(3) The remainder of the front could be lawn if it is large enough to justify cutting, but if it is a very small area cover it over with flagstones or concrete and leave a few spaces for standard roses or a shrub or two.

(4) Now the back of the house; a good rule is to treat small areas in a very formal way (i.e. in straight lines or circles) and large areas in an informal way. So let's decide on a vegetable garden and see what happens. Of course the whole garden will be immediately

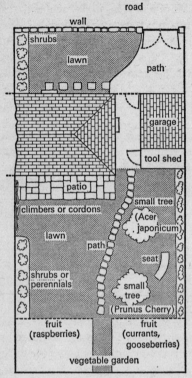

8. *A simple layout for the garden of a small semi-detached house.*

visible from the house so, rather than have the kitchen garden next to the house where it will dominate the situation, put it at the far end of the garden and again screen it with fruit or shrubs.

(5) The lawn, if it's not too narrow, can have shrub borders at each of the side walls and will need a path (able to stand the weight of a wheel-barrow) stretching from the back door to the vegetable-growing area. Unless the space is very limited a small tree such as a flowering cherry or a coloured *Acer japonicum* could be planted to break up the lawn, with spring bulbs around its base. In a very restricted area, a bird bath or small seat could be used instead. The points worth remembering are (a) if a tree is going to be planted,

put it in such a position that it cannot form an obstacle in the path and (b) be sure to put the tree where it will not shade the vegetable or fruit area and not so near the house as to spoil the view of the garden itself.

(6) If there is a wall between the gardens, you can fix a trellis at some point and let a climber (e.g. a rose) ramble up it. This helps to break the wall up and stop the garden looking like a long thin tunnel.

(7) In very thin gardens, with dividing walls as in rows of terrace houses, the light will almost certainly be bad. If your garden is like this cover most of the area with flagstones and simply leave a large central bed where bright colourful plants – such as petunias or roses – can be planted.

BOOK LIST

Gardening in Window Boxes and Other Containers: Fletcher, H. L. V. (Pelham Books)
Town and Roof Garden: Field, X. (Collins)
Garden Design: Crowe, Sylvia (Country Life Ltd)
Garden Making by Example: Taylor, G. C. (Country Life)
Garden Design: Midgey, K. (Penguin Handbook)
Design Your Own Garden: McCleod, Dawn (Duckworth)
Designing a Garden To-day: White, J. E. G. (Studio Vista)

5 The Lawn

Almost every garden has a lawn of some kind, for a nice green lawn not only looks nice but is also a place where children can play and, with luck, you can sit and relax over tea in the summer. A bad lawn is a source of constant work and worry but a good lawn, mowed regularly, is a very easy part of the garden to maintain.

Another important point is that lawns are a relatively permanent garden feature. Once a lawn is made it is very time-consuming and costly to re-make it or to remove it, so a great deal of care should be put into the planning stages in order to be sure that you have what you want where you want it and at a reasonable cost.

PLANNING THE LAWN

Most beginners think lawns are made of grass and that is that. They either forget or do not realize that there are a number of different types of grass and, depending on the purpose of the lawn and the dedication and purse of the gardener, good lawns can be made from many different grasses. Thus in a new house it is advisable to consider why you want a lawn.

Firstly, do you want it as a decoration, a nicely mown deep green sward in summer, free of weeds, and rather like the frame of a picture? A place on which the dog and the children are not allowed? If so, you will want the finest grasses and should be prepared to devote some time to weeding, edging, etc. You will also need a relatively expensive mower, for only the best tools can keep a lawn in a state of perfection.

But maybe all you want is a goodish bit of grass on which the family can play cricket or chase a ball. Maybe your wife will hang a clothes line across the lawn or beat a path across it to the side gate. It could be that you are only free to cut it at week-ends and have little time to weed it and keep it in good condition. In this case cheaper grass will do perfectly well and the lawn should be placed where it is easy for children to get to it, but where the ball (and most children play ball games) will not too easily get on the road and so be dangerous. A 'play lawn' for children or general family use should be near or next to the house but decorative lawns can be further away.

Finally, you may just want some grass to tidy up a corner; in that case, almost anything will do and it would be a waste of money to buy expensive seed.

Another point to remember in planning is that the *edge* of the lawn is the most difficult part to keep looking good. You should try therefore to be sure that your lawn is shaped and placed so that it is not too difficult to use an edging tool or shear, and also that the *length* of edges is kept to a minimum. Here you have to make another decision. A lawn in the shape of a rectangle has nice straight edges, is easy to keep tidy, but looks rather dull, whereas a lawn with curved edges, say surrounded by a shrub border, is nice to look at but much more difficult to maintain because of its greater length of edge.

PREPARING THE SITE

When you have decided the type and shape of lawn you want, the next step is to prepare the site. You may be simply converting a piece of a field and if so your task is very easy, although the result is always less than perfect. This type of lawn is dealt with later. But if you have moved into a new house you may be faced with a wilderness which it seems quite impossible to connect with the nice plan you have drawn on a piece of paper.

Firstly, clear the site of rubble, stones, pieces of wood and debris of any kind (the Housing or Cleansing Department of the local authority may help you here), for grass does not grow very high and it does your mower no good at all to hit a half brick at the first mowing. This clearance may take some time and patience but the lawn will be there for many years; it pays to be careful and painstaking at first as your troubles will be fewer later on.

When siting the lawn, try to choose a flat level situation as

The Penguin Book of Basic Gardening

slopes are very difficult to cut, and usually have a dry baked area at the top and a wet squelchy area at the foot. If your whole garden slopes then you could try to level it off with *top soil*, which can often be bought from a local builder. Once again, if you want a 'picture lawn', levelling is very important and should be done with a six-foot plank, spirit level and pegs; if you are the 'play' or 'coarse' lawn type, levelling by eye is reasonably satisfactory. If the lawn is small and on a quick slope, build a small retaining wall of precast concrete blocks (which you can later clothe with a climber) at the face of the slope and make the soil surface level behind the wall.

The most important point is drainage. If a lawn is badly drained, for example, by being on clay or under trees, it will quickly lose its grass and grow moss. To construct a very good lawn under such conditions you should ideally mix coarse ash with the lower six inches of soil, put a three-inch layer of coarse sand on top of that and then four inches of light loamy soil to form the surface in which the grass will grow. This is vital to ensure good drainage.

But most people cannot or do not really need or want to go to all this trouble unless they are on very heavy clay. It is often enough to dig a few herring-bone trenches about two feet deep and, say, six feet apart in the area where the lawn will be. All the old brick-bats, stones, etc. can be put in these trenches and the soil replaced. This will act as a simple drainage system provided you can remember the basic principle that water runs downhill and point the main trenches and the herring-bone feeders in the right direction. Many people provide a sump or outfall for the main drain by digging a deeper hole into which the water can flow and fill this also with rubble before resoiling. (You need not be afraid about putting bricks two feet under a lawn, for the area is unlikely ever to be dug and they will stay under for very many years). The principles of drainage are outlined in Chapter 1.

Finally, the surface soil should be prepared. The essential here is to enrich the top layers with well-rotted manure if possible – if this is not available use a dressing of lawn fertilizer at 2 oz. per square yard. The surface should be raked thoroughly, preferably after a shower of rain when the soil is a little damp so that any lumps break down easily. It is worth persevering until the entire area is broken down to a fine tilth. On a dry day the area should be made firm by treading and then the surface lightly raked again.

These are a lot of instructions and they may seem over-elaborate and fussy, but just remember that nearly all the work in a lawn comes in the initial preparation and if you do that well, the grass will take over for the next twenty years and your troubles will be few.

CHOOSING SEED

The best lawns are composed of a mixture of fine-leaved grasses which can stand a fair amount of drought and near-starvation. These grasses are the bents (Agrostis) and the fescues (Festuca). In their natural state these grasses form the closely cropped turf found by the sea or on a mountain and the more they are cut, and to a certain extent starved, the better they grow. They produce very fine lawns like golf course greens, but unfortunately under normal conditions in Britain they gradually disappear and are replaced by rather coarser grasses such as Annual Meadow Grass (*Poa annua*). Poa is the grass in the majority of British gardens and most people starting a new lawn should simply accept that in the end the lawn will be largely Poa anyway and therefore buy and sow a grass mixture based on this grass. Such a mixture contains finer grasses, but since it is based on common Poa it is cheap and perfectly satisfactory. The cheapness of this mixture (say 35p per lb.) means that the sowing rate can be 2 oz. per square yard and many weeds will be crowded out.

Many readers will have seen lawns on which the flowering spikes of one of the grasses stand up six or nine inches above the ground. These are the seed-heads of ryegrass and anyone who wants an average to good lawn should avoid this grass like the plague and buy 'ryegrass-free' mixtures. The ryegrass seed-heads are very difficult to cut and if they appear on a lawn they should be dug out as though they were weeds.

However, gardeners with a small corner to cover which will be used as a drying green would be pouring money down the drain to buy even ryegrass-free mixtures. Just buy the cheapest lawn seed you can and sow it quickly. This will provide a green covering and constant mowing will eventually make it a presentable area.

To summarize:
(1) For a very good lawn use a mixture of bents and fescues and sow at 1½ oz. per square yard.
(2) For a better than average lawn use a ryegrass-free mixture at 2 oz. per square yard.
(3) For a 'working' lawn use any lawn seed at 2 oz. per square yard.

SOWING LAWN SEED

The first thing to do is to calculate the size of the lawn. With a rectangular lawn this is easy, for the area in square yards is the length in yards multiplied by the breadth in yards. (Area in yards² = L × B in yards.) Many lawns, however, are not ideally shaped. There are

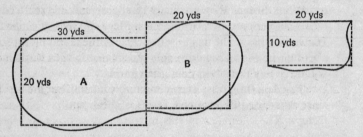

9. *The approximate area of irregular shapes can be measured by turning them into rectangles whose area can be easily calculated. The dotted lines in (a) and (b) indicate ways of squaring off the irregular shape.*

elaborate formulae which help you to determine the area of an irregular shape, but I think that the best way for the average man to determine the area of an irregular patch of ground is to treat it as if it were a rectangle or even two rectangles (see Fig. 9).

You may get too high a figure but unless the discrepancy is enormous this does not matter; it is better to sow seed too thickly rather than too thinly.

The actual process of sowing is important, but very simple if you follow two elementary rules. Always bulk up the seed by mixing it with at least an equal quantity of fine sand or soil – only an expert can sow 2 oz. per square yard and spread the seed evenly and thinly. It is much easier to sow 4 or even 8 oz. of a seed/sand mixture per square yard; if you get that evenly spread you will start off the lawn more uniformly.

The next thing to do is to divide your seed/soil mixture in two equal halves. Then try to cover the whole area with the first half. When you have done that, then repeat with the second half, this time sowing at right angles to the first sowing. If you walked north–south during the first sowing, walk east–west in the second. This prevents you from sowing the seed too lavishly at the beginning when you have a lot of it and then finding as you finish that you have to sow more thinly or, even worse, have run out of seed. Alternatively the area can be marked off in strips and the appropriate quantity of seed sown for each strip.

When the seed is sown it should be lightly raked in and if possible covered with a thin layer of fine soil or sand. Many experts then advise rolling it with a light roller. This is fine as it firms the surface and buries the seed, but be sure the roller is a light wooden one – a heavy iron roller will do a lot of harm.

The date for sowing a lawn is not very critical, but the best times are September/October or mid-March/mid-April.

EARLY CARE OF A SEED LAWN

Many weeds will certainly come up before the lawn seed has germinated and become established. Most of these are unimportant and will be killed when you start mowing the lawn. If, however, there are coarse *grasses* it is advisable to weed them out as they can be a pest for many years.

When the grass is about three inches long it should have its first cut. The first cut of new lawn grown from seed should never be done with a lawn mower for unless the mower is perfect (and very few mowers are) the grass plants may be pulled out at the roots and much damage done. Use shears or a scythe and let the clippings fall on the soil and stay there. If for some reason a mower must be used the blades should be set high and the grass box taken off. Thereafter regular mowing is needed but it is always better to keep the grass a little on the long side because a lawn which is very closely mown will tend to have the surface skimmed off it at the top of small ridges. Such skimmed areas will soon be bare and will be ideal places for moss and weeds to become established and ruin the look of the lawn.

MAKING A LAWN FROM TURF

If large quantities of good cheap turf are available from a local builder, garden centre or turf supplier (see Yellow Pages for the latter), this can be a quick way of getting a lawn. The best time for laying turves is in the autumn, preferably September or October, but nearly any time during the dormant season will do, provided the soil can be worked into a good condition. Otherwise preparation is the same as for a seeded lawn and should produce a flat, even surface, firmed to avoid future hollows and then raked fine to allow the roots of the turf grass to penetrate. Turves should be of an even thickness, usually $1\frac{1}{2}$–2 ins., and about 18 × 12 ins. in size. The turves should be laid touching each other, but with the joints staggered as on a brick wall or parquet floor. It is usual then to tread or beat them down to establish good contact between the bottom of the turf and the soil below, but if the area is flat and well raked this is not really necessary. Fine soil and sand should then be sprinkled over the whole area and brushed into the cracks between turves. This prevents drying out at the edges in hot weather and allows the roots to grow into these areas, binding the whole more tightly together.

MAKING A LAWN FROM A FIELD

It is surprising how easy it is to make a perfectly passable lawn from a meadow or pasture. Such a lawn will of course never be first-class but if the area is large or for play this may not matter. Naturally in the beginning it will contain many weeds of pasture and forage grasses but these will either mow out or fine down once the area is mown regularly.

The essential thing is to have a good power or a rotary mower. The latter is best as it can cut from any direction and the flailing action of the blades will slice through the toughest seed head. So all you need do is start cutting. The first cuts should not be too close and if the original herbage was long the cut grass should be raked away and either composted or burned. Successive cuts can be shorter until by the second year you should be cutting at the desired height.

Since this type of lawn is derived from an agricultural pasture the area will have been well fed and manured. *Do not feed* again for about four years by which time the grasses should be in a hungry soil which will encourage fine lawn grasses and not the coarser agricultural types.

FEEDING THE LAWN

There are many ideas about feeding lawns, but perfectly satisfactory results can be obtained by light feeding twice or at the most three times a year. The important thing is to feed early in the spring when growth is just beginning. In this way fine grasses are encouraged whereas agricultural grasses, which begin growing a bit later in the season than the fescues and the bents, face severe competition when they start their growth. A good guide is to feed in the first week of March in the south of Britain and a week later for every 150 miles north of London.

Any lawn fertilizer will do, but it is cheaper to buy sulphate of ammonia and calcined sulphate of iron and mix them with peat or sand in the proportion of ten parts sand: one part sulphate of ammonia: half a part sulphate of iron. Apply at 1 oz. per square yard. Another application of this dressing in late May, and, if growth has been vigorous, again in early August will do for the annual treatment. Additional autumn dressings are given to golf courses and bowling greens, but they may encourage disease during the winter, so amateurs who cannot take the necessary precautions can very well omit this dressing.

DRAINING AN ESTABLISHED LAWN

More than twenty-one years of answering questions about lawn problems have convinced me that most arise through bad drainage. This can kill grass and produce moss, weeds, algae and many other mishaps. If you move to a house with an established lawn which is badly drained you will have to make the best of a bad job. If your soil is clay, or very low-lying, you can also expect trouble.

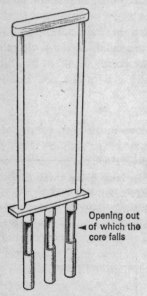

Opening out of which the core falls

10. *A hollow-tine fork.*

The best answer to the drainage problem is the 'hollow-tine fork' (Fig. 10). This is a fork with hollow tines (or prongs) which when pushed into the turf takes out little cores of about $\frac{3}{8}$–$\frac{3}{4}$-inch diameter. Spiking a lawn with a hollow-tine fork is very hard work as cores should be taken every nine inches, but it gives very good results as it provides hundreds of holes to improve both drainage and aeration. The deeper the holes the better the job, but that will depend on your eagerness and strength.

There is little point in making the holes unless you prevent them from collapsing, so when spiking is complete spread a thick layer of *very coarse* sand over the lawn. Brush this in so that it accumulates in the tine holes and so keeps them open. Within two months the holes will have disappeared from view as the grass will have filled them in on the surface but they will still be there as thousands of little drainage channels, each helping the grass to grow and the moss to decrease.

Hollow-tine forking should be done in the autumn after the last cut – by the spring the holes will no longer be visible and the lawn will look the better for it. If bare patches have developed, a little seed can be mixed with the coarse sand and the seed will then germinate in the holes and thicken up the lawn.

UNEVEN OR BUMPY LAWN

This condition means that the hollows in the lawn are missed by the cutter blades and the hills skimmed. The simplest remedy for small hollows and furrows is to apply a thick top dressing of finely riddled sand and compost over all the lawn in the autumn, enough nearly to hide the surface. The winter's rain will wash this into the hollows and the grass will grow through the new surface. If you want to lower a ridge or a small hill, make an H-cut in the lawn

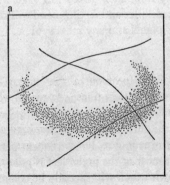 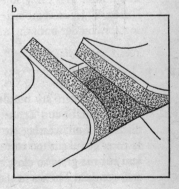

11. *Levelling a lawn.*

over the hill and fold back the two flaps so as to expose the bare soil (see Fig. 11). Then take away the offending soil and true up the surface, replace the flaps, tread it all down and cover with a good sprinkling of sand or fine compost. This method can of course also be used to raise low areas.

WEEDS

There are so many selective weed-killers on the market that no one need have a weedy lawn any more. Daisies, dandelions, clover, yarrow and all the common lawn weeds can be eliminated without harming the grass by one or two applications of the appropriate selective weed-killer. Put these substances on when the weeds are growing well – usually May or June – to get the maximum kill. Weed-killers should always be applied on a still day – wind causes spray to drift, possibly damaging not only your own but also your neighbours' gardens and you would be liable for any loss.

MOSS

Most lawns contain a little moss, but it only becomes objectionable when it begins to take over from the grass. It is often a sign of bad drainage or aeration, and hollow-tine forking will help the situation in autumn. You can also apply some mercurized turf sand in the spring. This is a combined weed-killer and fertilizer and will kill or severely hinder both the moss plants and any moss spores.

MOWING THE LAWN

Many gardeners are puzzled about how often and how close the lawn should be cut. There is no simple answer to this as it depends on soil, season, weather etc. – the only rule for the average domestic lawn is never cut too close. If in trying to avoid frequent cutting you cut the grass so close that most of the green leaf is gone, you will get dead patches in the lawn which will speedily be colonized by moss and weed. Close cutting also carries the danger of 'scalping' the top off little hills on the lawn surface, again allowing entry to weeds. Don't start any close mowing till May.

The more often a lawn is cut the better, for cutting discourages many coarse grasses and encourages the desirable fine-leaved ones. Mr Average, however, should settle for once or twice per week in the summer and less often during spring and autumn. In Britain in December, January, February and March lawns are usually very wet and the temperature is below that at which grass grows, so no cutting is needed.

Every winter mowers, especially motor mowers, should be sent to be sharpened and serviced – there is nothing more frustrating than to be all ready on a spring morning to give the lawn its first cut and to find that you cannot start the machine.

The appearance and even the health of a lawn and the enthusiasm of the gardener can be vitally affected by the type of mower he uses. A well maintained motor mower, of which there are now many on the market, makes cutting the grass a quick, easy job. A heavy mower, or one inadequate for the job, can so dampen enthusiasm that mowing is put off until the last moment and the lawn deteriorates.

There are three types of mower, each with virtues and vices.

(a) Cylinder Mowers

This is the standard, old-fashioned mower in which the cutting blades are borne on a cylinder behind which there is usually a roller. These are undoubtedly the 'quality' machines, and the lawns at Wimbledon and the greens at St Andrews are cut with cylinder mowers to produce the striped effect so beloved by suburbia. The quality of the mower, however, may vary greatly. The best cylinder mowers have eight to twelve cutting blades, ensuring a very even cut; poorer quality (and cheaper) machines may only have five. With this smaller number, some patches of grass are bound to be missed and the surface left uneven and so unsuitable for championship golf or tennis. The height is also important – in a good mower this can be adjusted with a lever, whereas on inferior machines it may require loosening screws or nuts and readjusting the blades and the sole plate.

Most cylinder mowers come complete with grass box into which the cut grass is automatically fed. This is useful on heavy soils, but on light sandy soils may be unnecessary – though no good lawn should have dead grass lying around on it, and gardeners should use a box most of the time for the best effect. If the grass is long, however, a box is a 'must'; long and especially wet grass lying on a lawn may kill the turf beneath and encourage disease.

Cylinder models may be either hand- or motor-operated, and nowadays motor mowers are so reliable that if you can afford one (and they can be very cheap) it is foolish to stick to the old 'push' type. The only exception to this is if you have a tiny irregular lawn on which the amount of turning makes a motor machine inefficient.

(b) *Rotary Mowers*

These have two or four blades borne on a circular metal plate revolving at very high speed. The plate revolves parallel to the surface of the lawn and so cuts the grass. The height of the plate in relation to the surface of the ground is variable so that the height of the cut can be adjusted. Rotary mowers can be dangerous because of the high speed at which the blades revolve and so are housed in metal casings protected on all sides except that next to the grass. All rotary mowers are powered, but in some only the blades are driven and you have to push; in others, including all the larger models, the engine both propels the machine and cuts the grass.

For rough work, e.g. a coarse lawn, paddock or field, the rotary mower is ideal. It will cut long grass which would choke a cylinder mower and can be used to keep a large area tidy with ease. In addition, a rotary will cut wet grass and is good on slopes.

On the other hand, few rotary mowers produce the closely cropped effect of the traditional mowers, and very few collect the cut grass. Recently, however, a new rotary has appeared on the market with an efficient grass-collecting system (unless the grass is very wet) and a roller behind the blades. This machine gives a close cut and a good appearance, and set at varying heights is a very good dual-purpose machine. For the finest lawns, however, there is so far no rotary which approaches the cylinder mowers.

(c) *Floating Mowers*

Lawn mowers which work on the hovercraft principle are now widely used and deserve comment. These are rotary mowers which are 'floated' off the ground surface on a cushion of air and so meet little or no resistance as they 'hover' over the grass. The rotating blades cut the lawn and in theory one has a very simple, light and effective mower.

In practice, however, there are snags. It is very difficult to attach a collecting system to small models of this type of mower, so it leaves cuttings in its wake; floating mowers cannot give a perfect finish although they may be very good for rough work; the recommended way of using this mower is to tow it behind you, and it is very difficult to see what you are doing unless you walk backward (which is dangerous), or go very slowly. There is the added danger of the extreme lightness of the mower – it moves over the surface of the ground so freely that it is possible to pull it across one's feet inadvertently and cause severe cuts. Stout shoes should always be worn when using a floating mower and the maker's instructions carefully followed.

This type of mower is, however, manoeuvrable. For example its ease of manipulation makes it ideal for steep banks and it will cut almost vertical slopes if used in broad sweeps from a fixed point at the top of the slope. It can also cut awkward corners and around trees and shrubs with ease. It will go right to the edge of a lawn and is a moderately efficient edging tool. Finally, it can be used to cut grass between concrete flags on a path.

This is not a tool to be used as the sole means of obtaining a good lawn, but as a good, easy, reliable mower for difficult slopes and awkward shapes it is absolutely first-class and it produces a reasonably satisfactory stretch of grass.

For all-the-year round instructions about lawn mowing and care see the Gardening Calendar starting on p. 260.

BOOK LIST

Lawns: Dawson, R. B. (Penguin Handbook)
Lawns: Dawson, R. B. (Amateur Gardening Handbook (Collingridge)
Turf Culture: Greenfield, I. (Leonard Hill)

6 Vegetables

Not long ago everyone knew how to garden and grow his own vegetables; you could hear boasts that so-and-so did not need to buy them from one year's end to the next. If one leaves out the cost of labour, growing vegetables is a very cheap way of getting food and also allows much more variety than fresh or frozen foods which, because of the requirements of marketing, tend to be rather uniform in size and flavour, and limited in variety. Many high-quality vegetables simply cannot be found in the shops because they are low-yielding, do not keep or travel, and so are not a very good proposition for a farmer who has to think of factors like labour costs. Golden Wonder potatoes, for example, are very rarely seen. In addition, new domestic deep freezers now mean one can not only eat one's own vegetables fresh in season, but also store away any glut for later in the year.

ORGANIZING YOUR VEGETABLE GARDEN

Most vegetables are best when grown steadily and quickly. Plants which are slow in reaching maturity are often tough and not so well-flavoured as those grown rapidly. A vegetable plot therefore needs a number of special qualities, as far as the area permits.

Firstly, it should be on a gentle south-facing slope. In this way it will get the heat of the early sun, water will not lie on the surface of the soil, and it will be protected to some extent from cold north and north-east winds. The sunniest and the best-drained area will naturally be the spot where growth begins and is most rapid so it should be reserved for early crops. Try also to avoid shade and drips from overhanging trees.

Secondly, if there is a choice of site, it is best to locate the vegetable plot near the kitchen, as vegetables have to be picked and gathered in all weathers and on a wet day it is much easier if the walk in the rain is short and dripping vegetables are not carried through the house. If you plan to grow a few herbs such as thyme or mint or parsley, station these immediately at the kitchen door, where the cook can pick a few sprigs whenever necessary.

Thirdly, the plot should be given straight edges if possible and provided with a good path or paths. The ideal shape is rectangular so that all the drills can be straight lines to make sowing or planting easy. Many small gardeners prefer to screen the vegetable plot from the rest of the garden and maybe even from the house; if you do this, arrange the screening plants (which can be low fruit bushes or cordons) so that they shed the minimum of shade per day.

Having chosen the best site for the vegetable garden it is important to think about crop rotation before digging or applying fertilizers – your whole soil treatment may depend on what system you adopt. Crop rotation basically means not growing the same crop in the same soil year after year. For example, if you grow potatoes every year in the same part of the vegetable garden, that area of soil will gradually be depleted of the food materials specially needed by potatoes and the rest of the soil fertility will be wasted. Secondly, potato roots feed at a particular level in the soil and so the layer of soil in which they grow will become nutritionally poor, instead of all the soil being used equally, and you will end up with a poor layer in what might be fertile soil. Thirdly, the pests and diseases which attack potatoes will always find potato plants immediately available and there will be a gradual build-up of trouble. Finally, there is a certain amount of evidence that plants excrete waste products and that if these accumulate through continued cropping with one plant they may very badly affect further growth of the plant. So when gardeners say that the soil is 'potato sick' or 'rose sick' they mean that continued monoculture (i.e. growing the same crop continuously year after year) has produced all the above effects to such an extent that the crop can no longer be grown economically.

All these troubles are avoided by adopting a rotation. There are many different types of rotation but generally a system which will permit the same crop to return to the same area of soil every three or four years is perfectly adequate. These are called three- or four-course rotations. The 'three-course' is the best for a small garden. The plot is divided into three areas and the system on page 98 followed.

A *four*-course rotation could be planned as follows:

Year 1:   Potatoes, spring cabbage; manure in autumn, no lime.
Year 2:   Peas, beans, leeks, shallots, celery; manure in autumn, lime.
Year 3:   Carrots, parsnips, beet, etc.; no manure, no lime.
Year 4:   Cabbage, cauliflower, broccoli, sprouts; manure, lime.

In each case there is a three- or four-year gap before the same crops return to the same area.

You may be thinking 'What about lettuce or radishes?' These can of course be grown in drills as an ordinary crop, but it is often easier and more economic of land to use them for 'intercropping', i.e. to use the space between the rows of, say, potatoes or peas. By the time the main crops are shading the ground between the drills the lettuce and so on are ready for eating. Lettuce, spring onions, radish, globe beetroot are all useful as intercropping plants.

Finally, something must be said about 'successional sowing'. If you choose one variety of pea or potato or any other vegetable, and sow the seed or plants all on the same day, the whole lot will be ready for eating roughly during the same week a few months later, thus giving you no peas throughout the year except for two weeks in July, when there is a glut. Successional sowing avoids this 'famine-and-glut' situation. There are two ways of spreading a crop over a longer period of time. The first is successional sowing proper, i.e. by sowing part of the crop at intervals throughout the growing season: if you plan to grow four rows of peas, you sow one row at the appropriate time, wait until the seedlings are showing through the ground a week or ten days later and then sow the second row, after ten days the third and so on. This not only spreads the crop but if you are attacked by drought, or pigeons, or disease, you may lose one or even two of your sowings, but you will be very unlucky indeed if you lose all four.

The second method is to vary the variety so that you have early, mid-season and late varieties. Thus early peas should be ready about ten or twelve weeks after sowing, while mid-season peas

YEAR 1

Plot	Crops	Treatment
A	Potatoes, Leeks, Swedes, Turnips	Manure heavily. No lime
B	Cabbage, Cauliflower, Sprouts	Manure in autumn. Lime in winter
C	Carrots, Parsnips, Beet, Peas, Beans	Little food necessary. No lime
	ONIONS	Manure
	Rhubarb	

YEAR 2

Plot	Crops	Treatment
C	Carrots, Parsnips, Beet, Peas, Beans	Little food. No lime
A	Potatoes, Leeks, Swedes, Turnips	Manure in autumn. No lime
B	Cabbage, Cauliflower, Sprouts	Manure in autumn. Lime in winter
	ONIONS	Manure
	Rhubarb	

YEAR 3

Plot	Crops	Treatment
B	Cabbage, Cauliflower, Sprouts	Manure in autumn. Lime in winter
C	Carrots, Parsnips, Beet, Peas, Beans	Little food. No lime
A	Potatoes, Leeks, Swedes, Turnips	Manure heavily. No lime
	ONIONS	Manure
	Rhubarb	

need twelve or fourteen weeks. You therefore sow earlies in March/ April and the main crop in May/June, and are sure of peas from mid-June until late August or September.

PREPARING THE VEGETABLE GARDEN

The standard practice is to prepare the kitchen garden during the autumn and winter so that all is ready for spring planting and sowing. Care should be taken not to dig in wet weather since this 'puddles' the soil or, more technically, destroys the soil structure. Digging in frost should also be avoided, for soil is a very good insulator against heat, and if you turn over frozen soil and put a frozen slab of earth eighteen inches below the surface, it will be late in the season before that layer of soil is thawed; plants whose roots go into it before it is completely thawed may suffer a check or even die.

It is very easy to rush into digging and think it is simply a matter of disturbing the soil and that will do. In a new garden – or even an old one – the whole process of vegetable growing can be made easier by good digging; the actual manual labour is also less onerous if digging is done the proper way. The worst problems occur on clay soils, which are heavy and wet and no easy matter to turn over. Drainage is sure to be bad here and this should be tackled at the same time as the plot is being dug.

Let us assume that you are starting from the very beginning with an area of rough uncultivated ground scattered with bricks, tin cans and so on. The first thing to do is to heap the bricks in a remote corner (they may come in useful for filling drains, bottoming paths, etc.). Then collect the broken wood etc., and burn it, and put the tins and bits of iron by the dustbin for collection. Any weeds or brambles should be scythed down or the weeds killed with paraquat (dosage on the packet). This weed-killer is harmless to the soil, has no residual effect and kills all green material in a week. Woody dead shrubs can be pulled out and burned and the top skimmed off either for the compost heap or for digging in.

There are two very important things about digging: get a good spade (see p. 8) and work slowly. It is a mistake to rush at it and

The Penguin Book of Basic Gardening

end up with a stiff back and incapable of working for a week. If the soil is clay or the garden is new then double digging is worth the trouble; if you have a light or sandy soil it is unnecessary.

The area to be dug should be marked off with a line and the digging begun by taking out a trench 18 ins. wide and 1 spit (10 ins.) deep. The soil from this trench should be heaped along the far side of the plot. For double digging the bottom of this trench should

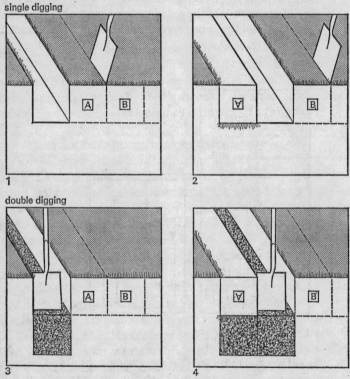

single digging

1   2

double digging

3   4

12. *In single digging (diagrams 1 and 2) a trench is dug and the soil taken to the other end of the plot. The next spit (A) is inverted into this trench leaving a second trench into which (B) can be inverted and so on. Double digging (diagrams 3 and 4) is exactly the same except that the next spit in the first trench is forked or spaded over before (A) is inverted on it. The base of the second trench is then forked over, and so on.*

now be forked a further 10 ins. deep and any manure or lime worked into this lower level (see Fig. 12). For single digging it suffices to scatter the manure over the face of the dug surface. You should then go back along the undug portion and start a second row about 6 ins. from the first. It is a great temptation to try to take big spade-fuls, but this is very tiring and in the end you will get through much more digging by taking 4–6-in. slices than by trying to move very large ones. If you are right-handed the best way to dig is to grip the top of the spade with the right hand and put the left hand well down the shaft. Hold the spade vertical and then, putting your left foot on top of the blade, force the spade vertically into the soil one spit deep (see Fig. 13).

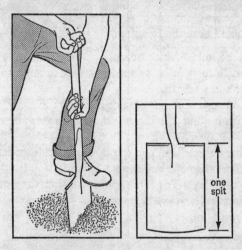

13. *The best way to dig.*

Many gardeners then lift the spadeful of soil and invert it in the trench, while others think it is quite adequate to break it up a bit without inverting. Certainly, if there are a lot of weeds, inversion may help to kill them but, if the soil is fairly weed-free, breaking up will do amply.

As you carry on digging the second row you will see that the soil from row 2 is going to fill trench 1, and that row 2 is now becoming trench 2, which will be filled by soil from row 3 and so on. This technique of moving the soil forward is very simple and leaves you with a trench at the far end into which the soil from row 1 should be put. The method also allows you to incorporate manure, fertilizers, lime, etc., into the soil and to remove any weeds or stones dug up in the process. It also gives the feel of the soil and shows any variation in it.

There are other digging systems, such as bastard trenching, but these are refinements and the beginner should stick to single digging except in the first year or on heavy clay soils.

Finally, never try to leave the dug soil smooth and tidy. It should be left as rough as possible and the weather, and especially the frost, will help to improve clay soils before the spring comes.

To sum up: there are a number of very important '*don'ts*' about digging which should never be forgotten.

(1)   *Don't* dig if the soil is wet or frozen.

(2)   *Don't* dig with a rusty or heavy spade. Be sure to buy a spade fitted to your size and strength.

(3)   *Don't* try to do all your digging in one day. Start off every year with one hour's digging and then increase that as you get more supple.

(4)   *Don't* take huge spadefuls. You can take two small spadefuls with much less effort than one large one.

(5)   *Don't* dig in thin shoes. To get the spade easily into the ground you need the oldest and heaviest boots or shoes you have.

SOWING AND PLANTING

Gardeners *sow* seeds and *plant* plants or tubers or bulbs and, although the two terms are often mixed, correct usage will be maintained here.

Seeds

Many amateurs buy seed by the packet and find it difficult to know how much is needed to sow a small patch. They usually overestimate in the beginning and are left with lots of unused seed which they keep for the following year in the hope that it will be all right. This is a false economy as it deteriorates. Seed is fairly cheap and fresh supplies should be bought each year. Information about quantities is given in the second part of this chapter, p. 111ff.

The best plan is to start with a catalogue on seeds and choose the varieties which are well flavoured and if possible early or very late – there is little point in having a garden full of cauliflowers or beans when they are at their cheapest in the shops.

Seeds need moisture to germinate and grow and the surface layers of soil may dry out very quickly. For this reason the seed bed should always be broken up, reduced to a fine tilth and firmed – only in this finely divided, but firm condition will the layers of soil close to the surface hold enough moisture for germination, yet allow the young seedlings to reach the light.

Depth of sowing is very important. Vegetable seeds are small and, when they germinate, the food contained in the seed must be sufficient to sustain the young plant until its leaves are above the soil surface and it is self-sustaining. If a small seed is sown too deeply, the seedling may never reach the surface and just die. There is no hard and fast rule for all vegetables under all conditions but, generally speaking, small seeds should be simply sown on the surface or in very shallow drills while larger seeds such as broad beans can be sown two or three inches down. (For further details about drilling, see p. 111ff.)

A common mistake is to sow the seed too thickly. If most of the seeds germinate (as they usually do) a nice-looking and dense green row of seedlings will emerge. Such a row is deceptive, as each tiny seedling is in fact struggling to survive in competition with all the others – each plant gets a reduced water and food supply and often reduced light. The lack of light is most significant as it causes the seedlings to be etiolated or drawn. Drawn plants are tall but soft and floppy and they are very vulnerable to disease. Sowing should therefore be done as thinly as possible with a single row of seeds along the drill.

No matter how thinly one sows seed, there is never enough room for all the plants to come to maturity and yield a crop, so they have to be thinned. The purpose of this is to reduce the number of plants and to space them so that each has sufficient room to yield the maximum crop. Thinning is not simply a process of pulling out unwanted plants – you should make sure that you are leaving the sturdiest plants (*sturdy*, not *tall*). In many cases, e.g. leeks, carrots or onions, the thinnings can be eaten as part of a salad. A common practice is to make an initial thinning to space plants at half the final distance apart and then a later one to establish the final distance.

In the case of carrots or onions, thinning should always be done with care and with the minimum of soil disturbance, for the carrot fly and onion fly are attracted by the scent of broken or damaged plants. Don't leave the thinnings lying among the crop, but take them away and put them on the compost heap.

Plants

With vegetables such as cauliflowers, sprouts, leeks, etc., the average gardener may not want to start with seed, but may buy plants from a garden centre or shop. A word or two about buying plants: again, do not be misled by size. Obviously you will not buy tiny, midget, poorly grown plants, but do be sure that the plants you do buy are sturdy and dark green (not light yellow). If you are buying plants such as tomatoes, choose them with short joints between leaves (internodes) and in all cases ensure that the roots are in a ball of soil or at least in a waterproof plastic bag. Many cases of plants bolting or going to seed are the result of young plants being allowed to dry out on the market stall and so suffering a severe check.

Planting must be done very carefully. Many gardeners simply dig a hole in the ground, drop the plant in, fill in the hole and move on to the next. This is a speedy method, but it leads to many failures. There is no point in being unnecessarily fussy about planting, but there are some obvious points which will make success more likely. Firstly, plant at the correct depth, making sure that the roots and the base of the stem at least are completely covered with soil. It is better to plant too deeply than too shallowly, but usually the soil level at which the plant has been grown can be seen and the hole should be just deep enough to accommodate the roots and have the soil surface at or above this level. The hole should be sufficiently deep to allow the roots to be well spaced and not cramped or doubled back on themselves.

A good routine for planting is as follows. Do the job on a day when the soil is moist. Using a trowel, make an appropriately sized

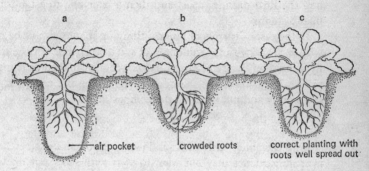

a   b   c

air pocket   crowded roots   correct planting with roots well spread out

14. *Planting out.*

hole, remembering that roots spread sideways as well as downwards; hold the plant firmly in the hole with the root extended; gradually fill with loose soil firming it occasionally with your hand or the trowel handle (see Fig. 14). When the planting hole is full firm down with your feet and water the plant. You should then have a good 'take'.

This may sound a lot of fuss about a very simple job, but with experience it can be done much more quickly than it can be written about and good, firm planting pays dividends when the crop is mature.

With cabbages or leeks a dibber can be used in place of a trowel. This is a short pointed stick about as thick as a spade handle (it is easy to make one from an old broken spade,) which when pushed into the soil leaves a neat hole. Cabbage plants are then dropped into the hole and the dibber plunged into the soil again about one inch from the original hole. If it is then levered towards the hole the soil drops around the cabbage roots and the hole is filled. It can then be trodden firm.

FERTILIZERS AND FEEDING

Chapter 3 (pp. 38–54) will have given you an insight into the value of fertilizers and so only a few practical points have to be made here.

For practical reasons it is best to add organic materials when the soil is being dug in the autumn. Ideally it should be well rotted, but it is often difficult to manage this and if you put the manure in in the autumn it will have all winter to break down. Organic materials can also be added to the surface as a mulch in early summer – this acts as a protection against drying out, the number of weeds is reduced and it can be dug in in the autumn to be ready for the next crop. You should spread the farmyard manure or compost throughout the whole depth of the row, so when digging don't lay the manure in the bottom of the trench, but scatter it on the face of the dug soil facing you so that it is spread at different depths.

Most gardeners also use so-called 'artificials'. These are chemical mixtures which give the plant a variety of food materials. Experts use special mixtures for different plants – any good store will sell special mixtures for roses, lawns, potatoes, tomatoes, etc. For beginners, a simple mixture such as Growmore or John Innes Base Fertilizer is sufficient.

This basic fertilizer is normally added to the soil a week or two before planting and should never be applied at the same time as lime. Quantities are usually given in ounces per square yard (oz./yd^2) – estimate the area to be treated and scatter the appropriate quantity as evenly as possible. In dry weather water well before putting on the fertilizer – this helps to dissolve it and carry the food materials down to the roots. If it is a small dose increase the bulk with a fairly large quantity of an inert material such as sand or compost, mix the fertilizer evenly through it with a shovel, and then spread the whole mixture; this prevents the first part of the area getting too much fertilizer and the later parts too little.

One is often advised to give a feed while the crop is growing. This is a bit difficult, as care has to be taken to avoid solid fertilizer landing on green leaves. It should be scattered by hand up the drills at soil level, preferably in the evening when dew may help to wash it into the soil, or before rain if you can judge this accurately.

WEED CONTROL

The best way of controlling weeds in a vegetable garden is hoeing. Most weeds can be killed chemically but many crops are equally likely to be damaged or even killed unless special precautions are taken to avoid splashing.

So consider hoeing first. The most useful type of hoe is the 'Dutch hoe' (see Fig. 15) which is pushed to and fro just below the soil surface. This cuts the stems of weeds or even uproots them. Used with care, a hoe can be a precision tool and good gardeners

15. *Using a dutch hoe.*

can hoe right up to the stem of, say, a cabbage, killing all the weeds but leaving the cabbage absolutely untouched. Most gardeners find it easiest to do their gardening in the evening when they come home from work, but hoeing should be done early in the day whenever possible. This does not apply to damaged or uprooted seedlings, which grow again if they are given a cool dewy night during which to recover; but if they are hoed in the morning and have to endure a whole day of wilting and bright sunshine their chance of recovery is very much reduced. Hoeing should also always be done in dry weather for, if there is rain, weeds easily develop fresh roots and start growing again.

Chemicals are fairly simple to use with shrubs, fruit bushes or paths but a few hints are needed for vegetables. Firstly, gardens infested with couch grass (twitch, scutch, quickens) should be treated when the ground is being dug – fork out the roots and destroy them and treat couch grass with Dalapon after the crop has been lifted. Secondly, you can use the method of 'pre-emergence' weed-killing; when you sow a crop there is an interval, about ten days or more, before the plants reach the soil surface, and in that time many weed seeds on the soil surface will have germinated and can be killed with paraquat. Some potato growers plant their tubers, wait until the first potato leaf appears just above the ground (indicating that the rest of the potatoes should be through in a few days) and then treat the soil with paraquat. This kills off all the weeds, does very little damage to the potatoes and the crop gets off to a clean start.

Finally, heavy mulching with peat, compost or even sawdust will smother weeds and help soil fertility. Make sure that your mulch does not actually touch the crop; if a tender crop such as lettuce or peas is being grown, you may be forced to protect the plants against slugs which have come in the compost. There are many slug killers on the market which, while not achieving complete control, will very substantially reduce damage.

CLOCHES

Cloches are long low sections of glass or plastic used to cover certain crops to shelter them from the elements. They do a number of useful things: the temperature under a cloche is always higher than outside so that the growing season can be extended by about two weeks at either end. This means that early crops can be sown under cloches some time before they could be outside and so give earlier yield. Lettuce and peas are often started under cloches.

Cloches also give some protection against cold winds and pests and diseases. It is, however, important to realize that they keep the rain off the soil and so there may be too little water for the plants unless the soil is moist to begin with and preferably rich in organic material. Since it is useless to have a high air temperature and a low soil temperature it is advisable to have the cloches in position for at least two weeks before the crop is sown or planted – this allows the soil to heat up and growth is then immediate.

If there is high wind the cloches must be firmly pegged down and, if possible, the ends sealed with board or plastic. This stops the wind from blowing in and making the cloches into a wind tunnel, and also helps to keep out small animals such as mice, which have been known to eat their way along a row of peas growing nicely under the cloches' protection. Growers often place a mouse-trap at each end of the cloches.

COLD FRAMES

A cold frame is a very useful addition to a garden with its multitude of uses. For example, it will protect tender plants in frosty weather, or grow early spring vegetables or half-hardy annuals for summer bedding. It can also be used for crops such as melons or early lettuce or for striking cuttings. In fact, it is a very easily made garden accessory.

The simplest frame is a wooden box with the bottom knocked out, placed on good soil and covered with a sheet of glass or polythene, providing a little protected area where tender things will flourish. Usually, however, frames have brick or wooden sides about three feet high at the back and about one foot at the front. This means that the glass or 'light' is sloping and allows condensation water to drain down to the base of the frame rather than dripping on the plants. In addition, the slope of the glass means that if you face the frame to the south or south-west it will get the maximum of light and heat.

There are a few rules about cold frames which will ensure that you get the maximum advantage from them.

(1) Be sure to give ventilation every day (except in severe frosts) by raising the light on to a block of wood or even lifting it off.
(2) In summer take the light off altogether.
(3) Feed the soil well and keep it moist but not wet.

(4) If you are building your frame, excavate the soil to a depth of about one foot and work in plenty of clinker or ash to be sure the drainage is good. The soil should be returned and fed for the crop in question.

From early February vegetables such as lettuce, carrots and radishes may be sown and later early cauliflower will do well. It is important only to use varieties which have been specially bred for frame culture to get the best results.

In frames, scrupulous cleanliness is essential, as old dead leaves lead to slug invasion and diseases such as botrytis; the soil should be changed each year and as leaves yellow and begin to decay they should be taken off the plants and put in the compost heap.

STORING AND KEEPING CROPS

Vegetables are best eaten fresh, but some crops can be safely stored for considerable periods. If the amount is relatively small the crop can be put in bags and stored in a cool (but frost-free) dark place. Onions and shallots can be made into 'ropes' by tying each onion by the neck and hanging them in a frost-free place. Other vegetables such as beans and peas can be deep-frozen, but their preservation is a culinary rather than a gardening problem.

Large amounts of potato-type vegetables can be stored in a

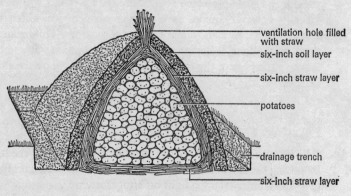

ventilation hole filled with straw
six-inch soil layer
six-inch straw layer
potatoes
drainage trench
six-inch straw layer

16. *Cross-section of a potato clamp.*

clamp (see Fig. 16) as follows. First the crop should be dried in the sun and any showing signs of damage or disease discarded – one bad potato, swede or carrot can rot the whole lot. Select an area which is level, well-drained and will not be flooded. Put on a thin sprinkling of lime (to improve drainage) and cover with straw to a depth of about 4 inches. Pile the crop on the straw to form a heap with sloping sides, and cover the whole with a 6-inch layer of straw. Place over the straw a 6-inch layer of earth, usually taken from a trench dug around the clamp. Beat this soil down smooth except for a few points at the top, where you should place a few vertical tufts of straw, rather like chimneys, to carry off moisture and gases. If well made, the crop will not get frosted and can be used right into the New Year; in fact it is a good idea to open the clamp at a few places in February to see that all is well – if there is no trouble you simply take out the vegetables you need and re-seal the clamp.

LIST OF VEGETABLES

In this section of Chapter 6 I have tried to give a summary of the cultivation of the common vegetables. Obviously, therefore, many rarer sorts and the niceties of growing giant vegetables for show are omitted. I trust that the directions are simple and the other details will help you to buy wisely and furnish your vegetable garden simply but well. A table of vegetable cultivation is also given on p. 128ff.

Beans

(a) Broad Beans

Broad beans are the hardiest of beans and like a well-drained soil into which manure has been dug the previous winter.

Planting: 1 pint of seeds will sow 60 feet of drill. There are two ways of growing broad beans. One, sow in the autumn, placing the seeds 2 ins. deep and 9 ins. apart with 18 ins. between the rows. If these are protected through the winter, either by cloches or in a relatively frost-free part of the garden, they will mature early. Two, seeds can be sown in March or April and simply allowed to come to maturity.

Cultivation: Beans are very much improved by applications of superphosphates at 1 oz. per square yard and sulphate of potash at ½ oz. per square yard to the soil before sowing. They should be hoed to keep weeds down, and after four clusters of flowers have appeared the tops of the plants pinched out. At this stage the plant is usually about 18 in. high. This pinching out is important as broad beans can be badly attacked by blackfly which damages both the young shoots and the developing pods. If the young tip is removed the blackfly cannot find a place to live and so the pods are unaffected. If there is any sign of blackfly give a dressing of Derris. If there is damage by mice set traps along the rows. Tall varieties should, of course, be staked (see p. 138).

Varieties: There are two types of broad bean: Longpods, suitable for winter (November) sowing, and Windsor, suitable for spring sowing.

Longpods:	Seville Improved Longpod	(early, heavy cropper)
	Masterpiece Longpod	(very good quality)
Windsors:	White Windsor	(very good quality)
	Harlington White	(heavy cropper)

(b) Dwarf, Kidney or French Beans

Planting: These are relatively tender plants and should not be sown out of doors until the risk of frost has passed. A half-pint of Dwarf Beans will sow 80 ft of drill and, depending on the area of the country, the sowings should be done from April until June. Seeds should be 2 ins. deep, 6 ins. apart with 18 ins. between the rows.

Cultivation: these are very shallow-rooting plants and need good drainage with lots of protection against direct sunlight on the roots. For this reason, well-manured soil and heavy mulching will always improve quality. Weeds should be kept down and nitro-chalk at ½ oz. per square yard applied during July.

Varieties:

Dwarf:	Masterpiece	(good quality)
	Black Prince	(heavy yielder)
	Canadian Wonder	(late to mature)

| Processor | (stringless) |
| Royalty | (heavy cropper, freezes well) |

For dry storing (haricot-type): Comtesse de Chambard.

(c) Runner Beans

These are grown for consumption in the late summer or early autumn but are eminently suitable for storage in a deep freeze, and so can be grown in quantity.

Soil: runner beans demand tender treatment. The soil should be light and well manured the previous autumn. A dressing of lime should have been given.

Planting: since this is not a hardy type of bean they are not usually sown out of doors until mid-May or early June, when the seeds should be put 2 ins. deep and 9 ins. apart in drills separated by 15 ins. An alternative is to place the seeds about 15 ins. apart in squares and train the plants to grow up bamboo canes rather like tent poles so that the canes meet in the centre and the beans hang down into the 'tent'. Lastly, you can sow two drills of runner beans 6 ins. apart, place stakes at intervals along this double drill and use wire netting supported by these stakes on which the beans can climb.

Cultivation: Since these are climbing plants, early staking is absolutely essential, for if the pods rest on the ground they will be damaged by insects or bruised by rubbing against hard surfaces. Beans like a dressing of nitro-chalk at 1 oz. per square yard while growing and, of course, weeds should be kept down by hoeing. If the weather tends to be dry, a good surface mulch will ensure continuous growth and prevent bud drop; if the weather is dry when the plants are in flower, spraying with a fine jet of water will help to set the flowers and so produce a crop of pods. Never leave old pods on the plants as this reduces the number of tender young pods which are the ideal ones for eating.

Varieties:

Tall:	Scarlet Emperor	(good quality)
	Prizewinner	(very good exhibition variety)
	Kelvedon Wonder	(early)

Small: | Kelvedon Marvel | (very early)
        | Dwarf Scarlet | (good quality)

Broccoli

Soil, planting and cultivation the same as for cauliflower (p. 118).
Broccoli is hardier and easier to grow.

Varieties:
Roscoff | (quality, cut November–April)
Early Feltham | (white head, mature January–February)
Early Purple
  Sprouting | (cut Christmas–March)

Brussels Sprouts

This is one of the best winter vegetables and deserves to be grown
much more widely than it is. It requires a long season of growth
and fairly good treatment.

Soil: Brussels sprouts yield most heavily in a good deep loam
which has been well dug and heavily manured the previous autumn.
In addition, a good basic fertilizer such as National Growmore is
often incorporated just before planting time at a rate of 2 oz. per
square yard. Like all other Brassicas, the soil for Brussels sprouts
should also be heavily limed the winter beforehand.

Planting: 1 oz. of seed will produce 2,000 plants. Brussels sprouts
can be grown from seed, sown in March and then transplanted to
the permanent site when the plants are about 3–4 ins. high in
May or June. It is much more common, however, for growers to
buy plants and simply to put them in the garden in late May–early
June, with about 2 ft between plants and 3 ft between rows. Each
plant should be carefully and deeply planted in the soil, preferably
at the bottom of a V-shaped drill and throughout the growing period
the soil should be kept as firm as possible. If Brussels sprouts are
grown in a light, puffy soil the sprouts open out and are not appe-
tizing – they are then said to have 'blown'.

Cultivation: since sprouts have to last through the winter they
should be fed in July and August, either with a liquid feed or with
1 oz. of potassium nitrate per square yard; weeds should be kept

down by hoeing and at every opportunity the soil around the plants should be made firm in order to prevent blowing. It is especially important to keep the soil firm in areas where there is a chance of wind-rock, as this often breaks the roots and so causes a deterioration in the sprouts.

The crop is usually gathered in winter, preferably after a frost. The sprouts should be cut and not pulled and one should always start at the base of the plant and work up. It is also good practice to collect a few sprouts from a number of different plants at each picking and not entirely strip one plant. Early sprouts can sometimes be picked in October but main crops can be picked until April.

Varieties:

Peer Gynt	(early)
Cambridge 5	(late, good quality)
Jade Cross F1	(very early, heavy cropper)

Cabbage

Soil: the recommendations given for cabbages apply to the whole of the cabbage family, the Brassicas, and so apply to Brussels sprouts, cauliflowers, broccoli, etc. In every case the ground should be heavily limed with up to 6 oz. of lime per square yard and should be dug in the autumn and allowed to consolidate for the whole winter so that it is not loose or puffy. A dressing of a good general fertilizer at about 2 oz. per square yard is necessary just before planting.

Early or Spring Cabbage

Planting: early cabbages are usually sown in late July or August and the plants put out in the garden in September–October. Beginners should buy good sturdy plants rather than try to rear their own from seed. Set the cabbage plants out in rows at intervals of 12 ins. with 2 ft between the rows. Make sure when planting that the roots are not bent or distorted under the ground and that the plants are very well firmed in by trampling around the base of the plant. Soil should be drawn up to the base of the stem. In periods of excessive frost the ground will become puffy and light and should be trodden down again to firm it.

Cultivation: very little needs to be done to spring cabbage other than to make sure that the plants are firm and, in February or March, when growth is beginning again, to give a light dressing of a general fertilizer or sodium nitrate at 1 oz. per square yard. These cabbages should then be ready to cut for eating in March–April.

Varieties:

Durham Early   (large heads)
Unwins Foremost   (good quality)
Ellams Early

Summer Cabbage

Soil: these do best in a rich soil in an open position, limed as for spring cabbage above.

Planting: good plants should be bought and planted out in April or early May at intervals of 12–18 ins. with 2 ft between the rows.

Cultivation: as there is usually a lot of weedy growth during the summer the crop will need hoeing to keep down weeds during the growing period. They may well suffer from cabbage root fly (maggot) or club root, in which case the first sign will be wilting during the heat of the day. These problems are very difficult to control or cure, but calomel dust around the base of the plant will help. If the trouble has appeared in previous years it is a good plan to dust the soil round the base of the plants with calomel dust when the plants are put in. In difficult districts summer cabbages are often planted at the bottom of a V-shaped drill and the soil then successively drawn up to the stem of the plant. This promotes the growth of roots from the stem and if earlier roots are attacked by root maggot or by club root the new roots will often carry the plant through the season.

Varieties:

Velocity   (early)
Favourite   (quality)
Primate   (good quality)
Golden Acre   (very early)

Winter Cabbage

Soil: as above.

Planting: winter cabbages are planted in July or August to ripen and be available during the winter. They are usually large plants and therefore should be spaced at intervals of 2 ft with 2 ft between the rows. Because they are large they are very likely to be moved by strong winds and need continual re-firming in the ground.

Cultivation: as for summer cabbage above.

Varieties:

January King   (quality)
Winnigstadt   (probably the most popular; cuttable in late July and lasts all through autumn and early winter.)
Christmas Drumhead (very reliable)

Carrots

Soil: carrots do best in light open soils which heat up quickly and have good drainage. The area should have been well dug and manured the previous year. If the soil is heavy, grow stump-rooted varieties; if light, long carrots can be grown successfully.

Planting: 1 oz. of seed will sow 100 ft. The first sowing should be made lightly about mid-April, in rows 15 ins. apart. The seed should be just below the surface in a very narrow drill. Thereafter weekly or fortnightly sowings can be made in order to obtain a successional ripening of the crop. If you allow from ten to twelve weeks between sowing and collecting the crop you will have an idea of the length of time which should elapse between successional sowings.

Cultivation: as the carrots germinate and grow you will see that you have sown too many seeds – the plants must be thinned in order to allow those which are left to make maximum growth. Thin in the first instance to leave about 4 ins. between the plants and then, a little later, once you have seen those carrots which are surviving best, increase the distance to 8 ins. The thinnings may be eaten in salads. Thinnings should never be left lying between the rows as this encourages carrot fly – a well-known destroyer of crops.

A basic general fertilizer should be applied at about 1 oz. per square yard along the row immediately after thinning – this will revive and encourage the plants which are left. The crop will also require weeding and this is best done by hand.

There are only two important 'don'ts': first, never sow carrots in soil which has been freshly manured; second, don't sow thickly because excessive thinning of the rows encourages carrot fly.

Varieties:

Early:	Early French Nantes	(quality)
	First Pull	(stump rooted)
Late:	James' Scarlet	(quality)
	Goldinhart	(freezes well)
	Long Red Surrey	(" ")

Cauliflower

This is one of the most difficult vegetables to grow well, but it is so popular that every gardener should at least try.

Soil: cauliflowers require a deep, well-dug, heavily manured soil. If you have a well-drained loam the results will be very good; clay soils are much more difficult. The best technique is to apply as much manure as possible in the previous autumn when the ground will benefit from double digging. Lime can be applied at the same time to improve the drainage.

Planting: 1 oz. of seed will produce over 2000 plants. Experienced gardeners grow their cauliflowers from seed, but most beginners prefer to buy plants. The ideal kind of plant at this stage should have three or four leaves. Before they are planted out give the ground a good dressing of compound fertilizer, at 4 oz. per square yard. Planting, in May or June, should be done carefully; make a large hole with a dibber or a trowel; spread the roots of the plants out in the hole; pack the soil firmly around the small plants and then water. They should be planted roughly 2 ft apart with 2 ft between the rows. It is often a good idea to sprinkle a small amount of calomel dust around the base of each plant to help control cabbage root fly and club root.

Cultivation: the real essential in growing cauliflowers is that they should grow steadily. In dry weather, therefore, you may need to water them. Weeds should be kept down by hoeing whenever necessary. When the head or 'curd' is formed a leaf should be snapped and bent over the top of the curd in order to keep it white and prevent it going either greenish or yellow in colour. Cauliflowers taste best if they are cut in the early morning.

Varieties:

Everyday Eclipse	(September cutting)
Snow King	(good quality, autumn)
Early Mammoth	(September cutting)
Autumn Queen	(very large, August cutting)
All the Year Round	(can sow at any time of year)

Leeks

The leek is the hardiest and the easiest winter vegetable to grow.

Soil: although they grow best on a rich, well-manured soil, leeks will grow practically anywhere provided a certain amount of humus has been dug in. It is also a good plan to treat the leek-growing area with bone meal at about 3 oz. per square yard. Leeks grow well in cold, wet conditions and can therefore be accommodated in almost any part of the garden though they are usually put in the area from which early peas or potatoes have been lifted.

Planting: 1 oz. sows a row of about 100 ft. Seeds should be sown thinly in shallow drills about ½ in. deep during March–April. Once the seedlings have reached a height of 4 ins. they can be transplanted to their permanent situation, probably in July or August. Another way of growing is to sow very lightly in drills in the permanent situation and to simply thin the plants to about 9 ins. apart in the row and the rows roughly 18 ins. apart. If the plants are to be transplanted they should be spaced 9 ins. apart. Transferring is very easily done. A hole 3–4 ins. deep should be made with a dibber and the leek simply dropped in. It should then be watered – this will cause the soil around the edge of the hole to crumble and cover up the roots, which can then be earthed up. As the leeks grow, continue earthing them up in order to encourage blanching. Leeks can be given specially made cardboard collars to keep the light off the base of the stem and so encourage the white appearance which is so much desired. As the leaves elongate, their tips should be trimmed three times during the growing season so as to encourage the formation of a large stick.

Leeks treated this way can be eaten at any stage, starting with the thinnings which can be used as a salad vegetable, right through the winter and even after fairly heavy frosts.

Varieties:

Musselburgh	(quality, will stand very hard weather)
Walton Mammoth	(early, short thick type)
The Lyon	(very long)

Lettuces

Average quality lettuces are not difficult to grow, provided the soil in which they are situated is organically rich and well-manured the previous autumn. Many growers, in fact, follow their leek crop with one of lettuce since the same conditions satisfy both.

Planting: 1 oz. seed produces 2,500 plants. Lettuce seeds can be sown from March until September, so by varying the variety you can have continuous cropping. They can be sown in a special lettuce bed or simply inter-cropped with other vegetables such as peas, beans, etc. The seed is small and should be sown $\frac{1}{2}$ in. deep, thinly in rows. They can then be successively thinned until individual plants are approximately 10 ins. apart and the rows 15 ins. apart; alternatively, they can be sown in another part of the garden and when they have germinated and are 2–3 ins. high transplanted.

Cultivation: the aim of good lettuce-growing is to produce lots of crisp green leaves and this is accomplished by maintaining a rapid rate of growth throughout the growing season. If there is any sign of drought you should water the plants and every three weeks give them a top dressing of either a spoonful of dried blood sprinkled around each plant or 2 oz. per square yard of general fertilizer scattered on the surface.

If the lettuces flop over, this is a sure sign of attack by root aphis. If this happens buy an insecticide containing Derris, and water it along the row.

Varieties: there are two types of lettuce: cabbage lettuce which have a solid heart and cos lettuce which consist of upright crisp leaves. Cos is rather more difficult to grow.

Cabbage: Attractie (early)
            All the Year Round (summer and autumn, good quality)
            Webb's Wonderful (spring and summer, excellent)
            May King (spring and summer, can be forced early in frames)
Cos: Little Gem (early, quality)
            Sugar Cos (early)
            Lobjoits Green (summer, very dark green leaves)

Onions

Onions are generally grown in a special area of the garden in which no rotation is practised as they need specially rich soil. This area should be enriched as far as possible with farmyard manure, and in order to ensure good drainage may be limed every fourth year. To ripen properly, onions need lots of sunshine – they therefore appreciate an open, sunny situation.

Planting: 1 oz. of seed will sow 100 ft. Seeds should be sown $\frac{1}{2}$ in. deep in March or April. The rows should be 12 ins. apart and once the seeds have germinated they should be thinned to 6 ins. apart. Another method is to plant tiny immature bulbs known as onion sets. These are planted to half the depth of the set, 6 ins. apart and 12 ins. between the rows in March and it is probably the easiest way to grow onions.

Cultivation: as the bulbs begin to swell, the plants should be fed preferably with a base fertilizer containing both phosphate and potash, and occasional doses of liquid manure; 1 oz. of nitrate of soda per yard of drill will also help to swell the bulbs. This feeding should be stopped about a month before the bulbs begin to ripen and, as the foliage gradually yellows, it should be tied together and bent back so as to face northwards. This exposes the neck of the bulb to the sun and hastens the ripening process. Growers are sometimes troubled by onions running up to seed, the so-called 'bolters' – this type of bulb should simply be removed. Onion fly can also damage the bulb, causing premature ripening and death. If this occurs, put calomel dust around the seedlings in early May in the following year.

Lift the bulbs in September, dry carefully and store in a cool, dry, frost-free place.

Varieties:

Autumn Triumph	(good quality)
Bedfordshire Champion	(good general maincrop)
White Lisbon	(salad onion)
Ailsa Craig	(quality, large bulbs, does not store well)

Peas

Soil: peas root very deeply and so prefer a soil which is rich in manure and has been limed quite heavily the previous winter. It should then be raked down in spring to provide a fine seed bed.

Planting: 1 pint of seed sows approximately 50 ft. Planting can be done over a long period of time, but in general it is best to plant the earlies in March–April and the main crop from April to June. It is also possible to plant in July or August but, if this is done, you must use early varieties of peas as these require less time to reach maturity than the main crop; in fact many growers plant early peas in the ground from which they have just lifted their early potatoes. Thus the ground is continually occupied and they get a very satisfactory second crop. Planting should be done by digging out a flat trench about 2–3 ins. deep and 18 ins. wide. The peas should be placed along this trench in three staggered rows about 4 ins. apart. The distance between the drills varies, depending on the height to which the variety of pea will grow. Thus, if you are planting Feltham First, which only grows 18 ins. high, you will need 18 ins. between rows, but a pea such as Onward, which reaches $2\frac{1}{2}$ ft should have $2\frac{1}{2}$ ft between the drills.

Early peas are often planted in fairly cold inhospitable weather and may take a long time to germinate. Under these circumstances they are very likely to be attacked by moulds or eaten by field mice, so ask for treated seed for the early crop. Old gardeners used to put gorse or holly along the drills of peas to ward off mice. The peas will germinate in about twelve days.

Cultivation: as soon as the peas come through the ground they are liable to be attacked by birds; to prevent this, stretch cotton thread between twigs to form a cover over the top and down the sides of the pea drill. If this cover is made about 6 ins. high it will very much discourage birds from pecking the plants and once they have grown more than 6 ins. high they are no longer attractive. Most pea varieties need staking as they are climbing plants – stout stakes should be driven in at each end of the row if it is short, and as frequently as seems necessary if it is long. Stretch string or wire netting between these for the peas to climb up. Do remember to be sure that the stakes are as tall as the variety.

No fertilizer is necessary during the growth of the crop, but in dry weather peas will benefit a great deal from a surface mulch of well-rotted compost or even peat. This helps to conserve the soil moisture and provides the kind of cool root run which peas like. Peas extract nitrogen from the air, thus supplying most of their own fertilizer, but if the soil is not very rich a dressing of superphosphates at about 1 oz. per square yard is useful. This is sometimes given in the trench at planting time but may also be given during the period of growth. Weeds can easily be kept down by hoeing.

Varieties:

Early:	Feltham First (18 ins.)
	Meteor (18 ins.)
	Kelvedon Wonder (2 ft, quality)
	Hurst Green Shaft (2 ft, excellent)
Main Crop:	Onward (2½ ft)
	Gladstone (3½ ft)
	Stratagem (3 ft, quality)
	Recette (2 ft, v. heavy, quality crop)

Potatoes

Soil: potatoes can be grown in any soil, but the best crop is obtained in a good rich loam. The soil should be well manured, preferably in the autumn, and there should have been no application of lime the previous year as it encourages potato scab. When planting scatter 1 lb. of a good potato fertilizer along each 20 ft of row.

Planting: 14 lb. of potatoes will plant roughly 120 ft. For early potatoes plant in mid-March; for main and late crops, April until mid-May is perfectly adequate. Take into account where you live and delay planting until you are sure that there is no chance of frost after the shoots are above the ground. The tubers should be planted in a furrow 4 ins. deep about a foot apart. Leave approximately 2 ft between the drills, increasing to 2 ft 6 ins. for large late varieties. Early potatoes should always have been sprouted and the number of sprouts reduced to two at most before planting.

Cultivation: once the shoots are 6 ins. through the soil draw the earth up to create a ridge; do this again at least twice during the growing season so that eventually the potato plant is growing out of the top of a quite substantial ridge. The reason for this is that the new tubers grow out of the stem and the more stem there is under ground the less chance there is of new tubers going green. This ridging is also a very good time for removing weeds. At each ridging, give a light dressing of a general fertilizer.

The early potatoes should be ready to lift in June–July and should be dug and used immediately in order to get the maximum flavour. Late varieties should be left in the ground until the haulms die down when they can be dug and spread out to dry. Diseased potatoes should be rejected, and the good sound ones can then be stored dry in a cool cellar in bags or else, if you have a large quantity, put in a clamp (see p. 110).

Varieties:

Earlies:	Epicure (quality)
	Duke of York
	Sharpe's Express (quality)
	Foremost
	Ulster Chieftain
Lates:	Majestic
	Arran Banner

Désirée
King Edward (high quality)
Pentland Crown
Craig's Royal
Golden Wonder (quality)
Maris Piper

Radishes

Soil: radishes are at their best when grown in rich shady moisture-retentive soil. Because of this and their short season of growth they are often used for inter-cropping between rows of peas or lettuce. The soil can be specially prepared by adding leaf mould or peat to produce a fine tilth in the surface layers.

Planting: they should be sown thinly in rows in shallow ($\frac{1}{2}$ in.) drills about 6 ins. apart. The minimum of thinning should be done and it is not advisable to sow outdoors before the beginning of April. The crop should not be in the ground longer than eight weeks, and so successional sowings at two-weekly intervals will ensure a succession of tender radishes.

Cultivation: to be at their best, radishes should be grown quickly and steadily. After germination, thin to about 3 ins. apart. In sandy soils in dry weather, watering may be necessary to prevent the crop going woody. They are attacked by club root and so should not be grown in infected soil.

Finally, as soon as they are of usable size they should be pulled, as older radishes are not only woody but also very hot and often hollow. They can be successfully grown in window boxes.

Varieties:

Scarlet Globe	(round, red)
Icicle	(white and long)
Wood's Early Frame	(rose, long)
Saxa	(spring and summer)

Rhubarb

Rhubarb is not strictly speaking a vegetable but it is usually grown in the vegetable garden. It is a perennial crop and so repays good initial cultivation.

Soil: rhubarb grows best in a light, deep, sunny open area. As much farmyard manure as possible should be dug in; if this is not available, use plenty of humus-rich compost.

Planting: most amateurs start with roots which should be planted in winter and certainly before March, and given a dressing of base fertilizer as soon as growth begins.

Cultivation: any seed heads which appear should be cut off and during the first year of growth very few sticks should be pulled. It is very easy to obtain early rhubarb simply by inverting a bucket over the young crown in February or March. Another technique for forcing rhubarb is to dig the root out in the early part of the winter and allow it to become frosted for three weeks; when re-planted it will come into yield early.

Varieties:
Prince Albert
Timperley Early

Swedes see *Turnips,* p. 127.

Tomatoes (Outdoor)

The tomato is a tender plant and needs a sunny, warm position, preferably in a south-facing border.

Soil: the soil should be rich in humus but should not contain any fresh manure – the best results are obtained by using a part of the garden which was heavily fertilized for a crop the previous year. Before planting, sprinkle 2 oz. per yard of tomato fertilizer along the rows.

Planting: short-jointed, dark green plants are best, and are put out from the end of May until the middle of June. Plant carefully in the soil 18 ins. apart with $2\frac{1}{2}$ ft between rows and give the ground around each plant a good soaking.

Cultivation: the plants should be induced to grow up a vertical string or tall stake. As they grow, take out side shoots by pinching between finger and thumb – side shoots develop in the angle made by a leaf and a stem and excessive numbers of these reduces yield.

One of the commonest faults in tomato growing is to try to get too great a yield. In the case of outdoor plants the top should be removed after four or five trusses have developed in the South, and after three or four in the North. As the fruit swells, a strain is put on the plant and so tomatoes should be given an additional feed as soon as the second truss has been set. Leaves which have turned yellow should be removed and in hot weather a mulch should be given around the base of the plants – take care that the mulching material does not touch the stems.

Varieties:

Sutton's Open Air   (early, hardy)
Outdoor Girl   (very early, specially bred for outdoors)
Ailsa Craig   (most popular, good quality but unreliable outside)

Turnips and Swedes

Soil: they can be grown in any soil but the best yields are obtained when manure has been dug in in the autumn and the soil well limed. It is also helpful to give a general fertilizer at 2 oz. per square yard before sowing.

Planting: 1 oz. seed will sow between 100 and 150 ft. Turnips are usually sown in April or May in thin rows 1 in. deep with the drills 12 ins. apart. Thereafter successional sowings can be made until June; you should then sow swedes with 18 ins. between drills.

Cultivation: as the plants develop, thinning will be necessary. For turnips which will be used in summer this should be done to produce 6 ins. between the plants; for winter swedes, which are very much larger, 9 ins. should be left. Both turnips and swedes are very susceptible to drought and should be protected against this by heavy mulching once the plants are well established. The seedlings are often attacked by flea beetle which eats the leaves, producing typically indented edges. This pest can be controlled by dusting the rows with an insecticide such as Derris. Early turnips for consumption in July and August should be used at once but swedes can stand a considerable amount of frost; in fact, it is often said that they taste better after frost. In very heavy soils, however, dig the

TABLE OF VEGETABLE CULTIVATION

CROP	RATE	SOIL	WHEN TO PLANT/ SOW	DEPTH OF PLANTING	SPACE BETWEEN PLANTS
Beans, Broad	1 pt–60 ft	Deep, well manured	Mid-Mar./ May	2 ins.	9 ins.
Beans, Dwarf	½ pt–80 ft	Light, rich, open	Mid-April/ June	2 ins.	6 ins.
Beans, Runner	½ pt–80 ft	Deep, well manured	Mid-April/ June	2 ins.	9 ins.
Brussels Sprouts	1 oz. = 2,000 plants	Deep loam, well limed, firm	Sow March, plant May/June		2 ft
Cab-bage, Spring	,,	Limed, manure in autumn, firmed	Sept./Oct.		12 ins.
Cab-bage, Summer	,,	,,	Plant out April/May		12–18 ins.
Cab-bage, Winter	,,	,,	Plant out July/Aug.		24 ins.
Carrots	1 oz.– 100 ft	Light, open, well drained	April/May	Below surface	4–8 ins.
Cauli-flower and Broccoli	1 oz. = 2,000 plants	Autumn dug, limed, well manured	Plant out May/June		24 ins.
Leeks	1 oz.– 100 ft	Specially humus-rich area	Sow Mar./Apr. plant out July/Aug.	3–4 ins.	9 ins.

VEGETABLE CULTIVATION, contd.

SPACE BETWEEN DRILLS	VARIETIES	USE	REMARKS
18 ins.	Seville Longpod White Windsor	June/Sept.	Pinch out tops after 4/5 flower clusters.
18 ins.	Masterpiece Comtesse de Chambard	July/Sept., dry for winter	Nitro-chalk at $\frac{1}{2}$ oz./yd^2.
15 ins.	Scarlet Emperor Dwarf Scarlet Kelvedon Marvel	July/Oct.	Stake firmly and give nitro-chalk. Never leave old pods on plant.
3 ft	Peer Gynt Cambridge 5	Oct.–Feb.	Keep soil firm and give a little feed in August.
2 ft	Durham Early Unwin's Foremost Ellams Early	March/May	Watch for wilting as sign of root maggot; if present dust with calomel around base.
2 ft	Velocity Favourite Golden Acre	July/Sept.	,, ,,
2 ft	January King Winnigstadt	Sept./Dec.	,, ,,
15 ins.	Early French Nantes James' Scarlet	July/Dec.	Do not leave thinnings around. Sow lightly.
2 ft	Early Mammoth All the Year Round Snow King	June/Nov.	Sprinkle calomel dust to control root maggot.
18 ins.	Walton Mammoth Musselburgh	Sept./April	Encourage blanching by earthing up.

CROP	RATE	SOIL	WHEN TO PLANT/ SOW	DEPTH OF PLANTING	SPACE BETWEEN PLANTS
Lettuce	1 oz. = 2,500 plants	Open, rich, organic	Sow Mar./ Sept. Plant out when 3 ins. high	$\frac{1}{2}$ in.	10 ins.
Onions	1 oz. = 100 ft	No rotation, very rich, deep	Seeds March, sets March/ April	$\frac{1}{2}$ depth of set	6 ins.
Peas, Early	1 pt = approx. 50 ft	Open and sunny, well manured	March/ April	2–3 ins.	4 ins.
Peas, Main	,,	,,	April/June	2–3 ins.	4 ins.
Potatoes, Early	14 lb.– 120 ft	No lime, well manured	March	4 ins .	12 ins.
Potatoes, Main	,,	,,	April/May	4 ins.	12 ins.
Rhubarb		Light, well drained	Winter/ March		18 ins .
Swedes & Turnips	1 oz. = 150 ft	Not demanding but prefer limed soil	April/May	1 in.	16 ins. swedes 9 ins. turnips
Tomato	1 oz. = 2,500 plants	Sunny, warm, old manure	May/June		18 ins.

SPACE BETWEEN DRILLS	VARIETIES	USE	REMARKS
15 ins.	Attractie May King Lobjoits Green Webb's Wonderful	May/March	Can be used as inter-crop. Feed with dried blood every 3 weeks.
12 ins.	Autumn Triumph Bedfordshire Champion	Sept./April	
Same as height of variety grown	Feltham First Meteor Hurst Green Shaft	June/July	Use treated seed.
	Onward Stratagem Recette	Aug./Sept.	Surface mulch, superphosphates at 1 oz./yd².
2 ft	Epicure Duke of York Ulster Chieftain	July	Keep soil well ridged at least twice.
2 ft 6 ins.	Pentland Crown Désirée	Oct./March	Lift and store as soon as haulms die back.
2 ft 6 ins.	Prince Albert Timperley Early	April/Nov.	Feed during growth. Cut off flower heads.
18 ins.	Turnip – Golden Ball Swede – Champion	July/March	If any root maggot apply lindane or calomel.
2 ft 6 ins.	Sutton's Open Air Ailsa Craig Outdoor Girl	July/Sept.	Pinch out side shoots. Feed as tomatoes swell.

swedes before the soil becomes water-logged, dry them off and store them in a cool cellar.

Varieties:

Turnips: Early Snowball
            Golden Ball (quality)

Swedes: Purple Top
            Champion (quality)

BOOK LIST

Vegetable Grower's Guide: Oldham, C. H. (Crosby Lockwood)
Vegetable Gardening: Simons, A. J. (Amateur Gardening Handbook, Collingridge)
A Kitchen Garden: Furner, B. (Arthur Barker)
A Concise Guide to Vegetable Gardening: Mead, Cicely (Muller)
Down to Earth Vegetable Growing: Hills, L. (Faber & Faber, Garden Book Club)
The Vegetable Garden Displayed: (Royal Hort. Soc. London)
The Complete Book of Vegetables and Herbs: Genders, Roy (Ward Lock)

7 *Flowers*

Growing flowers was once the most popular side of gardening but with the advent of the amateur home gardener and because of the time involved it suffered a decline in popularity. Recently, however, the demand for cut flowers has led to a fresh interest, and most shrub borders now have small flowers at their edges. The old-fashioned bedding-out techniques have gone to be replaced by an increased use of perennials, but although changes have taken place, the cheapest and in many cases the simplest way to get lots of bright colour in the garden is still to grow flowers.

'Flowers' is an omnibus word and includes a very large number of different kinds of plant as well as an enormous number of different species and varieties. For example there are *annuals* which can be sown outdoors in spring (say April and May) to flower the same summer; *hardy annuals* which can be sown in autumn and can withstand the normal winter frosts; *half-hardy annuals* need some protection from frost and are usually planted when the risk of very low temperatures is passed; *'tender' annuals* must be grown indoors all the time.

It will be clear that *annuals* exist for one season only – after flowering they seed and then die down. In subsequent years, however, they may emerge as weeds among some other flowers – anyone who has grown nasturtiums knows that they come up and flower every year, self-seeding all over the place. (Such self-sown plants can be a boon to the casual gardener or a curse to the tidy one but they amply justify the definition of a weed as 'a plant in the wrong place'.) Each autumn and winter, therefore, you have to clear away the dead plants and sow again the following spring.

Biennials are sown in one season when they make a lot of leaf growth. They rest through the winter, flower the following year and then die down. One of the commonest biennials is the foxglove which is planted out in the autumn to flower the following year.

The other great group, sometimes known as 'the gardener's friend', is the *perennials* which once established go on for several years. They usually die down in the winter, in the sense that the soft stems and leaves wither, but the roots stay alive and in the spring start to produce new leaves, stems and flowers. The length of life of perennials varies; some are treated as biennials, and kept for only two seasons, but well-established clumps of, say, Michaelmas daisies may last for five or six years. In the end, however,

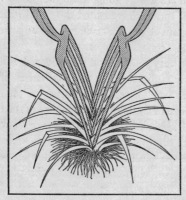

17. *Dividing a fibrous-rooted perennial plant.*

they must be replaced or divided – two forks are sunk back to back through the middle of the plant into the ground and then levered apart (see Fig. 17). This can be done almost as well with a spade and fork or even a trowel and fork. You can also take cuttings and layers of many perennials such as carnations or dahlias by treating them just like shrubby cuttings and rooting them in John Innes or vermiculite. Details are given later, p. 182.

The final major group of flowering plants is that which contains fleshy storage/reproductive structures such as *bulbs*, *corms* or *rhizomes*. Here we find daffodils, iris, lily of the valley, lilies and gladiolus. These are excellent as cut flowers, and, in addition, many of them flower when there is little other colour in the garden, cheering everyone up at the end of a dreary winter.

All these types of plants will be dealt with in more detail later in the chapter. First there are some general things to be said and it will save a lot of time if they are said here.

PLANNING A BORDER OR BED

By definition a border should be at the edge or border of the garden, but beds demand very much the same treatment so they will be considered together. The first piece of advice is to make a plan. This is not essential if you are simply going to fill the border or bed with annuals – although if these are well sited the result is better – but a plan is really important if you are trying to create a trouble-free perennial border to last for ten years or more.

A single flower can look very solitary and a mixed bed of flowers growing higgledy-piggledy is just a mess; to avoid either of these you have to plant flowers in clumps. The number of plants per clump will vary with the size of the clump and the size of the flower, but to get any effect at all, even with moderately large plants such as iris or lilies, three is the minimum and about ten the maximum. You can therefore draw the outline of your border on squared paper and simply fill in areas with the names of the plants you intend to grow, as below (Fig. 18):

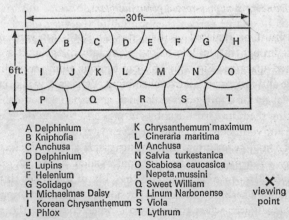

A Delphinium
B Kniphofia
C Anchusa
D Delphinium
E Lupins
F Helenium
G Solidago
H Michaelmas Daisy
I Korean Chrysanthemum
J Phlox
K Chrysanthemum maximum
L Cineraria maritima
M Anchusa
N Salvia turkestanica
O Scabiosa caucasica
P Nepeta mussini
Q Sweet William
R Linum Narbonense
S Viola
T Lythrum

X
viewing
point

18. *Plan for a border of twenty perennials which will be viewed from the right and front so that the tallest plants are to the back and left.*

Position

Borders or beds often site themselves and you may have little choice in the matter, but if you have a choice, try to get a wind-free area, for few flowers have sturdy stems and a strong wind or constant draught can do a lot of damage. Of course, it is often possible to grow shrubs as a windbreak, or even to shelter weaker plants by growing them in the lee-side of taller, bushier ones, but this limits your freedom of planting so try to avoid windy or draughty areas. One of the worst places is a narrow passage between two adjacent houses, as wind is often funnelled through the gap and there is usually a lot of shade and dampness, so only special flowers such as lily of the valley will survive.

On the other hand, although like other plants flowers do best in good open sunlight, many can grow quite well in shade, and you need not be afraid of a shady area provided it is not dominated by great trees such as beech, lime or pine which take all the food from the soil and create problems of drip as well as shade. A list of plants tolerant of shade is given on p. 162.

Try to have the border or bed, if it is at all possible, running away from the house and not across the line of vision, for this tends to stop the eye going any further and so seems to shrink the garden. In a large garden this limiting of the view may be done intentionally to allow you to move from one region to another, but in a small garden it is a real mistake. You must have seen many tiny front gardens made to look even tinier by having a bed in the centre when a continuous expanse of grass or even a standard rose would have been much more effective.

Shape

It is simplest to plant borders or beds with straight edges but beds in a lawn can have curved edges and of course round or elliptical beds are perfectly all right – except that you run into the problem of maintaining edges. Although straight *edges* are best, it is wrong to arrange your *plants* in straight lines. Gone are the days when a soldier-like line of tulips marched down the garden, headed by a single line of alyssum or geranium. Nowadays most growers prefer the effect achieved by group planting with the area occupied by the group having an irregular outline as in the specimen plan (Fig. 18).

Feeding

Many borders have one side facing the garden, and the other a wall or fence or hedge. In filling such a border remember that hedges are very hungry so plants near them should be well fed, and that walls, etc., may produce problems of shade and even wind turbulence. If you want to hide the wall or fence plant a few clumps of tall perennials or even shrubs in front of it, or have a simple climber going up it such as Virginia creeper or *Hydrangea petiolaris*. Borders near walls should be well mulched each year, for rain driving against the wall trickles down and soaks through the soil, draining away its goodness. A wall may also protect a border from prevailing rainy winds and thus create an area of drought. So watch out for dryness.

WHAT TO GROW

What to grow and where to grow it are the questions that bother most beginners. These are difficult questions and have to be settled basically by your own taste and inclinations, but as usual there are some guide lines. Your choice of plant must be influenced by height and colour, for although some gardeners like to see a uniform bed with only one colour such as blue or white, others think this is insipid and prefer a more interesting range of colour. Border designers often work with what are called 'colour triads'. These are groups of three colours which together create a pleasing effect. Such groups are red, yellow and blue, or using secondary colours orange, violet and green; yellow, pink and blue is also an attractive combination. Don't let such ideas tie you down – for contrasts are often very effective – just keep them in mind when you plan.

Some gardeners prefer to grow a mixed border, i.e. one containing annuals, perennials and even a few shrubs, although it is probably less work to make a bed or border solely of perennials and shrubs. Beds of annuals alone are not very popular today though wonderfully bright effects can be obtained by bedding out lobelia, asters, nicotiana, petunias, etc. Remember too that in a mixed border with shrubs, perennials, annuals and a few bulbs you can have flowers nearly all the year round.

The size of the plants should always be taken into account, with the taller plants at the back and smaller plants as you approach the edge of the border, until you reach the front where you can grow small carpeting plants. It is a good plan too, to vary the height of the tallest plants at different points on the border and even to have a few groups of tall plants coming forward in sweeps to prevent a 'lined-up' appearance. For example, although all the tallest plants should be at the back, have a few different heights in these tall plants to avoid the appearance of a thicket or a fence. Of course, if you are planning a bed and not a border, then the tallest plants should be in the centre with the smaller ones graded down to the edges.

A very crowded bed can raise all sorts of problems of weeding, so space the shrubs and perennials well apart. This permits easy weeding, room for the permanent occupants of the bed to spread out, and you can always fill in at any time with annuals or bulbs. Many bulbs such as crocus or snowdrop are finished by the time the other plants start to grow, so that a fair number of these can be planted since they will not be competing for ground space.

Staking

Finally, in many cases there is bound to be the problem of staking; tall annuals or perennials are too weak to resist wind by themselves and need support. The best time to stake is when the plant is about a foot tall and does not really require support.

In staking any plant there are a few essential things to remember. Always be sure that the stake does not damage the roots. The best and surest way to do this is to have the stake firmly embedded in the hole before you plant the tree or shrub. The roots can then be spread around the stake and little or no damage will be caused; hence the saying 'you plant the stake first'.

You may however be staking sweet peas or herbaceous plants and here it is best to use bamboo canes and tie each plant to a cane; alternatively the canes can be used to form the corners of cages within which groups of plants will find support, or you can stretch twine or netting between canes along rows of such plants as sweet peas. Moveable metal rings can be bought for carnations and you simply attach the ring to the stake and the plants grow within the ring.

Many growers find canes very artificial-looking and prefer to use branched twigs pushed into the ground when the plants are young. As the plants grow through the twiggy branches they will get support and at the same time hide the twigs.

SOWING SEEDS

Many seeds sown outside in their permanent homes will germinate and grow perfectly well if left alone. Beginners often wonder about the depth of planting – if seeds are sown too deeply they may never reach the surface; on the other hand, if they are sown too near the surface, frost and drought may kill the young tender plants. There is a very simple rule-of-thumb for this; the seeds should be sown at a depth of about three to four times their own diameter. In a light sandy soil use the higher figure and in a good moist soil the lower figure.

Details of sowing outside are as follows:

(1)   Make sure the surface of the seed bed has been reduced to a fine tilth by digging and raking to get rid of all lumps of soil and stones.

(2)   Mark out the area to be occupied by the plants.

(3)   With a line stretched between two pieces of stick, mark out shallow drills of the appropriate depth by drawing a trowel or the corner of a hoe or spade over the surface. Straight drills make for easier sowing and weeding, and if the area is planned to be irregular the formality will be lost when the plants grow.

(4)   The seeds should then be sown thinly. If large, you can put each seed in its appropriate place, but since most seeds are small take a pinch between the finger and thumb and carefully sprinkle along the drill. It is important not to sow too thickly, otherwise you will have a great deal of thinning to do and the plants themselves will suffer by being too crowded in their early stages, which makes them long, floppy and weak.

(5) Most seeds must be covered, but fine seeds only require a little sand or soil sifted over the top. Larger seeds can be covered by pulling in the sides of the drill, not enough to make a ridge but simply levelling the surface.

(6) On most soils, and especially on very light sandy areas, a sprinkle with a watering can will help to firm the seeds by settling the soil around them in the drill.

Tender annuals or even half-hardy annuals will not survive outside until the seedling stage and so must be raised under some form of protection such as a cold frame, or even a sun lounge or window sill. You can make a simple cold frame (see p. 109) in which you can raise seedlings not only of flowers but also of vegetables such as lettuce – and when the good growing weather comes you can transplant the seedlings and your plants will start growing at once to give you earlier results. The alternative is to sow outside and then wait for maybe two weeks before growth really begins.

If you use a cold frame you should be sure that it contains good fine soil; it is often worth buying or making a good seed compost and simply using it as the soil in the frame. If you are sowing indoors, pots, boxes or plastic trays should be filled with John Innes seed compost (see p. 245). To germinate the seeds in boxes or pots you need only a few inches of soil, for the roots do not go down very deep, and as they grow bigger you have to transplant them anyway. Water the soil well, scatter the seed thinly over the surface, cover with a thin sprinkling of soil, then cover the box with a sheet of glass or polythene plus a few sheets of newspaper to conserve the moisture and reduce the light, and put in a warm place.

As soon as germination takes place and green shoots appear above the soil, the covering of glass or polythene and paper should be removed and the plants allowed plenty of light and air in order to produce sturdy growth. If there is a real threat of frost outside, replace the glass in the cold frames at night for protection. Regular watering may be necessary, but it is better to under-water as excess moisture provides the ideal conditions for a very common disease called 'damping off'. This is caused by a fungus which thrives in the damp humid conditions one always gets if seed is sown too thickly and pots overwatered. If your seedlings begin to damp off, it is best to throw them out, wash the container with a good disinfectant and start again with clean soil. You can weed out infected plants and save some of the others by letting the soil dry a little but this is so often a waste of time that it is better to accept the situation and cut your losses by starting again.

PRICKING AND TRANSPLANTING

Many flower seeds are tiny and it is impossible to sow them thinly enough to ensure that when they germinate each seedling will have sufficient space in which to develop properly. For this reason, most seedlings must be 'pricked out' into boxes. This means transplanting the seedlings to a box where they will continue to grow until they are big enough to be transplanted to their permanent positions in the garden. At the same time it gives you the chance to select only the best seedlings for pricking out and to discard the others to the compost heap.

Let us say that you have sown the seed in a plastic plant pot and there is now a multitude of seedlings developing which need pricking out; the first problem is 'when should this job be done?' If you examine the root system of a seedling, you will find that it consists of a main root with a few branch roots; the older the seedling, the larger and the more branched the main root becomes. If the root is allowed to become long and much branched, then as you transplant the seedling you are bound to break some of these fine roots and so injure the delicate young plant. So the solution to the problem is to prick out seedlings as soon as possible after germination, and the ideal time is as soon as the first 'true' or 'rough' leaves appear.

Most flowering plants have two seed leaves or cotyledons which supply the seedling with food until the true leaves are formed. Cotyledons are very simple in shape and so are easily distinguishable from the true leaves, which appear soon after the cotyledons and are smaller editions of the adult leaves. The germination of most seeds can be described as follows. First of all the young root emerges. This you cannot see since it is underground, but very soon the young plant emerges from the soil and the two green cotyledons expand. The plant grows on a little and two adult leaves appear. Pricking out should be done at this point, though you should not wait until the adult leaves are fully expanded; in fact, the best results are obtained by pricking out as soon as possible.

The process can now be put into a succession of steps:

(1) A day before you prick out, give the seedlings a good soak to be sure that they are not short of water before you transplant them.

(2) Fill a box with J.I. seedling compost (J.I. 1) or its equivalent, making sure that this compost is well watered and firmed down after placing in the box.

(3) Make sure the surface is flat and smooth and then press the edge of a ruler into the surface, leaving a thin line. Repeat this at right angles to the first pressing to mark the surface of the compost with two rows of parallel lines, each 1 or 2 inches apart depending on the size of the seedlings. Where lines intersect each other a seedling can be planted.

(4) Make planting holes at these points with a small dibber or pencil, making the holes big enough to take the complete root system.

(5) Uproot the seedlings by pushing the pointed edge of a wooden label or an old knife into the soil under the roots and gently levering them up.

(6) Separate out the individual seedlings: Seedlings should *never* be handled by the stem – tease them apart gently, holding them by the leaves. The stem of a seedling is very delicate and any bruising can cause death or serious damage, while the leaves and even the roots are much tougher.

(7) Lift each seedling by its leaves and place it in the hole, which should be deep enough to allow the seed leaves (cotyledons) to rest on the soil surface, then firm around the seedling with the point of a wooden label to make sure that the young roots are in contact with the soil.

(8) When you have planted a seedling at each intersection of your parallel lines give the box a sharp tap or shake to settle the soil back down again, and water the surface lightly with a fine spray.

(9)   Place the box in shade for a day or two to give the seedlings the chance to recover, and once growth has begun again bring them out into maximum light to grow on.

You may wonder why you should go to all this fuss and why not plant these seedlings outside straight away after germination. The reason is that seedlings outside are in a cold hard world with rain, rough soil, cold winds, insects and so on, all of which may damage them. By pricking out in the way I describe you are taking the seedlings through their tenderest stages under ideal conditions and the chances of success are very much greater.

Plants which are to be grown indoors as house plants can be pricked out into small pots (4½ ins.) three or four per pot, and after some growth can be thinned down to a single plant which of course should be the strongest.

PLANTING OUT

Before plants grown inside in a greenhouse, porch or even window ledge can be put outside they require a period of acclimatization known as 'hardening off'. During this period, the safe constant indoor conditions are gradually made more like those the plants will meet outside so that the shock of going straight into the garden is reduced. This hardening-off process can be done in many ways; the boxes can be moved from a heated to an unheated greenhouse, or they can be put out in a cold frame, or if they are already in a cold frame the glass cover (the light) of the frame can be lifted during the day. If you have grown the seedlings in the porch or the house you can simply carry the boxes out during the day or increase the ventilation by opening doors and windows.

Once hardening off is over and, in the case of tender annuals, the threat of frost has gone, the plants can be put in their permanent position. The time of year to do this varies according to the plant; many biennials such as wallflowers will be planted out in November, while other more tender ones such as geranium or salvias will not be outside until May or even later. Usually you will find short but exact accounts of the timing of sowing etc. on seed packets and these instructions should be carefully followed.

The border or bed should be carefully prepared, especially if you are hoping to use it for trouble-free perennials. Annuals are much less demanding since they only occupy the ground for a short time, but even they will benefit from being grown in good soil. Therefore dig in some manure or compost before planting out. Where possible group the plants as described under 'Planning' (p. 135), making sure that there is enough space for the plants to develop properly. Allow six to nine inches between small plants at the front of the bed and two or three feet between tall species at the back or in the centre of an island bed.

Young seedlings are very attractive to slugs – if there is any sign of them use a scattering of slug pellets based on metaldehyde. These are poisonous to children and dogs so be very careful in using them.

WEEDING

In a bed of mixed annuals, perennials and a few shrubs it is dangerous to use chemical weed-killers as they may also kill the plants. In many cases, therefore, you will have to resort to hand weeding or hoeing.

Hand weeding is often regarded as the last resort – a back-breaking task which should only be done if all else fails. Fortunately it is only necessary with very difficult weeds such as couch grass, mare's tail or bindweed, but if you find it necessary to hand weed, then do it thoroughly the first time and preferably *before* planting – if the job is only half done you will have as many weeds in two or three weeks and you might as well have left it alone. Doing it thoroughly can mean that to get rid of, say, couch grass you should fork the soil over very carefully picking out every piece of stem or root you see and burning it. Do *not* put it on the compost heap – a well-made compost heap is very useful but if you allow weeds and weed seeds to be in the heap, then as you spread the compost you are also spreading weeds.

Hoeing is much easier and simply involves pushing the tool to and fro just below the surface of the soil. The modern two-sided hoes are light and very good and the movement of the blade cuts

A garden with a sense of mystery

Two climbing plants: rose 'Lawrence Johnson' above,
fast-growing clematis montana below

Two garden pools

Every inch in this
small space has been
used to create a
leafy green bower

A carefully planted
border and trellis in a
London garden

Two winding gardens
giving a feeling of size
and surprise

Left Two simple, straight gardens

Covered walks can create a 'room outside'. The garden above has been designed to need minimum care

A garden on a bunker

the weed below soil level so that root and shoot are separated and die – though in many cases you may just temporarily uproot the weed seedling and it may re-root in the cool of the night or in the next shower of rain. The secret of hoeing therefore is to try to do it in the early morning, especially on a day that looks like being hot and dry when all the weeds should be dead by nightfall.

Weed-killing by chemicals is the easiest work of all: mixtures, such as Weedol, based on paraquat are very useful chemicals with a very wide spectrum of action to kill all green plants except mosses. It acts by being absorbed by the green leaves in daylight and so upsets the biochemistry of the leaf that the plant dies. This means that if you can keep the chemical off any green foliage the plant will be unaffected, so, to avoid damaging plants you want to keep, use a special plastic spray boom on your watering can – they're quite cheap. With this boom (sometimes called a trickle-bar) the spray can be directed very accurately and it is simple to use para-quat around shrubs or even perennials to kill weeds. This chemical is immediately absorbed and broken down by the soil so that there is no accumulation of toxic substances or danger to later crops in the same soil. Gardeners should keep a special watering can for weed-killers to minimize the danger of accidents; if you have only one watering can, be careful to wash it out very thoroughly before putting it away.

Many weed-killers are very poisonous, so make sure that you label each bottle or tin clearly, and keep them on a high shelf or in a locked cupboard well out of the reach of children. Most accidents occur through poisonous liquids being put into lemonade bottles, so on no account do this.

Weeds can also be controlled here by mulching with leaf mould, compost or FYM; this should be done in May or June depending on the soil and the weather. If the function of the mulch is weed-prevention, a layer at least two inches thick is necessary or stronger weeds will grow through.

TWENTY HARDY ANNUALS

COMMON NAME	SCIENTIFIC NAME	HEIGHT	COLOUR	MONTH OF FLOWER-ING (1-12)	REMARKS
Marigold	Calendula	1-2 ft	Yellow/Orange	7-10	Seeds very freely, wide range
Cornflower (Sweet Sultan)	Centaurea	1-3 ft	Blue/Rose	6-9	There are very beautiful F1 hybrid strains
Clarkia	Clarkia	1-2 ft	Wide range	6-9	Prefers sunny light soil
Cosmos	Cosmos	1-4 ft	Red/Pink/White	7-10	Good cut flower, some half-hardy
Californian Poppy	Eschscholtzia	9-12 ins.	Yellow/Red	6-9	Flowers freely in a sunny spot
Godetia	Godetia	9 ins.-3 ft	Wide range	7-8.	Thin well on ordinary soil
Cloud plant	Gypsophila elegans	1-2 ft	White/Red	7-9	Good cut flower
Sunflower	Helianthus	2-10 ft	Yellow	7-9	Good cut flower
Larkspur	Delphinium	3-5 ft	Blue	7-9	Very good cut flower, many fine new varieties

Love-in-a-Mist	Nigella	1–2 ft	Blue/White	7–10	Floral decoration plant, very easy
Mignonette	Reseda	1–2 ft	Yellow/Red	6–8	Very fragrant
Nasturtium	Tropaeolum	Climbs	Yellow/Orange	7–10	Very easy to grow but can run rampant
Nemesia	Nemesia	5–18 ins.	Blue/Red	7–9	Good edging plant
Baby blue-eyes	Nemophila	6 ins.	Blue	5–9	Very good edging plant
Black-eyed Susan	Rudbeckia	1–3 ft	Yellow	7–9	Good cut flower
Soapwort	Saponaria	9 ins.–3 ft	White/Pink	5–8	Cut flower
Stock	Matthiola	6 ins.–2 ft	Red/Yellow/White	7–9	Very fragrant, cuts well
Sweet alyssum	Alyssum	3–9 ins.	White/Pink	6–10	Good edging plant
Toad Flax	Linaria	6 ins.–1 ft	Lilac/Red/White	6–10	Very dependable
Scabious	Scabiosa	1–3 ft	Blue/Red/Yellow	7–10	Very many varieties

In addition you might try asters, poppies, candytuft (iberis), echium, lavatera, mallow. For sweet peas, see p. 160.

ANNUALS

There is such a wide range of size and colour in annuals that it is impossible to give anything like a complete list, so I will just make a very limited selection of easy-to-grow species. Remember that hardy annuals should be sown out of doors in the place where you want them to bloom. After germination they should be thinned to a reasonable distance, depending on the size of the adult plant which may range from a few inches to ten feet, and when the flowers are over they should be dug out and put on the compost heap to prevent some species from spreading seed all over the garden.

HALF-HARDY ANNUALS

This is the group of annuals which are susceptible to frosts and are therefore sown and germinated under protection such as a greenhouse or cold frame. Generally they require a temperature of about 55–70°F for germination, which means that in a cold greenhouse conditions are not usually right for sowing until March/April. You should prick them out as young as possible, harden off the seedlings for about two weeks and put them outside as soon as the danger of severe frost is over.

PERENNIALS

These are more or less permanent occupants of their part of the border and if grown extensively will considerably reduce the amount of work you have to do. They are very useful as cut flowers since a large number have long tough stems.

Most perennials can be planted at any time during the winter, but the best time is during the second half of September and the whole of October – though if your area is cold and wet it is better to plant in early spring, i.e. March/April. In all cases wait until the soil is in good condition rather than putting the plants in very wet or very dry soil. You should always plant a little below the depth at which the seedling was growing in order to allow for a certain

TWENTY HALF-HARDY ANNUALS

COMMON NAME	SCIENTIFIC NAME	HEIGHT	COLOUR	MONTH	REMARKS
Ageratum	A. x hybrid	1 ft	Blue/Pink	6-8	Sunny position
Antirrhinum	A. majus & hybrid	1 ft	Red/White/Yellow	7-10	Seeds freely
Aster	Callistephus	6 ins.–3 ft	Very good choice	8-10	Very many types and forms
Cockscomb	Celosia plumosa	1–2 ft	Yellow/Red	8-9	Outside in June
Cobea	Cobea scandens	Climber	Blue	7-10	Outside in June
Ipomea (Morning Glory)	I. Rubro-caerulea	Climber	Bright Blue	7-10	Beautiful climber
Lobelia	L. erinus	6 ins.	Blue/Pink/White	7-10	Also trailing varieties
Love-lies-bleeding	Amaranthus caudatus	2 ft	Red	7-9	Long red spikes
Marigold (African)	Tagetes erecta	2–3 ft	Yellow/Red	7-10	Lovely easy flowers
Mesembryanthemum	M. criniflorum	3–6 ins.	Brilliant colours	7-9	Dwarf edging
Nicotiana	Nicotiana affinis	2–3 ft	White/Red	7-10	Scented
Petunia	Petunia hybrids	1–2 ft	Wide range	7-10	Very vivid and attractive
Phlox	P. drummondii	6 ins.–2 ft	Wide range	7-10	Prefers heavy soil
Purslane	Portulaca grandiflora	3–6 ins.	Red/Yellow/Violet	7-10	Prefer poor dry soil
Salvia	S. patens	6 ins.–1 ft	Red/Blue	9-10	Vivid spikes
Salpiglossis	S. hybrid	2 ft	Red/Yellow	7-9	Sunny borders
Thunbergia	T. alata	Climber	Yellow/Purple	7-9	Sheltered porch
Vervain	Verbena hybrids	6 ins.–2 ft	Range	6-10	Good in window boxes
Viscaria	V. candida	1 ft	Red/Blue/Pink	7-9	Makes good drifts
Zinnia	Z. elegans	1–2 ft	Wide variety	7-10	Cuts well

amount of soil settlement, and the plants should be carefully firmed in especially after frost.

As mentioned on p. 138, staking may be necessary if the plants are tall, but if you choose plants carefully you can avoid having to stake altogether. If it is necessary, you should do it early, certainly before the plants begin to flop over. Canes may be used, but with some plants like pyrethrum it looks much more tidy and natural to use branched pea sticks in a circle around the plants and connect the sticks with twine or, if you have enough pea sticks, encircle the plants completely and avoid string altogether.

After a few years you may notice that the flowers are getting smaller. This should be remedied by either thinning the number of flowering stems or by dividing the clump and re-planting in a new situation. In thinning you should reduce the number of stems at least a month before flowering to allow space for the remaining stems to grow as well as increasing the share of soil food which each stem can obtain. Division should always be done if there are clear signs that the centre of a clump is becoming weak or straggly. You divide *early* flowering perennials in the autumn and *late* flowering ones in the spring, choosing the young outer part of the clump for re-planting and discarding the hard woody central mass.

Digging or even forking among perennials is best kept to a minimum, and weeds should be controlled by hoeing. It is almost unnecessary to winter-dig such a plot; a shallow forking or even a deep hoeing will provide all the soil movement that is necessary and will avoid damaging roots.

In many cases mulching is advised as a means of maintaining soil fertility but this can act as a source of weed seeds and should only be used if you are sure the compost is weed-free. If you have any doubts at all, use a complete fertilizer and top dress with peat.

BULBS

A wide range of plants are grouped together under the general term of bulbs, although this includes plants which produce corms, rhizomes and tubers. In fact the term bulb is, very roughly speaking, normally used for any swollen part of a plant used for propagation.

The difference between these terms need not concern us here since we are only interested in growing flowers from them. Nevertheless, it does mean that there are some differences in their treatment and I will indicate these as I go along.

When you buy most plants of this type they have been prepared by the grower in order to flower in their first year. What happens to their flowering capacities in future years is entirely up to you and the treatment they receive in your garden. They all like a good well-drained soil with a lot of organic matter. If your soil is heavy or wet then either don't expect a great deal of success or be prepared to set the bulbs on sand and cover them with sand; this is the only way of getting good growth. A dressing of bone meal at planting time at 2 oz. per square yard will also help.

There are two schools of thought about planting bulbs; some like to use them as edging plants or in beds, and some like their bulbs in grass or else just informally situated in drifts. Both schools have some right on their side, as the larger types such as hyacinths, large tulips, etc. are best in formal situations but little bulbs such as crocus, snowdrop or winter aconite and daffodils are best in groups.

The usual practice for informal drifts is to throw the bulbs down gently and just plant each one where it falls, only making adjustments to ensure at least the width of two bulbs between adjacent bulbs.

Bulbs growing in grass or under trees where they can be left to naturalize are very attractive and will often increase in number over the years. For this to occur the plants must be allowed to grow and their foliage must die down naturally. In a lawn this means it is the middle of June or even later before you can cut the grass, so that if you plan to naturalize bulbs in a lawn, limit them to a corner of the grassed area. Many bulbs will naturalize among shrubs and add a lot to a relatively cheerless spot in early spring if you plant cyclamen, winter aconite, scilla, crocus, etc., among the shrubs.

Planting

Plant bulbs in a hole about twice the size of the bulb and dust in some bone meal before planting. The depth of planting will vary

TWENTY PERENNIALS

COMMON NAME	SCIENTIFIC NAME	HEIGHT	COLOUR	FLOWER-ING MONTH	REMARKS
Achillea	*A. filipendula*	5 ft	Yellow	6–9	Good cut flower
Wormwood	*Artemisia lactiflora*	5 ft	Cream white	7–10	Stands shade a little
Michaelmas daisy	*Aster novae-belgii*	Varies	Many	8–10	Very many varieties
(choice varieties are Blondie (white), Bishop (purple), Alpenglow (rose-red), Erica (purple), Royal Velvet (purple))					
Spiraea	*Astilbe x arendsii*	2–3 ft	Purple/Pink/White	6–8	Loves moist soil
Campanula	*C. latifolia*	3 ft	Violet/Blue/White	6–9	Most beautiful but soon over
Koreans	*Chrysanthemum Koreanum*	2–3 ft	Wide Range	8–10	Very popular
Delphinium	*D. belladonna*	3 ft	Blues	6–8	Rich soil, use slug bait
Carnations (Pinks)	*Dianthus allwoodii*	1 ft	White/Red	6–9	Like lime, very scented
Bleeding Heart	*Dicentra spectabilis*	3 ft	Red and White	5–6	Very good drainage, but worth trouble

Fleabane	*Erigeron hybridus*	3 ft	Rose/Purple	6–9	Divides easily
Gypsophila	*G. paniculata*	1–4 ft	White	7–9	Floral decoration flower
Christmas Rose	*Helleborus niger*	1 ft	White	12	Beautiful winter flowers specially if protected
Lupin	*Lupinus* Russell	3 ft	Rainbow	5–7	Do not allow to seed
Paeony	*Paeonia sinensis*	4 ft	Red/White	5–8	Rich soil, stake well
Polyanthus	*Primula vulgaris elatior*	1 ft	Wide range	3–8	Many varieties in rich soil
Polygonum	*P. amplexicaule*	4 ft	Pink/Red	7–10	Spreading and tough
London Pride	*Saxifraga umbrosa*	1½ ft	Pink/White	4–7	Spreading, easy, grows in shade
Potentilla	*P. fructicosa*	2–4 ft	Yellow	6–8	Shrubby, good borders
Veronica	*Hebe spicata*	1–3 ft	Blue/Pink	6–8	Many varieties and sizes
Violet	*Viola*	6 ins.–1 ft	Yellow/Blue/Black	5–9	Wide range, includes pansies

with the size of the bulb and the heaviness of the soil. For example, a small bulb such as snowdrop in a light soil may be planted 4 ins. deep in normal conditions but only 2 ins. deep in a heavy soil, whereas a larger bulb such as a gladiolus should always be 4 or 5 ins. deep, but in heavy soils should have sand below and above it. The hole should then be filled and firmed over.

The time of planting also varies but the general rule is that spring- or winter-flowering species should be planted in September–October, summer-flowering plants such as gladiolus or alstroemeria in March–May, and autumn-flowering bulbs, e.g. autumn crocus, in July.

After-care

The care of bulbs really hinges on the fact that the food which is going to nourish the flower of the following year is manufactured by the leaves and stored in the bulb. Thus, when a daffodil flowers it completely exhausts the bulb from which it grew and next year's flower will develop properly only if ample food is made by the leaves *after flowering*. It is vital, therefore, that every opportunity should be given to the leaves to work to their maximum before they die down. If you do not want the seeds (and very few people do) then remove the spent head immediately after flowering so that no food is wasted in producing unwanted seeds. At the same time give a light top dressing of sulphate of ammonia at about 1 oz. per square yard. Then leave the foliage to die down naturally. If this is impossible, lift the plants carefully with lots of soil and transplant them to a trench in an inconspicuous part of the garden. There they can ripen and die back and the bulbs be re-planted in the autumn.

Some bulbs, such as dahlias or gladioli, should be lifted in the autumn each year since they are susceptible to frost. Clean off soil, dry out well in the sun and then store in cool, dry conditions for replanting the following spring.

Indoor bulbs are discussed in Chapter 10, p. 253.

SOME SPECIAL FAVOURITES

Chrysanthemums

This is one of the most widely grown of all flowers and its culture has become very specialized. The beginner won't want to enter his blooms for flower shows, though this may come later, so he will stick to the outdoor, hardier types. Unless you have a greenhouse, varieties have to be selected very carefully since the fact that they flower so late in the year makes chrysanthemums exceedingly vulnerable to wind, rain and frost. I shall assume that there is no greenhouse available but that you have a cold frame.

Varieties to flower in September or October should be planted in May in groups of three or four in soil which has been well dug, even double-dug if you are on clay, in order to ensure good drainage. Good well-rotted farmyard manure should be dug into the top spit – chrysanthemums are generally not very deep-rooted and must be fed near the surface. If you want large blooms, give 2 oz. per square yard of bone meal as a supplement when you plant.

Chrysanthemums are almost never grown from seeds, but usually from rooted cuttings. You can buy these from local nurseries and should arrange to receive them in early May. They should be planted when the soil is in good condition by digging a hole with a trowel (not a dibber) and giving the roots plenty of room to spread. Plants should be at least 18 ins. apart and each plant should be well staked and tied. They should be well firmed down and the tops pinched out or 'stopped'. This is done by simply removing the tip of the plant by pinching it between finger and thumb. This encourages the development of side shoots and, in a few weeks, instead of a leading shoot bearing what is usually called the 'break bud', there will be a number of side shoots each with a crown bud. This process should be repeated towards the end of June – after the second stopping, the plant will become much more bushy and produce a greater number of flowers (see Fig. 19).

Stopping is one of the great arts of chrysanthemum-growing, for by simply removing the terminal buds you can control the number of flowers which the plant will bear. A plant has only a limited

TABLE OF BULBS

NAME	SOIL	TIME OF PLANTING	DEPTH	COLOURS	TIME OF FLOWER	REMARKS
Anemone	Sandy	Jan./April	2 ins.	Red/Blue	March/Oct.	Vary flowering time by alteration in planting time
Chionodoxa	Loam	Sept./Oct.	3 ins.	Blue	March	Very attractive colour
Colchicum	Humus-rich	July	3 ins.	Yellow/Violet	Sept./Oct.	Leaves in spring
Crocus	Light	Sept./Oct.	3 ins.	White/Yellow/Purple	Feb./April	Different planting times for autumn flowering species
Cyclamen	Under trees and shrubs	June/July	1 in.	Pink/Purple	Feb./April	Leave to naturalize
Eranthis (winter aconite)	Sandy loam	Sept./Oct.	2 ins.	Yellow	Jan./March	Very early and easy
Fritillaria	Shade	Sept./Nov.	2 ins.	White/Spotted	Apr./May	Very beautiful
Gladiolus	Open sunny well-drained	Mar./April	4–5 ins.	Many colours	July/Sept.	Good cut flowers

Hyacinthus	Well-drained	October	4 ins.	Many colours	Apr./May	Fragrant
Iris (bulbous)	Well-drained	Sept./Oct.	4 ins.	White/Blue/Yellow	June/July	Very handsome
Iris (rhizome)	Humus-rich	May/July	Surface	Many colours	Apr./June	Cut flowers
Lilium (A very large and varied group. Special books should be consulted)	Well-drained	Aug./Oct.	4 ins.	Many colours	June/Sept.	Shade lovers
Muscari (Grape hyacinth)	Well-drained	Aug./Oct.	3 ins.	Blue	Mar./April	Good naturalizer
Narcissus (daffodil)	Humus-rich	Aug./Sept.	2–4 ins.	Yellow/White	Mar./May	Varied forms
Scilla	Shade	Sept./Oct.	2 ins.	Blue/Pink	April/May	Good drifts
Tulip	Well-drained	Oct./Nov.	4 ins.	Many colours	Apr./May	Good cut flowers

quantity of food material available to develop its flowers so if you want a few large flowers, or even one very large flower, then you stop accordingly. The good amateur who simply wants cut flowers for the house will allow four or five flowers to develop and remove

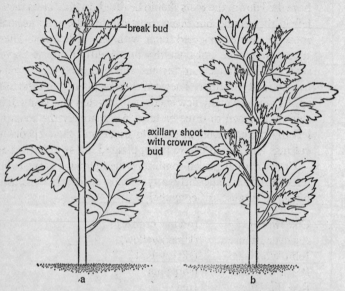

19. *Chrysanthemum plants: (a) with terminal break bud, (b) terminal break bud removed and new shoots appearing in the axil of the leaves. Each of these new shoots bears a crown bud.*

the rest of the buds. But stopping the plant not only means altering the number of flowers; it also delays the development of flowers, so by careful disbudding you can fix the week in which the flowers will be at their best. This, of course, is only important to exhibitors whose blooms must be perfect on the exact date of a flower-show; in most gardens, such meticulous stopping and timing is quite unnecessary.

In very industrial areas or regions of high wind it is not uncommon to lift outdoor chrysanthemums, put them in pots and bring them into the house to bloom. If you are considering this, be sure to give the soil a thorough soaking the day before you lift the plants and then, to reduce the shock of transplanting to a minimum, lift the plants with a very big ball of soil which will more or less fill the pot in which you intend to plant them.

In November, when the flowering season is over and the plants have died down, the roots should be lifted. In mild areas they can be left in the ground but severe frost can kill them, so normally the roots are planted in a cold frame with very little water. There they spend the winter, not bone dry but slightly damp to prevent the roots from completely drying out, and with good ventilation except in very frosty weather. They can then be planted out the following spring when so many new shoots will develop that you will have to thin them down to three or four. Alternatively the roots may be left to develop shoots in the cold frame and these shoots used as cuttings and rooted before being planted out as described above.

Under normal garden conditions the following varieties are very reliable and are sufficiently early for most parts of Britain, since they bloom in August or September:

Chatsworth   (orange bronze)
Ashover Beauty   (lemon yellow)
John Woolman   (silvery pink)
Peach Blossom   (soft pink)
Red Bill Riley   (red)
Sweetheart   (red pink, very early)
Zenith   (purple red)

Dahlias

Dahlias are usually bought as tubers and should be planted after all risk of frost has passed about 4 ins. deep in well-drained humus-rich soil. They prefer an open sunny position but will tolerate a little shade.

As the plants develop they need little or no attention although the taller types, e.g. cactus-flowered dahlias, may require staking since they will reach three or four feet in height. For this reason most people prefer the smaller varieties.

They will flower in August and September and the plants should be cut down only when frost comes. In mild places I have seen them go on until November or even December. As soon as they are frosted the tops should be cut off, and after two weeks the tubers lifted and dried. They can then be stored over winter in a cool frost-free dry place wrapped in newspaper or in a box. These tubers can then be re-planted the following spring directly into the garden or allowed to develop shoots in a cold frame. The shoots are used as cuttings to increase the stock. Alternatively the old tubers can simply be separated in April/May as soon as the buds are clearly visible.

Beginners should buy a collection of different varieties rather than a single variety to see the range of form and colour. Most catalogues list collections which can be bought either as tubers in January or as plants in May. A mixed selection of six varieties costs 50p–£1, depending on the types.

Sweet Peas

The sweet pea is one of the most desirable of flowers in many different ways for it has colour, scent, makes a good cut flower and is not very difficult to grow. It demands good soil preparation with lots of organic material dug into the top spit. Expert growers double dig a special sweet pea trench which they manure very heavily in the autumn. In early spring, the surface soil can be lightly forked over and broken down. In mild areas the seeds can be sown outside in March, but in colder, wetter places April is soon enough, and in many bad areas, or for late flowers, May is all right.

The seeds should be sown thinly and about one inch deep, and to ensure good plants many experts sow in pots under glass as early as October/November in open well-drained compost and over-winter them in a cold frame. The plants can be put out in April in double rows – i.e. two rows of plants close together (1 ft), then a wide gap (3 ft) before another two rows.

Staking is most important as sweet peas are essentially climbers and each plant as it grows should be tied to a support. (Sweet peas will cling to supports by tendrils, and the amateur can rely on these to hold them up. Professional growers remove the tendrils and so the plants must be tied to the supports.) One of the best ways of supporting sweet peas is to use a frame of wire stretched between posts. The best results are obtained by constantly removing the side shoots which appear in the angle made by a leaf and the stem. These are known as axillary shoots and if allowed to develop unchecked they reduce the number and quality of the blooms.

As soon as the flower buds appear liquid feeding should be begun – good results are easily obtained by syringing the plants with a foliar feed except in very wet weather, when a dry compound fertilizer can be dusted along the rows. As soon as the flowers open they should be cut for the house.

BOOK LIST

A Concise Guide to Flower Growing: Witham Fogg, H. G. (Muller)
The Complete Flower Grower: Shewell-Cooper, W. L. (Faber)
Encyclopaedia of Chrysanthemums: Bennett, M. (Pearson)
Annual and Biennial Flowers: Balfour, A. P. (Penguin Handbook)
Unfamiliar Flowers for your Garden: Darnell, A. W. (Collingridge)
Growing Cut Flowers: Witham Fogg, H. G. (Blandford)
Summer Flowers: Brown, R. (Ward Lock)
Perennial Flowers for Small Gardens: Hunt, P. (Arthur Barker)
The Garden Flowers: Witham Fogg, H. G. (Blandford)
Hardy Perennials: Lloyd, C. (Studio Vista)
Collins Guide to Border Plants: Perry, F. (Collins)
Bulbs: Roy Genders (Robert Hale)

TABLE OF FLOWERS FOR DIFFERENT SITUATIONS

(PERENNIALS (see p. 148)

Clay Soils

Aster	Erigeron	Polygonum
Astilbe	Geranium	Primula
Caltha	Hosta	Salvia
Campanula	Iris	Sidalcea

Chalky & Limestone Soils

Alyssum	Dianthus	Lathyrus
Anemone	Geranium	Linaria
Aquilegia	Gypsophila	Paeonia
Campanula	Hypericum	Prunella
Centaurea	Iris	Scabiosa
Clematis		

Shady or Woodland Areas

Anemone	Dicentra	Polygonum
Aquilegia	Geranium	Primula
Astilbe	Hosta	Saxifraga
	Lobelia	

Windy Positions

Alyssum	Malva	Sedum
Anemone	Potentilla	Stachys
Centaurea	Scabiosa	Valeriana
Geranium		

Moisture-Loving Plants

Astilbe	Mimulus	Rudbeckia
Caltha	Phlox	Salvia
Hosta	Polygonum	Sidalcea
Iris	Primula	Trollius
Lobelia		

Town Gardens

Aquilegia	Hypericum	Primula
Campanula	Iris	Salvia
Chrysanthemum	Lobelia	Sidalcea
Dicentra	Lupin	Veronica
Geranium	Polygonum	Viola

Ground Cover (*choose dwarf spreading varieties*)

Ajuga	Hypericum	Prunella
Armeria	Lamium	Stachys
Dianthus	Origanum	Veronica
Geranium	Polygonum	Vinca

Cut Flowers

Achillea	Chrysanthemum	Gypsophila	Polygonum
Aquilegia	Delphinium	Helianthus	Rudbeckia
Aster	Dianthus	Lupin	Sidalcea
Campanula	Erigeron	Paeonia	Stachys
Centaurea	Gaillardia	Phlox	Trollius

Scented Flowers

Clove Carnations	*Lilium auratum*	Stocks
Freesias	Lily of the valley	Sweet peas
Honeysuckle	Mignonette	Sweet scabious
Jasmine	*Matthiola bicornis*	Thyme
Lilac	Roses	Violets
	Sage	Wallflowers

8 *Shrubs, Trees and Hedges*

More and more people are growing shrubs and trees. There are many reasons for this but I think a combination of ease and beauty is probably the most important. In addition there are now many more varieties suitable in size for even the smallest garden. The character of a garden used to be determined by its herbaceous borders and rose beds. These were a riot of colour in summer but a source of work and worry for the rest of the year. One of the great advantages of shrubs is their range of times of flowering plus the fact that many have not only attractive flowers but also coloured fruits in winter and flaming autumn foliage. The modern garden is *not* a collection of flowerbeds and borders but increasingly a place of green lawns, with very few beds, maybe a shrub border and specimen shrubs or trees growing out of the lawn. It is much more restful – a place for relaxation and children's games rather than double digging and bedding out.

Firstly, don't be put off by cost. A shrub or a tree is more expensive than a packet of seed, but a rose bush costing, say, 50p will give pleasure for ten or fifteen years. A rose bush must be pruned but there are many shrubs which, once planted, will need little or no attention for years. This means there is a great saving in digging, weeding, sowing and so on. Once you have arrived at a general plan a fixed sum of a pound or two can be spent on shrubs or trees each year and the garden will slowly take shape. You can also propagate from your own plants and exchange rooted cuttings with fellow gardeners.

Care should always be taken in the choice of shrub and in the place where you plant it. It is very easy to obscure an ugly view or building with a few *well-placed* shrubs or trees, but a *badly-placed* tree may spoil a very nice view. A few shrubs can also help to focus attention on some special feature so that the eye is taken to a pleasant vista without anyone realizing that this has been carefully planned.

To do this and get the best value from your planting, stand with your back to the house and look out and survey the neighbourhood. Pick out the eye-sores and the pleasant views. Then go to each window in turn inside the house and try to imagine the garden with trees or shrubs at the chosen places. Put all these views together and you will come up with a shrub or tree-planting plan.

But before you plant anything there are a number of points to remember. Firstly plant only a few shrubs to begin with – these will act as guides to the eventual plan. Not only is this cheaper, but it will discourage you from crowding shrubs or trees so that they cannot grow to their full extent and show their maximum shape and beauty.

Secondly, it is not enough to find out the common or even the scientific name of a shrub; you must also be sure of the variety or cultivar (cultivated variety) you want. For example, most people know the mountain ash or rowan tree, whose scientific name is *Sorbus aucuparia*. It is a tree about fifteen feet high with a slender trunk and a roughly spherical crown of branches. As such it is a very attractive focus of attention and is often used at the foot of a garden to provide privacy from adjacent houses. But there are a number of varieties of *S. aucuparia*: for example, Pendula is a weeping form with branches trailing down to the ground which is useful as a low screen but not as a tree; Hilling's Spire is upright with branches parallel to the main trunk so that it does not have the spreading crown of the usual rowan. This is very good in a small garden where upright growth is important, and a wide spread of branches could be an embarrassment. (For a list of trees and shrubs see p. 185).

The third thing to remember is that while trees and shrubs may provide privacy and a screen against neighbours they also occupy quite a lot of ground and create shade. Shade may be tolerable in an open lawn or at the foot of the garden, but near the house it may darken rooms and make them damp, so consider all the possible consequences before you plant a tree near the house.

Remember too that you have neighbours, and that shade may darken part of their garden and lead to hard feelings. If you think your planting may produce problems ask for advice or simply have a chat with the interested parties before you embark on anything ambitious. Shade affects the growth of other plants so you must consider what you are going to plant underneath at the same time as you consider the tree or shrub.

Finally, always take great care if you are planting anything large or permanent near a path or pavement. As the shrubs grow they may obstruct the footpath and lead to trouble with the local authority. Many enthusiasts start off with a love of shrub roses which are easy to grow and require no pruning – all in all, the beginner's dream. But they have thorns and if grown near a road or path will not only snag stockings and dresses but can actually be dangerous if long branches with thorns whip over the pavement on a windy day. So when planting thorny or spiny plants think carefully about their final size and shape.

PREPARATIONS FOR PLANTING

Soil

The ideal soil for all shrubs is a deep loam with good free drainage. However, practically no-one has this so you must make the best use of what you have. Shrubs and trees are generally long-lived so it is good sense to prepare the ground carefully before you plant; this may seem a nuisance at the time, but once the tree is planted it may occupy that space for twenty years, and you will never need to dig or cultivate the area again. Good preparation not only ensures that the tree or shrub will take root but encourages better growth for many years. So first of all choose the site, remove any large stones or rocks and burn any old tree stumps or dead wood – – pests and diseases can spread from a decaying stump to a living tree and shorten its life considerably. The ground should then be well dug (double digging is advisable) and a quantity of leaf mould or compost incorporated in the planting area. This is especially important in sandy soils which can be very dry in the summer unless they have moisture-holding humus – young trees which have not had time to develop good roots may simply die from drought.

If on turning the ground over you find that the soil is shallow with a layer of rock or heavy clay within one foot of the surface, you will have to reconsider carefully. Even a small tree or large shrub is a heavy object and is held erect by the roots, so that the tree can retain its upright position despite the buffeting of high winds. If the soil is very shallow roots may not be able to grow deep enough to support the plant. So you will have to break up the heavy clay to allow the roots to penetrate, prepare a special hole for planting, or choose small or even dwarf varieties whose roots will be able to hold a three-foot shrub or tree firmly in position.

Planting

Most beginners dig a small hole and stuff the shrub into it, perfectly content so long as the roots are covered. If you are lucky you may get away with this half the time, but generally the tree will die. So, a golden rule in tree or shrub planting is to prepare a large hole deep enough to allow the soil mark on the shrub to be just below the soil surface and wide enough to contain the roots with little bending or coiling. Too shallow planting may expose the roots to frost and drought, and too deep may not allow the air around the roots which is so necessary for good health. The soil you dig from the hole should be placed to one side and mixed with leaf mould or compost. Then you are really ready to begin.

In some cases special planting holes may be necessary, for example if you try to grow a rhododendron on a chalky soil. In such a case the expert would dig a very large hole, maybe even line it with polythene, and then fill it with a mixture of lime-free soil and peat before planting the shrub. Beginners, however, are well advised to practise the old adage of 'horses for courses'; if your soil is not suitable for, say, rhododendrons you should simply not grow them but concentrate on the kinds of shrub your soil can grow well.

When to Plant

It is important to plant at the correct time of year, and the reason for this is simple. Plants lose water from their leaves in great quantities in the process known as transpiration, and this water is taken from the soil by the roots and simply passed up the stem to the leaves. If the roots are damaged or if they are inadequate in any way the leaves will be short of water, will go limp and wilt and the plant will die. When you buy a shrub the roots are often wrapped in sacking and sometimes enclosed in a ball of soil. You remove the sacking and plant the shrub. It takes a long time for the roots to start growing again and make sufficiently intimate contact with the soil to enable them to absorb water, and if there is a dry spell or even a lot of wind immediately after planting a lot of water will evaporate from the leaves and the plant may die.

To avoid this, trees and shrubs are usually planted after the leaves have fallen or, better still, in the late autumn or early spring when the plant is dormant and losing little or no water. This gives it a chance to settle in the soil and for the roots to start growing again before the leaves appear in spring and put a strain on the water supply. On the other hand, evergreen trees and shrubs such as holly or conifers, which do not shed their leaves in winter although they become semi-dormant, are best planted in spring in about April.

These planting times are very important – plants can easily be lost if they are moved at the wrong time. Recently, however, the garden centres have started selling container-grown trees and shrubs. These plants are *not* dug out of the soil but have been grown within the containers so that when bought the root system is perfect. In many cases the whole purchase can be put into the planting hole as the container may be made of paper or even peat which will rapidly rot away in the soil and the plant will continue growing with no interruption of root action. Container-grown shrubs and trees can therefore be planted at nearly any time of year, although it is unwise to plant when they are in full flower, as this is a time of stress for the plant when the minimum of movement is advisable. Apart from this there are few risks in planting container-grown material, though it is always wise to follow the pattern advised for ordinary plants.

Planting Procedure

Let us assume you have some shrubs which you want to plant in late autumn. The hole in the ground is ready, the soil for refilling the hole is mixed and the plant is lying on the ground beside you.

You then carefully remove the packing, trying not to disturb the ball of soil around the roots. If there is no soil around the roots you should look for any sign of broken roots, and if you spot any trim them back with scissors or secateurs.

If the plant is container-grown you simply put it in the hole but if its roots are exposed you should try to ensure that they are well spread out at the bottom of the hole. This spread of roots means that as they grow the plant will be securely anchored against wind from any direction and will draw its food supply from all around the plant and not just one place. Many young trees and shrubs will need staking for a year or two until the roots are well established – plant the stake at the same time as the shrub, driving it firmly into the soil at the base of the planting hole with the roots arranged around it. Stakes driven in after planting can damage roots.

Next, gradually fill in the hole with the soil/compost mixture a little at a time, shaking the plant gently and treading the soil down now and then to make sure that the soil and the roots are firmly in contact with each other. Continue filling the hole and treading it down until there is a little mound around the base of the tree – the soil level will eventually settle and fall. Give the newly planted shrub a good watering to wash the soil into any fine cracks or spaces around the roots, and that is that.

Small trees planted in lawns should always have a circle of bare earth cut out around them. This is easily done at planting time and allows the tree to be fed within the circle without encouraging heavy growth of grass. You can also cut the grass around the circle with a mower which does away with the long grass against the tree trunk which cannot be mown and must be cut with shears. The clear area around the tree also stops you banging the plant with the mower. Of course you have increased the length of edge, and you will need to weed the cleared area, but this is a small price to pay for good trees and shrubs. You can also grow spring bulbs or small annuals around the base of the tree.

To summarize:

(1) Prepare the hole carefully and make it large.
(2) Spread the roots and plant the stake too.

(3) Fill the hole slowly with a rich compost/soil mixture, making the soil firm as you go along.
(4) End up with a good watering.
(5) After severe frost visit each shrub and refirm the soil around it.

For a list of shrubs suitable for a range of differing conditions see p. 205-207.

HEDGES

Hedges are nearly always trees or shrubs cultivated in such a way that their height is kept down and adjacent plants merge branches. The general principles of spacing do not apply in planting a hedge since the idea is to prevent the plants reaching their full size or true shape.

The soil under hedges tends to be poor, for not only are there many plants in a small area but you are continually cutting bits off the plants, taking the clippings away and burning them so that the food in the soil is always in danger of being seriously depleted. It is very important therefore that the soil in which a hedge is to be grown should be well dug, composted and even given some additional slow-acting fertilizer such as bone meal before planting.

Many trees and shrubs can be made into hedges – far more than the usual privet and its golden variety. With careful attention privet makes a very good hedge, but so do many other plants, and if you are interested in moving away from the standard pattern a list of suitable shrubs for hedging is given at the end of this chapter (p. 206). Nowadays mixed hedges are becoming more and more common and some very good combinations of flower and leaf colour can be produced. For example, *Prunus cerasifera pissartii* can be mixed with privet, beech with privet, and many of the berberises and cotoneasters blend well. I have seen *Jasminum nudiflorum* used in a mixed hedge and in all cases the general effect is good. If you decide to grow a mixed hedge try to match species of roughly the same vigour and height so as not to have to prune at different times of the year. It is also not very advisable to mix evergreen and deciduous plants since evergreen, of which holly is a good example, will outgrow the deciduous plant and maybe kill it.

The ideal hedge should be dense enough to keep out dogs and cats (maybe even small boys) and should not be thin at the bottom as this produces draughts of cold air at ground level which may do damage to other more tender plants. To produce a uniformly dense hedge the plants should be cut to half their height immediately after planting. This encourages the growth of side shoots and so helps to thicken the hedge. Continue cutting back frequently in the first few years to half height in spring and removing new wood each summer. This means sacrificing height to begin with, but unless you do so you will never get a good thick hedge.

Young hedges may need clipping back three or even four times in the first few years, but as the final height and thickness is reached the number can be reduced. Two clippings are usually perfectly adequate for a fully grown deciduous hedge, one in spring and the other in August. Evergreen hedges, on the other hand, should always be pruned in spring when new growth will rapidly remove their bare shaved look. Ideally a hedge should be tapered upwards and not have a flat top on which snow can lie and cause damage. This tapering also helps to thicken out the sides and so produce a denser hedge.

Many gardeners thicken their hedges by pushing some of the cut pieces into the ground after the autumn pruning. These act as cuttings of half-ripe wood which will root by the next spring. Of course a large number die but some always strike and then you have a new plant thickening the base of the hedge.

Before leaving hedges, I must repeat that they should only be planted after careful thought, as they do cast shade and tend to deplete the adjacent soil of foodstuffs. If you feed the hedge too well the task of keeping it under control can be very difficult, so plants near it must be able to withstand shade and poor soil. There are sprays on the market which are growth deterrents and will inhibit the growth of hedges for some months. This means less pruning though you should remember that any reduction in growth also means a reduction in the formation of basal and side shoots so that the hedge will never become thick and solid.

CARING FOR TREES AND SHRUBS

Staking

One of the main reasons for growing trees and shrubs is that they save work. This does not mean that once you have planted them and they are growing you should neglect them entirely. For example, you need to be careful in the way you stake young shrubs. It is very important that this is done carefully and well, for a badly tied tree will tend to chafe its bark on the tie and if this is made of wire or rough string the tree may be killed. Special broad ties can be bought for trees and shrubs but as they are expensive many amateurs wrap the wire or string with sacking or rags to produce a soft surface which will not grind the bark away, or they fix a ring of soft rubber (old bicycle tyre) or rags on the tree where the tie goes around it. Ties should be checked every year for tightness and as the tree grows they will need to be loosened. The tie should be tight enough to allow the tree or shrub a little movement, but not much – a tree which rocks violently will suffer root damage and may die.

Labelling

At the same time check your labelling of the plant. There are many different types of label, from the metal plates you see in parks at the base of specimen trees to the little wooden labels you put in plant pots. The best for most shrubs or trees is the metal tag that can be tied to the twigs or branches on which the name of the shrub, both scientific and common, is written in soft pencil. Do not use ordinary ink as it will wash off in the first rain; biro is all right but it does not last so long as pencil. I try to label each shrub twice in case one becomes illegible or is lost. This may seem a bit fussy but it is maddening not to be able to put a name to a tree in your own garden, and your memory may be unreliable after a year or two.

Feeding

If the soil has been well enriched before the tree or shrub is planted you won't need to feed it again for two or three years. On the other hand most trees or shrubs show marked benefit from an annual

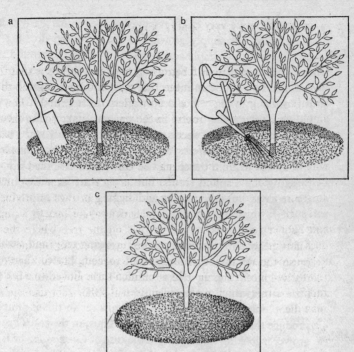

20. *Mulching:* (*a*) *Remove 2–3 ins. of surface soil taking care not to damage the roots.* (*b*) *Give the exposed soil surface a good soaking.* (*c*) *Replace the soil and spread the mulch 2–3 ins. thick on top. Do not pack it up to the stem of the plant. The mulch material prevents water evaporating into the air.*

dressing of compost, leaf mould or peat. This mulch properly applied has a number of advantages; it adds humus to the soil and helps to maintain free drainage; it acts as a protective layer on the soil surface (many trees and shrubs have their feeding roots near the surface and in a period of drought these delicate roots can be killed); it ensures that the soil does not heat up excessively and gives the plant 'a cool root run'; it also acts as a weed smother – many weed seedlings buried beneath two or three inches of compost never reach the surface and simply die, while those which do come up can be very easily removed as their roots are not deep in the ground but simply growing in the loose top dressing. Most people mulch by simply scattering compost on the ground around the plant, but there is a better way as shown in Fig. 20.

A further point should be obvious from what has just been said; it is difficult to dig or hoe deeply around shrubs and trees without killing or damaging roots. So if you have weedy shrub beds try either to smother the weeds or kill them chemically with paraquat; if you are driven to hoeing or even forking try to imagine the roots spreading out from the shrub like the spokes of a wheel. To avoid breaking these spokes (roots) fork *along* the line of the roots and *not across it*. But keep forking and digging as a last resort.

Pruning

Many people are discouraged from growing trees and shrubs because the details of pruning seem so complicated. They aren't really – most pruning is just common sense linked to a little (very little) observation of your plants.

People do ask 'Why prune?' The answer to this is simply 'To produce the kind of effect you want'. Thus, in the case of roses the grower is looking for flowers, in the case of *Cornus alba* he is trying to encourage young growth with bright red stems, and in the case of apples he wants fruit.

Pruning is tree surgery and is best done in winter when the tree or shrub is dormant. Then the plant can be closely inspected without leaves and flowers getting in the way and in the cold weather there is much less chance of infection getting into the pruning wound. The first job in winter is to remove the dead wood and burn it. Dead wood should be pruned or if necessary sawn off; if the death of any particular branch is due to disease you thereby lower the chances of the disease spreading to other branches. A word of warning here: if you prune off a diseased branch and then move on to tidy up a healthy one you will spread the disease on the secateurs, so give them a wipe with a duster soaked in disinfectant as often as you think they may have been contaminated.

Make sure the cut is clean and if possible close to the main trunk or branch; make the cut surface elliptical by extending top and bottom edges. Use good sharp secateurs, as jagged edges are difficult to heal and, if water gets into a split branch and freezes, the branch will split further. If you have to leave large wounds after removing a major branch the cut surface should be protected with creosote or tar or one of the special proprietary paints (see Fig. 21).

The second job is to prune the plant 'to shape', which really means that you make it grow in the manner you want and not as

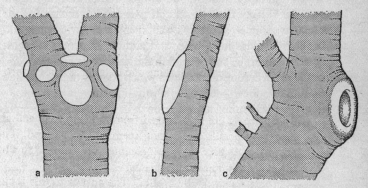

21. *Pruning thick branches: (a) Cut off the branches as close to the surface as possible. (b) Make the cut surface elliptical by extending top and bottom edges; coat with a preservative paint. (c) Healing starts from the edges producing a raised rim which eventually meets in the centre.*

nature directs. To do this you make sure that you have branches growing out all round the tree, i.e. that it is not one-sided. Badly placed or spindly branches should be cut off flush with the trunk. Sometimes ordinary shrubs suddenly develop a shoot very much more vigorous than the others. If left alone this 'bull shoot' will begin to dominate the shrub, getting most of the food and water and perhaps causing the rest of the plant to dwindle and die. Such an overgrowth should be removed or drastically shortened. Any weak or damaged shoots should be taken out.

Apart from the above, you will find that most shrubs and trees can look after themselves and, if things are going well, then it is best to leave them alone. Pruning is not necessary every year and it should only be done when needed.

The Penguin Book of Basic Gardening

Lastly, if you want flowers you may need to prune for this, as well as doing the normal winter pruning.

Trees and shrubs can be divided into groups for pruning:

(1) *Shrubs which flower in winter or early spring*
Examples: *Forsythia suspensa, Clematis montana,* Winter Jasmine etc.

If you think for a moment you will realize that early spring shrubs must be bearing their flowers on twigs and branches formed the previous summer, and if you want many flowers you must encourage lots of twigs in summer and autumn. It would be senseless therefore to prune such shrubs in the latter half of the year, for this would mean cutting off the wood which is going to bear the flowers. So prune your early-flowering shrubs immediately after the flowers fall. This will stimulate new growth in summer and autumn and thus increase the quantity of flowers.

It is easy to say 'prune immediately after flowering'; the real question is how much to cut off. If you look at any branch of a shrub you will see that the tip is soft and green and as you look back towards the main stem there will be a ring marking the end of last year's growth (the old wood) and the beginning of this year's growth (the new wood) (Fig. 22). If left alone *this* year's *new* wood will become *next* year's old wood, the flowers will continue to be borne on the new wood at the ends of the branches and will get further and further away from the main stem. In order to stop this and to keep the flowers where you want them you prune this group of shrubs by cutting each branch back almost to the old wood, but not quite. New shoots will arise near this point and the flowers will be borne there.

(2) *Shrubs which flower between April and July*
Examples: Lilacs, Cotoneaster, Spiraea etc.

This type of shrub also flowers on old wood, but if you prune immediately after flowering you will probably remove a lot of wood which would flower next year, for *this* year's flowering shoots and *next* year's flowering shoots are growing at the same time. So the treatment here is very simply *leave them alone.* You should, of course, remove dead wood and shoots that are getting too big, but otherwise

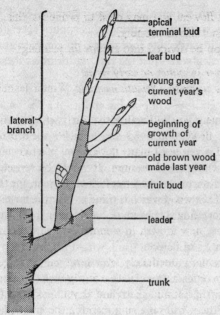

apical
terminal bud

leaf bud

young green
current year's
wood

lateral
branch

beginning of
growth of
current year

old brown wood
made last year

fruit bud

leader

trunk

22. A shoot showing leaders, laterals and the difference between old and new wood, and leaf and fruit buds.

this group of shrubs is the lazy gardener's dream, for they require little or no pruning.

(3) *Shrubs which flower from July until late autumn*
   Examples: Buddleia, *Clematis jackmanii* etc.
These flower on shoots which have grown since spring, i.e. on new wood. Pruning must therefore be done in the *winter* so that when spring comes the new shoots can grow uninterrupted. So in December/January you cut the flowering stems of the previous year back nearly to the old wood; this will encourage lots of new growth in early spring. (See also point (1) p. 178.)

(4) *Evergreen shrubs*
   Examples: Holly, Berberis, heaths and heathers, conifers.
These normally require little or no pruning and should only be

trimmed to keep them within the necessary bounds. Such cutting as is required is best done in spring; this applies specially to heathers which tend in gardens to lose their tight compact growth unless given a trim each year—just the tips, with garden shears.

(5) *Trees*

Fruit trees need a special type of pruning and will be dealt with in Chapter 9; here I just consider decorative trees, such as flowering cherry, in the small garden. Once again we ask the question 'What do we want?' and the answer usually is 'a shapely tree, not too tall, which flowers at the appropriate time of year'. Therefore choose your trees carefully after reading the catalogues listing height, time of flowering, and any other points of interest. The list at the end of this chapter (p. 185) should serve as an introduction to the range and variety.

Good trees always have a single trunk with a balanced top and you should never buy a tree with more than one stem. If for some reason the main stem or leader gets broken, a number of shoots will grow out from below the break; one of these should be selected and trained as the new leader even if this means tying it to a stake to make it vertical. The other shoots should be cut off so that all the food material goes into the new leading shoot.

Most garden, as distinct from forest, trees will branch at some height up the trunk – it is the development of these side branches which produce the shapely head. As the tree grows it should be watched for any branches which are growing excessively and would unbalance the tree. If any appear, they should be trimmed back and if the distortion of shape is too great the branch should be removed.

To sum up, the golden rules in pruning are:
(1) Only prune if you have a good reason.
(2) In the case of flowering shrubs, observe the time of flowering and prune accordingly.
(3) Burn all old and dead wood.
(4) Paint large pruning wounds with some protective substance.
(5) Most important, be sure your secateurs are sharp.

PROPAGATION

One of the greatest pleasures for everyone is to get trees and shrubs for nothing. This is easy if you know a little about plant propagation. There are four types of propagation of which only one, *cuttings*, is of major importance. The other three will therefore be dealt with briefly:

(1) *Seeds*

Propagation by seed is nature's way and in theory is the easiest and best, but many trees and shrubs are sterile and produce no seeds. Others are hybrids and produce seeds which do not breed true. This means that the plants grown from seeds will not necessarily be as good as the parent and you may waste years nurturing a seedling only to find that when it flowers it is not what you want. So collect and, if you like, grow seedlings for interest but do not expect reliable plants from many of them. (For details on growing seeds and seedlings see Chapter 7, p. 139.)

(2) *Division*

This very simple method of increasing numbers involves dividing a parent plant into two or more daughters. It is only possible with shrubs which produce many stems and roots, e.g. spiraeas. In spring the clump is split with a sharp spade or simply torn apart, ensuring that each piece has undamaged roots and stems. These are then planted and watered and although they may take a year or so to settle down will eventually become good plants. Division cannot of course be used on trees or shrubs with a single stem, though there is an artificial imitation known as layering.

(3) *Layering*

This method encourages a tree or shrub to produce two or more root systems. Briefly a long whippy branch close to the soil surface is chosen and a sloping cut is made about half-way through this branch on its undersurface, about a foot from the tip. A pocket of soil near this branch is enriched with leaf mould and sand to ensure good drainage but adequate moisture, and the shoot bent down in a

U-shape making sure that the cut part is under the soil in the prepared pocket. It can be kept there by putting a stone on top or by simply pegging it down with a forked stick. The tip of the branch will protrude above the ground (see Fig. 23).

Layering is best done in the spring and it usually takes 6–12

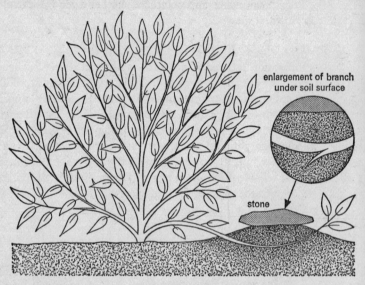

enlargement of branch under soil surface

stone

23. *Layering*.

months before a new root system has developed from the cut area. This will be obvious as the tip of the layered shoot will start to grow again. Once this happens the stone and the compost can be removed and the layer with its new root system separated from the parent and planted elsewhere. There is no need to restrict yourself to one layer per plant – commercial growers often use specially prepared parent plants from each of which many layers can be taken in any one season.

There is a variation of this method known as air layering (Fig. 24) which can be used if there are no branches near enough the ground to act as ordinary layers. You choose an actively growing young branch and make a slanting cut in an upward direction half way through or even less. Don't make the cut too deep or the cut end will simply die and drop off (some growers prefer just to remove a little circle of bark from the branch about ¼ in. wide). If you use the 'cut' method wedge the cut open with a piece of matchstick or twist of sphagnum moss.

You then take a polythene sheet and wind it several times round

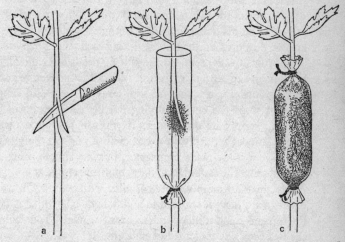

24. *Air Layering:* (a) *The upward sloping cut about 1–2 ins. long reaching nearly to the centre.* (b) *Polythene tied round the branch several times with the lower part below the cut and tied firmly to the branch.* (c) *The cylinder of polythene packed with moss or peat and sealed top.*

the branch until the base of the cylinder is below the cut. Tie or tape the lower edge to the branch firmly. The cut will now be inside the cylinder which should be filled with damp sphagnum moss, peat or even moist leaf mould. The top can now be sealed with tape and the layer is in a little container of its own. The polythene lets air through but retains moisture and in a few months, if your technique is good, you will see the new roots appearing under the polythene. The branch and its new roots can then be separated from the parent and planted out.

Many dwarf shrubs such as heathers layer naturally and of course you can also divide them.

(4) *Cuttings*

A cutting is a part of the plant which is separated from the parent and stimulated to produce its own root system. This is the chief method of propagating trees and shrubs and although there are tricks to every trade and some shrubs are notoriously difficult, the general method is simple (see Fig. 25). In addition, friends do not usually object to your taking a few twigs from a special shrub and these can be made into cuttings. Enthusiasts always carry a sharp knife and a polythene bag when visiting each other's gardens.

For roots to be produced the cutting needs a certain amount of heat, plenty of air and moisture. In fact the modern technique of rooting cuttings in a fine mist or spray is successful simply because it stops the cutting drying out before it produces enough roots to supply its own water. If you can provide a reasonably humid atmosphere, say in a box with a glass or polythene top, you have a ready-made propagator, but any simple container will do providing the essentials of light, moisture and heat are available. Many amateurs simply use a pot filled with compost in which the cuttings are placed, slip it into a polythene bag which is closed at the top and stand it in a porch or near a window. You should open the bag each day to get rid of stale air.

Since root production needs air, the compost must be light and open; a mixture of equal parts of coarse sand and loam or compost or peat is perfectly adequate. If you cannot get these then vermiculite or soilless composts are nearly as good. This mixture should be pressed down but not compacted and the cuttings inserted using a thin rod such as a pencil to make a hole a little wider than the cutting. The cutting should be planted so that its base is in contact with the soil and not left dangling in the hole, otherwise it will die. The production of roots is hastened if the base of the cutting is dipped in a hormone rooting compound before it is inserted in the medium.

Cuttings should always be taken from twiggy side shoots. This enables them to be pulled from the main stem with a small piece of the old stem still attached. This is called a cutting with a 'heel' and the heel helps roots to develop. If the heel is too long it should be trimmed with a sharp knife or scissors. There used to be great dispute about whether the cutting should be taken above or below a leaf-joint or node on the parent plant, but this is a relatively minor point through there is some reason to believe that a cutting just below the joint is best.

The cutting should not be too long. Two or three inches is adequate although ten to twelve inches is not too long. It is advisable to reduce the number of leaves on longer cuttings until there is only the bud at the tip and two or three pairs of leaves. In all the operations use a very sharp knife otherwise bruising or splitting can damage the cutting.

There are three main types of cutting, depending on the time of year at which they are taken. The differences in treatment are very small but attention to detail will produce better results.

(a)   *Soft cuttings* are taken from the tips of soft green growing shoots and are sometimes called 'tip' cuttings. They are usually taken in spring or early summer and because they are soft they need to be protected against excessive water loss by being rooted in a propagator or polythene bag, and given bottom heat if possible.

(b)   *Half-ripe cuttings* are taken with a heel in July or August and are the ones most often used commercially. These can be rooted ('struck' is the technical term) outside provided they are placed in a sheltered shady spot. Shelter can be very simple – a cloche or bell jar is most efficient but I have seen many cuttings rooted under jam jars.

(c)   *Ripe- and hard-wood cuttings* are taken from ripe wood of the current season's growth, preferably in September/October. Such cuttings, about four to six inches long, can be tied together in bundles with wool (it is believed that they stimulate each other to produce roots). Since they are usually leafless the problem of water loss is eliminated. Many of these can simply be inserted outside in a light open soil in a sheltered spot or in a cold frame. There they can stay all winter and many will have rooted by late spring. There will be losses but also many gains.

One of the greatest temptations facing the beginner is to examine his cuttings to see if roots have been formed – this often kills them. Once a cutting has been inserted it should be left alone until the development of the terminal bud or of side buds shows that growth is occurring. Only then should the new plant be carefully dug up, grown in a suitable area for a year or two and then planted in its permanent situation.

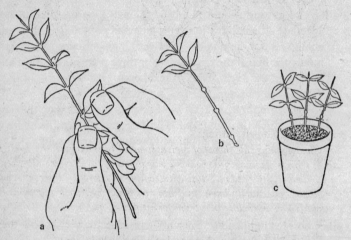

25a. *Taking a privet cutting: (a) Cut a length of stem and remove the bottom leaves. (b) Cut the stem at an angle with a sharp razor blade just below a leaf junction and remove all except the top two or three pairs of leaves. (c) Fill a plant pot with a mixture of coarse sand and peat and insert the cuttings with about one-third of their length below the surface, well down. Keep the pot in a cool, shaded place and take care that it does not dry out.*

Summary

(1) Be sure to use a light open compost for rooting cuttings. Some growers prepare a special trench a few feet long and fill it with the soil/peat mixture.

(2) Your knife or secateurs must be very sharp.

(3) Remember if possible to take a heel with the cutting.

(4) Reduce the number of leaves to the bud to two or at the most three pairs.

(5) Use a hormone rooting powder.

(6) Although you should have your cuttings in a sheltered spot,

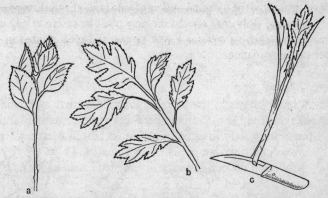

25b. Taking a soft cutting:

a) Choose young side shoots of typical stems in June-August. b) Detach them with a clean cut just below a leaf junction. c) Remove all except a few leaves, slit base and dust with rooting powder. d) Insert in a pot or box of open, sandy loam. e) Firm and water soil well and place in a cold frame or enclose in a transparent plastic bag.

they do need light and so a north-facing aspect is very good – they are unlikely to dry out there and the light is adequate.

(7) If you use a home-made propagator, polythene bag or even a jam jar remember to open the top every day to allow plenty of air into the container.

LIST OF EASY SHRUBS AND TREES FOR SMALL GARDENS

Acer

This is a group of sycamores and maples, most of which are too large for the small garden, but some smaller Japanese varieties have bright red beautiful foliage and can be highly decorative. Best grown as an individual shrub in a sheltered or even shady corner. Since many Japanese maples are grafted they are not easy to propagate.

Soil: they prefer rich, well-drained but moist conditions and rarely succeed in open windswept areas. Plant when dormant.

Pruning: very little is needed except to shape and open out the plants in January/February.

Varieties: Acer palmatum atropurpureum, leaves crimson all summer. 12 ft, £4.
Acer japonicum aureum, soft yellow leaves and slow-growing. 15 ft, £2.

Arbutus unedo

A small (20–30 ft) tree suitable for milder parts of Britain. It is evergreen and in the autumn produces white flowers and fruit very like a strawberry in appearance. At its best in winter, when both flowers and fruits are present. Costs approx. £1.30.

Soil: will do well in peaty or limestone soils under moist mild conditions.

Pruning: cut back old stems in May, but otherwise just keep the plant in shape.

Aucuba japonica

Well-known shrub often mistaken for laurel. It has large leaves like those of rhododendrons, but these are often mottled with yellow and may even appear speckled. The flowers are small and inconspicuous but female plants will produce red berries which last until the summer. The yellow colouration of *A. japonica* leaves is due to a virus disease. This virus will not spread to other species of plant and so it is perfectly safe to grow. It is one of the few instances where a diseased plant – in this case mottled – is of greater value than a healthy green one. The virus does not appear to shorten the life of the shrub.

Soil: will thrive in almost any soil even if drainage is poor, and although it will grow in the sun, better leaves are produced in shade.

Pruning: once established it is very difficult to kill *Aucuba* by pruning so that they can be clipped and shaped to form a hedge or simply grown as a shrub. Over-large specimens can be cut back to about 18 ins. off the ground. They will shoot again from the base and can be re-shaped. Pruning can be done at any time of year but in the case of hedges April or early May is best.

Varieties: A. japonica crotonoides, leaves heavily mottled. 10 ft, £1.20.
A. japonica sulphurea, leaves with broad yellow margins, 6 ft, £1.95.

Azaleas

See Rhododendron, p. 201.

Berberis

There is a very wide range of species of berberis, some evergreen and some deciduous, some with brightly coloured flowers and fruits. Species are available to grow in almost any soil or light condition. Many species have long thorns and so are used as hedging plants, to keep out children and animals.

Soil: almost any soil is suitable though they may be adversely affected by waterlogging. Will grow on both lime and lime-free soils.

Pruning: as in most shrubs old branches or shoots should be cut back to ground level. Many species produce occasional over-vigorous shoots (bull shoots) and these should be cut back to the main branch from which they grow. Otherwise shape evergreen species in March/April and deciduous species in January/February.

Varieties: from many species I have selected:

B. beaniana, a compact deciduous bush. Yellow flowers in June and purple berries in autumn. 6 ft, 75p.

B. darwinii, a common evergreen glossy species. Red flowers in April/May and blue berries. There are many varieties of this. 10 ft, £1.10.

B. stenophylla, evergreen and probably the most beautiful. Makes an excellent hedge. Bright yellow flowers all along the stem in April/May. Berries in August. Can be cut and shaped to almost any form. 8 ft, 65p.

B. thunbergii, a deciduous species with bright red foliage in autumn. The flowers are single and not very attractive but fruits are bright red and stay long after the leaves fall. Makes a good hedge. 6–8 ft, 90p.

Propagation: layers or cuttings. Seed should be sown in boxes of sand in November and left outside to freeze until the late spring when germination will occur.

Buddleia

Very attractive to butterflies and may be literally covered with them in summer. They are easy to grow and free flowering, especially if they have an open sunny position.

Soil: need a good soil, but will survive on both chalky or light seaside soils.

Pruning: prune according to the time of flowering; i.e. if they flower in spring prune immediately after flowering, but if in June or later pruning should be done in early spring or even late winter.

Varieties: B. alternifolia, a beautiful shrub which will weep down to a lawn with scented purple flowers in May/June. Remove suckers if they arise. 10–12 ft, £1.15.

B. davidii, a strong-growing, fragrant shrub with purple flowers. 12–15 ft, £1.

B. globosa, flowers in golden orange balls in May/June. 15 ft, £1·05.
Propagation: hard-wood cuttings.

Calluna

This is the true heather, and under appropriate conditions is one of the hardiest and most easily grown ground-cover shrubs. There are innumerable varieties of colour, texture and size.

Soil: it prefers a poor moist soil which is usually acid. If the soil is too rich it will lose its typical appearance and become leggy and upright instead of bushy. It is a lime-hater and should not be grown on a chalk or limestone area.

Pruning: does not need pruning in the ordinary sense but should be clipped in late winter to encourage new flowering shoots.

Varieties: C. vulgaris H. E. Beale, pink double flowers in October/November. 2 ft, 38p.

C. vulgaris C. W. Nix, bright crimson flowers in August/October. 2 ft, 38p.

C. vulgaris alba, true white heather, flowers in September. 38p.
Propagation: division, or by tip or half-ripe cuttings.

Camellia

Dark glossy evergreen shrubs producing very simple but shapely red, pink or white flowers in early spring. They are hardy but the flowers often get damaged by frost so that the full beauty of the bloom may never be realized. Camellias are lime-haters and should occupy a sheltered part of the garden. In dry weather they should be sprayed with a fine water mist. A good cool-greenhouse plant.

Soil: their roots must always be in moist, but not wet soil, so a rich peaty or humus-containing soil is ideal. In summer most growers mulch the shrub heavily with peat and compost.

Pruning: none is required other than a shortening back immediately after flowering in April to keep the bush in shape.

Varieties: C. japonica, a wide range of single and double white and red varieties. 3 ft, £2.50–£4.50.

C. williamsii, very free-flowering from February–April. White, pink, red varieties. 5 ft, £2.75.

Propagation: difficult but can be layered.

Ceanothus

Mostly wall shrubs with attractive little blue flowers in spring or summer. They are not self-clinging and should be provided with a trellis or wire framework. Contains deciduous and evergreen varieties. Fairly slow growing.

Soil: a well-drained soil in a sunny situation is ideal. Thus south or south-west walls should be chosen if possible.

Pruning: varies according to the time of flowering. Cut back the longest shoots immediately flowering is over in spring varieties, but in late-flowering – e.g. Ceres or Autumnal Blue – remove dead wood and shorten long shoots to 6 inches from main stem in February/March.

In the case of climbers, shorten side shoots back to a few inches from main branches as soon as flowers die.

Varieties: C. dentatus, evergreen, blue-flowering in May. 80p. *C. hybridus,* a wide range of varieties mainly blue and pink, in flower from July/October. £1.20.

Propagation: half-ripe cuttings in sand in August/September.

Chaenomeles

This is the plant once called 'Cydonia', 'Japonica' and 'Quince'. They are very hardy and produce their pink or red flowers early in spring in full sunshine. Good wall shrubs and can be clipped to form a hedge.

Soil: they will grow in practically any soil and almost any situation.

Pruning: in all cases (shrubs, against walls, hedges) shorten as soon as the flowers die. In the case of wall shrubs this pruning should be severe.

Varieties: C. speciosa, flowers from February until April. Has thorns and makes a good hedge or a wall shrub. Atropurpurea is dark red and Pink Lady a clear pink. £1.20.

C. japonica, a small spreading and spiny shrub.

Brilliant red flowers and apple-like fruits which can be made into jelly. £1.20.

Propagation: hard-wood cuttings will root, but layers are most satisfactory.

Chimonanthus

Flowers in January/February and has fragrant yellow-brown flowers, hence name winter-sweet. The leaves are dark green and rough. It will stand full exposure to frost or sun but is best against a wall or fence.

Soil: not at all demanding, but will die if waterlogged.

Pruning: shorten flowering branches back in March, but in free-growing bushes only thin if required.

Varieties: C. praecox (fragrans) var. *luteus* has light-yellow flowers. 5 ft, £1.50.

Propagation: layers in spring, see Figs. 23-4.

Cistus

Rather small evergreen shrub which bears many flowers during early summer. They can be used in rockeries or as edging plants, and have a pleasant smell when the leaves are bruised. Sometimes called the rock rose.

Soil: best on a thin dry soil such as on a retaining wall. They are not completely hardy and may be killed back in frost but will usually recover.

Pruning: in early years remove longer shoots to maintain a dwarf compact habit, but after five years no further pruning is needed.

Varieties: C. laurifolius, the hardiest species, with rough dark green leaves and white flowers with yellow bases. 6 ft, 65p.

C. × purpureus*, best in mild and coastal areas. Large red flowers. 4 ft, £1.05.

Propagation: half-ripe cuttings.

Clematis

One of our most easily grown free-flowering shrubs. All the species like lime and will climb very rapidly over walls, trellis or even up another tree. Some are evergreen.

Soil: said to like a warm head and cool feet so they should be planted in moist humus-rich soil to which limestone has been added. The base of the plant should be shaded by mulching or by other plants and the head left free to climb.

Pruning: when first planted cut hard back to force bud growth and then prune each branch again in March/April. Once established, prune early flowerers (*C. montana*) when necessary, but late flowerers (*C. × jackmanii*) should be cut back nearly to old wood in February.

Most species can be cut hard back if they get out of hand.

Varieties: there is a very wide range of clematis species and varieties and one should consult a specialist catalogue for accounts of the great range in colour and form.

C. × jackmanii, very large dark purple- and pink-flowered varieties flowering in July/September, e.g. Crimson King, Gipsy Queen (purple). £1.20.

C. montana, very popular garden climber with smaller white/pink flowers in May/June. £1.30.

*The name *C.* x *purpureus* signifies that the seed was obtained from *Cistus purpureus* but the pollen came from another unknown species of Cistus, so that the seed is not true-breeding for *C. purpureus.*

C. tangutica, bears yellow flowers in September/October and has attractive seed heads. £1.20.

Propagation: usually by layers.

Cornus

Small trees or shrubs with attractive fruits and flowers. In some species the bright red bark is very effective even when leaves have been shed.

Soil: prefers a humus-rich soil and is almost indifferent to sun or shade.

Pruning: if the species is red-barked, prune heavily in April to encourage fresh bright growth; the others only need pruning to shape.

Varieties: C. alba has the best bark and the variety Spaethii also has variegated leaves. The flowers and fruits are not very conspicuous. 6–8 ft, 90p.

C. florida, large white flowers with good autumn leaf colouring. 10–20 ft, £3.

Propagation: layers.

Cotoneaster

A very large family of easy-to-grow shrubs. The flowers are small white and pink and fairly inconspicuous in May/June but they bear masses of berries ranging in colour from black to red and yellow. Many varieties are evergreen and others have rich autumn colours. They can be grown as isolated shrubs, hedges or wall shrubs.

Soil: if put in their first position as young plants they will grow in almost any kind of soil.

Pruning: most species require little or no pruning and if left alone will only need cutting to shape when necessary.

Varieties: C. frigida will stand industrial pollution and bears bright red berries in winter. Deciduous. 12–15 ft, £1.50.

C. horizontalis – as its name implies this shrub grows along the ground and so can be used to clothe a bank or hide a manhole cover. The variety Variegata has silvery leaves and all have scarlet berries. 2–4 ft, £1.15.

C. salicifolia a graceful bush with slender pointed leaves whose undersurface is white. White flowers in summer, dark red berries in winter. It makes a good specimen bush on a lawn specially if the variety Pendula is chosen. 8–12 ft, £1.05.

Propagation: layers or half-ripe cuttings.

Crataegus

Hawthorns have a deserved reputation for toughness but prefer open sunny spots where they form well-shaped low trees.

Soil: any good soil.

Pruning: none except to shape.

Varieties: C. oxycantha is the common hawthorn but many very decorative varieties have been produced. Try Punicea with scarlet berries (£3) and Rosa Plena (£3.20) with double pink flowers. 15–20 ft.

C. × *carrierei*, hybrid with large white flowers and very large berries. Practically thornless. 15 ft, £3.50.

Propagation: the decorative types are grafted so cuttings are not very satisfactory. Seed.

Cytisus

The ordinary broom now has very many rich and varied colours. Broom should be planted very young and never transplanted, and their permanent positions should have a light or even poor soil. Once established they give a show of flowers very quickly.

Soil: virtually anywhere not waterlogged.

Pruning: immediately after flowering trim off the flowering shoots with shears – this helps to prevent old plants going straggly.

Varieties: C. × *kewensis*,* a dwarf variety which bears masses of yellow flowers. Ideal for a wall or rockery. 6–12 ins., £1.10.

C. scoparius, Scotch broom has a wide range of colours, e.g. Firefly (gold and red), Lord Lambourne (scarlet and cream), Sulphureus (deep yellow). 6–8 ft, £1.10.

Propagation: Seeds. Cuttings very difficult unless in mist.

* See footnote, p. 191.

Daphne

One of our earliest shrubs, bearing masses of purple or pink flowers in February/March. It is not an easy shrub to establish and likes good light and clean air.

Soil: moist, well-drained, preferably with a little lime.

Pruning: none.

Varieties: D. mezereum, a very wide range of cultivars bearing pink to red flowers which appear in February before the leaves. It also carries red berries. Usually dies after about six years for no apparent reason. There is a white variety, Alba. 2–5 ft, £1.29. *D. odora* should only be grown in milder areas but has highly scented pink; white, red and purple flowers and is evergreen. 3 ft, £2.55.

Propagation: seed.

Deutzia

A free-flowering graceful shrub which can be grown well in half shade.

Soil: rich moist soil with good rainfall.

Pruning: Only cut out distorted and thin old wood after flowering every 2–3 years.

Varieties: D. gracilis – the typical flower is white but variety Carminea is dark red and Mont Rose pink-purple. 4–6 ft, £1.05.

Propagation: soft- or hard-wood cuttings or seeds.

Erica

A small shrub with a wide range of colours (red, pink, white, purple) and a very varied flowering time. In fact it may be said that at any time of year some varieties of erica will be in flower. They are very good as edging shrubs, in a rockery, but only few can be grown in isolation. Instead of flower beds, beds of heather (ericas) are gaining in popularity largely because of the reduction in labour once they are established and the range of colours of flower and foliage available. Although called heathers, they are really heaths.

Soil: they do not like lime (though the many varieties of *E. carnea* will tolerate it), and grow best in a rather poor peaty and sandy soil.

Pruning: usually no pruning is necessary but for the best results those varieties which bloom in autumn should be lightly trimmed in February to preserve the dwarf appearance.

Varieties: E. arborea, (Tree Heath), with white scented flowers. 6 ft, 90p.

E. carnea, ordinary winter-flowering heath with a large number of varieties e.g. Springwood White, Springwood Pink flowering December/March, King George V with rosy red flowers November/February. All *carnea* varieties will tolerate lime. 1 ft, 38p.

Propagation: soft-tip cuttings under mist and in cold frame. Layering. Does not transplant very well.

Euonymus

A small tree with attractive foliage both in summer and autumn. Some species e.g. *E. europaeus* harbour blackfly in winter which will infect beans in summer so should never be grown near a vegetable garden. It is tolerant of light shade. Sometimes called the Spindle or Wayfarer's Tree.

Soil: very undemanding and will tolerate lime, but the better the soil the larger the shrub.

Pruning: very little other than to keep in shape.

Varieties: E. europaeus has attractive fruits and the variety Atropurpureus has purple foliage. 6 ft, £2.40.

E. japonicus, a beautiful shrub but only hardy in mild districts. Dark evergreen leaves and pink fruits. 10–12 ft, £1.10.

Propagation: evergreens by cuttings, deciduous by seeds or cuttings.

Forsythia

A very easily grown shrub very popular for its massive production of yellow flowers in early spring. Even before the flowers open outside, a spray cut and brought into a warm room will open in a few days.

Soil: will do well in any soil and in sun and shade.

Pruning: as soon as flowering is over, new wood should be cut back to a few inches of old wood.

Varieties: F. suspensa can be grown in a north-facing position. 6–10 ft, £1.05.
F. intermedia spectabilis, strong, free-flowering and needs virtually no pruning. 7–8 ft, 90p.

Fuchsia

Very beautiful red/purple flowering shrub common in coastal and mild areas where it can be grown as a hedge. Most species are killed by frost and are therefore more suited to greenhouse cultivation.

Soil: well-drained, light or loamy.

Pruning: in cold areas frost will kill the shrub back to the ground but if dead wood is removed the shrub will grow again. In mild areas all you need to do is shorten the side shoots in February.

Varieties: F. riccartonii has red/purple flowers. 4–6 ft, 80p.

Propagation: soft-wood cuttings in heat.

Hamamelis

The witch hazel is a very reliable shrub, producing yellowish flowers in mid winter. Although not very conspicuous and rather tattered-looking, the flowers are scented and therefore worth having.

Soil: is quite at home in the shade and likes a moist soil with a good humus content.

Pruning: none except to shape after flowering.

Varieties: H. mollis, easily grown with bright yellow flowers. 10 ft, £3.20.
H. japonica, a large number of varieties, some with good autumn foliage. 15 ft, £3.

Propagation: layers.

Hydrangea

A very common shrub often grown as a house plant. Most species will succeed in mild areas but in frosty parts some protection may be necessary if regular flowering is to be obtained. Can tolerate some shade.

Soil: should be rich in humus or if not the base of the plant must be mulched and shaded in summer.

Pruning: remove dead wood in winter and cut back young growths to good buds in February/March (but see *H. petiolaris*).

Varieties: H. macrophylla, the common hydrangea, of which there are many varieties all requiring winter protection. Blue, red, or white flowers. 2–4 ft, 75p.

H. petiolaris, a climbing species, is equally good on a north or south wall. It does not need a trellis or wire since it is self-clinging and should only be pruned if it gets out of hand. 20 ft, £1.20.

Propagation: half-ripe cuttings.

Hypericum

An easily grown plant with large yellow flowers. Can be used for a ground cover (say on a rocky bank) or as an erect small shrub. Mostly evergreen but may lose their leaves in severe winters.

Soil: will thrive in any soil and even in shade.

Pruning: when plants seem to have died, if they are severely cut back in March they often come again from the base. Otherwise most bushes should be trimmed a little in February and old wood removed.

Varieties: H. calycinum (Common Rose of Sharon) has showy yellow flowers even in shade. Cut back each spring, and you can use as ground cover. 1 ft, 30p.

H. patulum, evergreen with autumn tinted leaves and large flowers. Variety Forestii with crimson leaves in autumn is worth trying. 4 ft, 90p.

Propagation: cuttings in August.

Ilex

Well-known hollies. Modern varieties have variegated leaves and berries ranging from yellow to deep red. There are male and female trees and you need one of each for free berrying although there are a few bisexual varieties also. Slow to establish. Grows slowly and can be clipped to make a hedge.

Soil: medium loam is best and they will stand atmospheric pollution.

Pruning: can be cut to any shape in April or August. Hedges may require clipping at both times.

Varieties: I. aquifolium var. *fructo-lutea*, yellow berries. £2.
I. argentea-marginata, silver edges to the leaves. £2.
Golden King, deep red berries and golden mottled leaves. Up to 50 ft, £1.90.
Propagation: seedlings usually found around parent tree.

Jasminum

Wall shrubs whose most popular species are those which flower in winter. Some are sweetly scented.
Soil: prefer open, well-drained in a sunny situation.
Pruning: winter-flowering species should be cut hard back immediately after flowering.
Varieties: J. nudiflorum, Winter Jasmine, with bright yellow flowers. Very hardy and will scramble over fences or even up a west wall. 10–15 ft, £1.10. (West wall means *facing* west.)
J. officinale, a highly scented summer, white-flowering species. 15 ft, £1.10.
Propagation: cuttings in autumn.

Lonicera

This is the group of honeysuckles which have been popular for so long because of their fragrant flowers and the ease with which they can be grown. They are mainly climbers and twiners and can be used to mask an unsightly wall or to scramble along a hedge.
Soil: all species prefer a soil containing leaf mould, but the shrubs (*L. nitida*) will survive very well in a lighter soil in sun.
Pruning: in general remove old or thin shoots after flowering. Where climbers get too straggly they can be cut back nearly to old wood.
Varieties: L. periclymenum, the native honeysuckle, with many white heavily scented flowers. £1.20.
L. fragrantissima, smaller flowers but very sweetly scented early in year. March/April. 8 ft, £1.20.
L. nitida, small evergreen species with tiny leaves. Can be pruned to make a very tight compact hedge. Best in coastal and southern areas. 4 ft, 70p.

Propagation: cuttings in October and semi-hard cuttings in July/ August.

Magnolia

Very beautiful small trees. Difficult to establish but worth the effort. Most species flower in early spring so they require protection except in south or coastal areas.

Soil: a good loam with quick drainage is best, but will also thrive in light soil provided they are heavily mulched in summer.

Pruning: should be kept to a minimum and only done if needed to shape tree during the growing season.

Varieties: M. grandiflora, very fine evergreen wall shrub with 6–8-in. white scented flowers, beautiful dark green glossy leaves. 20 ft, £3.20.

M. sieboldii, evergreen with white flowers. Flowers best in light shade in May/June. 10 ft, £2.80.

M. soulangeana, most popular magnolia, bearing tulip-shaped white/pink flowers before leaves. It is probably the hardiest and can be grown against a wall or as a shrub. There are many varieties with differing shades of colour. 20–30 ft, £4.

M. stellata, good for small garden, bearing many scented white flowers in March/April. Should be mulched each year with peat. 10 ft, £4.

M. wilsonii, a small shrub which is attractive against a house for the flowers hang downwards and so should be seen from below. 12 ft, £3.20.

Propagation: layering (takes two years).

Mahonia

Often included with berberis. Small evergreen spiny-leaved shrubs which grow well in shade. Yellow flowers and blue berries. Can be grown as ground cover.

Soil: very undemanding.

Pruning: only if necessary.

Varieties: M. japonica (bealei), beautiful evergreen bearing long clusters of sweetly scented yellow flowers in winter. 5 ft, £2.40.

Propagation: seed or layers.

Malus

Flowering crabs with a wide range of white/red flowers and bright red and yellow apples. Some also have coloured foliage and are ideal as a small decorative tree in a small garden. Can be bought as a bush, or as half standard.

Soil: any good soil provided drainage is adequate.

Pruning: prune to shape tree but be sure to keep the centre open and eliminate crossing branches.

Varieties: M. × eleyi, copper foliage, deep crimson flowers and scarlet apples. Has won prizes for fruit and flowers. 20–25 ft, £3.50.

M. floribunda, the Japanese crab, with much variation in flower and fruit colour. John Downie has beautiful fruits from which delicious jelly can be made. 20–25 ft, £3.60.

Propagation: since most are grafted on crab or apple stocks this is not recommended.

Philadelphus

The Mock Orange has sweetly scented flowers in long arching cream white branches. It is easy to grow in a sunny position, and can tolerate chalk.

Soil: any reasonably good soil.

Pruning: thin after flowering in May/June. Can be cut hard back if it overgrows, but you lose a season's flowers this way.

Varieties: P. coronarius, most popular species, with white flowers. Belle Étoile has red markings on the petals and Virginal is double. 8 ft, £1.05.

Propagation: cuttings will root easily in light shade.

Pieris

A very ornamental shrub whose foliage is bright red when young and which bears long sprays of bell-like flowers resembling lily of the valley.

Soil: prefers a deep humus-containing soil. A lime-hater.

Pruning: very light if any.

Varieties: P. japonica, evergreen with red leaves in spring and free-flowering. The variety Forrestii is even more brilliant if given a sheltered spot. 6 ft, £3.

Propagation: half-ripe cuttings in August.

Prunus

A group embracing flowering cherries, plums, almonds, laurels. They are all hardy and a wise choice will repay itself many times over.

Soil: any soil will support them, but a good loam is best. Many, especially the plums, do well on chalk.

Pruning: all species are liable to a disease called silver leaf which enters through pruning wounds. They should therefore be pruned as little as possible and only to shape the trees.

Varieties: P. avium flore pleno bears many white flowers in April/May. Japanese cherries are very popular and have a wide range of single and double white, pink and red varieties. 25 ft, £2.

P. cerasifera is the Myrobalan which can be grown as a tree or a hedge; Pissartii has dark copper leaves and red flowers. 15 ft, £2.80.

P. communis, almond white flowers in February/March 20 ft, £3.60.

P. laurocerasus, cherry laurel, is a common evergreen resembling some rhododendrons. Tolerates deep shade, bears purple fruits. 5–20 ft, 75p.

P. persica, ornamental peach with pink- or red-flowered varieties e.g. Russels Red; Clara Meyer is double pink. 20 ft, £4.

P. subhirtella autumnalis flowers November/March. 15 ft, £4.

Propagation: not advised.

Rhododendron

One of the largest and most popular types of garden shrub, ranging from a few inches high to 30–40 ft. There is such a variety of colours, shapes and types that it is impossible to do them justice in a paragraph. A few general notes will therefore be given. Species and varieties can be bought for any situation from a good catalogue or better still from a garden centre which should be visited in May/June to see them in flower. Note that azaleas have identical likes and dislikes. They are at best in slight shade and should not be too exposed to early morning sun or high temperature. They will flourish on a north-west aspect and never do so well facing due south. They cost £2-£7.

Soil: lime will not be tolerated. The soil should be humus-rich and well drained; at planting time, enrich the soil locally with compost or peat. Rhododendrons are surface rooters and can be severely damaged in periods of drought if the surface soil dries out. A good technique therefore is to top-dress the area around the shrub with a thick layer of peat, compost, spent hops, bracken, or any humus-rich material each spring.

Pruning: this is very rarely necessary except to cut back almost to ground level if they overgrow. Unless they are grafted shoots will spring very freely from the base. Dead flowers should be removed.

Propagation: cuttings only root very slowly and propagation should be left to experts.

Rhus

Easily grown small shrubs and trees noted for foliage colours. Good for a small garden.

Soil: any except water-logged.

Pruning: cut back *R. typhina* to old wood in March/April. For the others only prune to shape if necessary.

Varieties: R. cotinus, called 'smoke tree' on account of its mass of tiny grey flowers. Var. *folis purpureis* has dark purple-red foliage. 8 ft, £1.60.

R. typhina, Stag's Horn Sumach, small tree whose long leaves turn bright gold and red in autumn. It produces erect cone-like structures which are often covered with crimson flowers. 15 ft, £1.20.

Ribes

Popular shrubs known as flowering currants. They are very undemanding both as regards soil and light. Their flowers are very attractive in April/May.

Soil: almost any.

Pruning: only if necessary but can stand any amount of cutting.

Varieties: R. sanguineum, many varieties, with a range of pink/crimson flowers and green/yellow leaves. 8 ft, 80p.

Propagation: ripe cuttings in July.

Note: in early spring before the flowers have opened, branches can be taken into the house where they will flower in a vase. If this is done they usually come out white.

Rosa

See separate section on Roses, p. 207ff.

Sorbus

The rowan or mountain ash is a small tree suitable for a medium-sized garden. They have white flowers but are usually grown for the masses of attractive yellow/red berries in the autumn.

Soil: a sunny spot in almost any soil, but preferably well drained.

Pruning: only to shape.

Varieties: S. aucuparia, the type has scarlet fruits but *Xanthocarpa* has yellow berries – £3; Pendula is a weeping tree – £4; Hilling's Spire an almost vertical tree – 10–15 ft, £3.50.

Spiraea

Rather neat small shrubs with flowers in sprays. Summer-flowering, deciduous, easy to grow.

Soil: almost any and grows well on chalk.

Pruning: most species should be cut back nearly to old wood in February, but the few spring-flowering varieties should be done immediately after flowering.

Varieties: S. arguta, pleasant shrub with white sprays in April. 6 ft, £1.05.

S. japonica, red-flowering species. Anthony Waterer has large flat flowering heads. 5 ft, £1.10.

Propagation: late-wood cuttings or by division or natural layers.

Syringa

The lilac is very popular with a wide range of colour in showy flowers. They generally have a limited life of 15–20 years but are easy to grow. Since many of the better varieties are grafted, care should be taken to destroy suckers as soon as they appear.

Soil: sun-lovers which do in any soil. Annual mulching helps.

Pruning: remove dead flowers and straggly shoots. If it overgrows it can be cut well back with the loss of a year's flowers.

Varieties: Charles Joly, deep red purple double flowers. 15ft, £1.75

Congo, red single. 15 ft, £1.75.

Jan van Tol, pure white single. 15 ft, £1.75.

Miranda, pink. 15 ft, £1.75.

Propagation: layers, but watch out for suckers. If possible avoid grafted stock which is cheaper to buy but can be unsatisfactory over the years.

Veronica (*Hebe*)

Small blue-flowered shrubs whose ideal home is by the sea. They do moderately well in any clean-air area if a little shelter can be provided. Can be made into a hedge but are difficult to keep tidy.

Soil: well-drained and if possible sunny.

Pruning: none except removal of old flowers.

Varieties: V. brachysiphon has white flowers and is very hardy. 5 ft, 90p.

V. elliptica, commonest variety, with pale green leaves and purple flowers. 3 ft, 60p.

V. speciosa, the parent of many varieties, e.g.:

Autumn Glory, purple. 3 ft, 90p.

carnea, pink. 3 ft, 90p.

Simon Deleaux, crimson. 3 ft, £1.15.

Propagation: cuttings.

Viburnum

Many species and varieties of this widely-grown shrub. Flowers can be had from October (*V. bodnantense*) until June (*V. opulus*) and there are varieties for all soils and shades. Easily grown.

Soil: most garden soils but preferably a well-drained loam.

Pruning: prune evergreen species in April if necessary. Deciduous types should only be tidied by removing dead wood.

Varieties: V. bodnantense, very beautiful, winter-flowering, fragrant rose/cream flowers. Needs occasional mulching with peat or leaf mould. 10 ft, £2.

V. fragrans, winter-flowering with white buds and bare branches. Prefers sunny sheltered spot but once established is excellent. 12 ft, £1.90.

V. opulus, Guelder Rose, has clusters of white flowers in June and some varieties e.g. Compactum also bear red berries. Some show bright autumn colours. 12 ft, £1.

V. tinus, winter-flowering evergreen which grows well in heavy shade. 10 ft, £1.60.

Propagation: half-ripe cuttings.

Wisteria

A very beautiful climbing wall shrub with long sprays of pale purple flowers in May/June.

Soil: needs a deep rich soil and a sunny position so it is best to prepare the site with rich compost before planting.

Pruning: may be allowed to grow indefinitely but if growth is too extreme the young shoots should be shortened to 2 or 3 buds in winter. Makes a very good espalier.

Varieties: W. sinensis, long sprays of scented purple flowers. Alba is white. £3.20.

W. venusta, shorter but more scented sprays of creamy white flowers in May/June. £3.50.

Propagation: layers.

SPRING-FLOWERING SHRUBS

Forsythia × intermedia
Forsythia suspensa (Wall)
Chaenomeles speciosa
Ribes sanguineum
Berberis stenophylla
Spiraea thunbergii
Spiraea arguta
Cytisus burkwoodii
Cytisus scoparius (Donard Seedling)
Weigela (Bristol Ruby)
Pieris japonica forrestii

AUTUMN SHRUBS WITH GOOD FOLIAGE

Hamamelis mollis
Acer osakazuki
Rhus typhina

Berberis aggregata
Cotoneaster bullata
Cotoneaster lactea

Pernettya mucronata
(Donard White)

WINTER-FLOWERING SHRUBS

Chimonanthus
fragrans
Cornus mas
Daphne mezereum
Erica carnea
and vars.

Hamamelis
mollis
Jasminum
nudiflorum
Mahonia

Prunus subhirtella
autumnalis
Viburnum tinus,
× bodnantense,
Viburnum fragrans

SHRUBS FOR TOWN GARDENS

Acer negundo
Aucuba
Broom (Cytisus)
Chaenomeles
Cornus
Deutzia

Forsythia
Hypericum
Jasminum
Laurels
Lilacs
Mahonia

Philadelphus
Prunus
Rhododendron
Rhus
Ribes
Viburnum plicatum

HEDGE PLANTS FOR TOWN GARDENS

Beech (Fagus)
Cotoneaster
Crataegus

Lonicera nitida
Chaenomeles
Cornus alba sibirica

Prunus laurocerasus
Pyracantha
Symphoricarpus

UNUSUAL HEDGES

Berberis, many forms
Forsythia

Gooseberry
Rosa

LIME-HATING HEDGES

Andromeda
Azaleas and
Rhododendrons
Camellia

Daboecia
Erica
Kalmia

Pernettya
Pieris
Vaccinium

SHRUBS FOR CHALKY SOILS

Berberis	Cytisus	Prunus
Buddleia	Deutzia	Rosa
Chaenomeles	Forsythia	Spiraea
Cistus	*Hypericum calycinum*	Syringa
Clematis	Laburnum	Veronica
Cornus	Philadelphus	

SHRUBS FOR PLANTING IN SHADE

Aucuba in variety	Hypericum	Skimmia
Azaleas	Lonicera	*Viburnum tinus*
Bamboos	*Mahonia aquifolia*	Weigela
Cornus	Pernettya	
Euonymus radicans and *japonicus*		

ROSES

Types of Roses

Roses are so rewarding that they deserve the best treatment and soil preparation. Most roses have a long flowering season and such a range of colour, scent, size, fruits, that there is scarcely a garden without them. They are usually divided into a number of groups of which the following are the most important:

(1) *Hybrid teas* are the most common type of rose grown today. Most varieties bloom from June until the autumn, producing large flowers either one on a stem or in small clusters of two or three. They are usually planted in beds but may stand alone. Many hybrid teas can be grafted on a tall single stem and are then called standards or half standards.

(2) *Floribunda* and *polyanthus* roses differ from hybrid teas in having smaller flowers in much larger clusters. At one time it was easy to distinguish the two groups but with the present trend towards larger blooms the difference is becoming less obvious. Floribundas are larger, stronger bushes and when grown close

together in beds they give a mass of colour for months. They can be pruned to form a hedge.

(3) *Climbers and ramblers* have similar habitats. Climbers are often climbing forms or variations of hybrid teas while others are climbers in their own right. They are not self-clinging and need support, but they can be trained on a trellis or arch or even along wires to cover any structure. Ramblers have the same climbing habit but bear sprays of flowers which are valuable for decoration. Ramblers usually branch a lot at the base whereas climbers have a single stem at ground level.

(4) *Shrub roses* are of mixed origin, some being very old roses with masses of simple but attractive flowers, others specially bred modern varieties. They are all very vigorous and are usually grown as specimen shrubs or in small groups. Although the flowers are not so showy as hybrid teas and many have a short flowering season, they have a unique delicacy and many produce beautiful autumn colours and fruits.

(5) *Miniature roses* are suitable for borders or rockeries, and can be treated as polyanthus – i.e. like category 2.

Preparation and Planting

All types of rose do best in a sunny well-drained area, but they are tough and will survive fairly unfavourable conditions. As always, make sure the ground is well prepared with animal manure, especially on light sandy soils, and the bottom of the planting hole broken up to ensure good drainage. The roots should be well spaced. Standards and half standards will need staking.

All bought roses (with the exception of shrub roses) are grafted on a root-stock (usually brier) and the point of the graft can be seen as a rather swollen area at the base of the stem (see Fig. 26). In planting, this junction between the root stock and the top of the plant (the scion) should be just below soil level – if this area is exposed to wind-rock or severe frost damage, disease may get in and the rose will die of canker.

You will probably either buy container-grown roses or get them in a pack from a multiple store or through the post. As usual the container-grown plants present no problem other than those of normal good planting. The others should be unpacked and, if they have dried out in the post, set in water overnight. If the soil is too wet for planting or if there is a prolonged frost the roots can be buried in a shallow trench. This is known as 'heeling-in', for the soil should be trampled firmly around them; they will come to no harm whatever the weather. If there is severe frost it is advisable

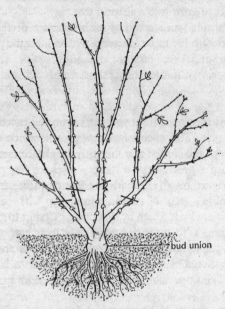

bud union

26. *A rose bush planted with the graft or bud union below the soil surface. Cut back as indicated by the lines just above a good outward-pointing bud.*

not to unpack the roses or else to bury their roots in a bucket of damp peat in the garden shed.

Once roses have been firmly planted and staked (if necessary) they must be pruned as shown in Fig. 26. If you are planting in winter, hybrid teas and floribundas should be cut back to half their size to reduce wind-rock. In March they should again be cut back to within a few inches of the root stock, making sure that the topmost bud points outwards so that when it develops you will have a spreading bush and not one whose branches cross each other in the centre. Climbing hybrid teas need not be pruned so drastically but should still be shortened back to about 2 ft, while ramblers can be cut hard back to a good bud about 6 ins. above the graft. Standard roses should also be pruned nearly to the graft (which in this case is near the top of the plant) and care taken to ensure that suitably placed buds are left to grow into a shapely tree.

Top dress the shrubs with compost each summer preferably after rain, and if growth is not satisfactory, put on a good general fertilizer or even a special rose mixture at about 2 oz. per square yard in the early spring just after the final pruning.

Annual Pruning

If you want the best from your roses you must prune all except the shrub roses every year. This encourages new growth which bears the flowers and keeps the shrubs at a nice tidy height. Remember again the importance of good sharp secateurs – roses are very prone to die-back and a jagged rough cut tends to encourage this disease.

When you examine a stem of rose in winter you will see that there are many dormant buds which by the spring will start to grow; the essence of pruning is to cut each branch back to an *outwardly-pointing* bud. The cut should be made about a quarter of an inch above the bud and should be a steeply sloping cut which will shed water like a roof. The slope should be in the direction away from the bud (Fig. 27).

There used to be a school of thought which held that pruning of established roses should be done in November, so-called 'winter-pruning', but the best modern growers prefer to shorten the bushes back in late autumn to stop wind-rock and then to complete the actual pruning in March or even early April in the North – for the amateur, this is particularly important in windy areas with heavy frosts. In any case you should not prune until the danger of *severe* early frosts has passed.

Pruning starts by removing all weak and all dead shoots. Shoots crossing in the middle of the bush should also be cut out, for the ultimate aim is to create a bush with all the main branches growing outwards away from the centre of the bush.

There are so many axioms about pruning that it is pointless to repeat them all, but remember the saying that 'growth follows the knife'. This means that, for every branch you remove, many otherwise dormant buds will be stimulated to grow and you will end up with an increase in the number of branches and in the size of the bush. Therefore if you have a strong vigorous rose such as Peace

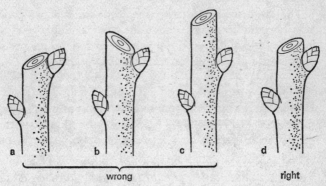

a   b   c   d

wrong   right

27. *Pruning cuts:* (*a*) *Cut too close to bud.* (*b*) *Water would drain on to the bud and cause it to rot.* (*c*) *Cut is too far away from the bud and so dieback might kill it.* (*d*) *Cut slopes away from the bud and is not too close.*

you should prune lightly, but weaker varieties should be severely pruned (see Fig. 28).

Hybrid tea roses should be pruned as above in March/April to produce a neat compact bush by reducing all the branches to within 9 in. of the grafted point. As the shrub ages this becomes more difficult, but try to prune as low as possible provided three or four buds are always left to inaugurate new growth.

Floribunda roses should be pruned like hybrid teas but not so severely. It is usually enough to cut weak shoots back very severely but only to remove about one third of the strongly growing shoots. Really old branches should be cut back to a good outward-growing side shoot and the side shoot then cut back to about 3 ins.

Standard and half standard roses are really hybrid teas on a long stem so the same pruning principles apply; but always make sure that the buds which are left are so distributed that the bush will be shapely, especially if it is a weeping variety.

Finally, *climbing roses* usually flower on side shoots, i.e. ones coming off the main stem, so the aim of pruning is to produce as many side shoots as possible. This is done by removing old or dead wood and by cutting back existing side shoots to within two or

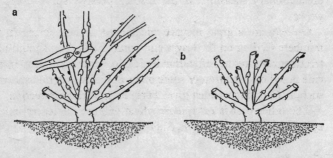

28. *Pruning a rosebush: (a) Shorten the branches back to an outwardly pointing bud in March or April. (b) The finished bush. Note the slope of the cut which is always away from the bud below.*

three buds of the main stem in March. These buds will grow and and bear flowering branches. Climbing roses often become bare at the base; if this happens care should be taken to prune any basal shoots to leave buds which will develop eventually into flowering shoots. *Ramblers* are very strong growers which will stand severe cutting back each autumn once flowering is over. In some cases fresh growths may have developed about a foot above ground level – if so the old growths should be cut back to this point.

Rose Problems

There are two main rose diseases and two pests which the beginner should be able to recognize and to treat.

The first disease is *black spot*, which as the name implies is a purplish-black discolouration of the foliage. This increases in size and the leaves die and fall off. Black spot is a disease of clean air caused by a fungus (*Diplocarpon rosae*) and the treatment is to remove infected leaves and burn them, and spray with a Captan or

Orthocide fungicide every two weeks during the growing season. The other disease is *rose mildew* which is recognizable as a greyish powder on twigs and leaves. Where mildew is common it is advisable to plant resistant varieties such as McGredy's Yellow, Canary, Pinocchio, etc., or to spray with Dinocap, Karathane or Benlate as soon as the first signs of disease appear, or even in May as a precautionary measure. If the disease persists spray every two weeks.

Greenfly are a great menace and appear in late spring in vast numbers feeding on the leaves and young buds. You should begin treatment before the infestation builds up, spraying with an insecticide based on Menazon or some other partially systemic substance such as Malathion which gives fairly long-lasting protection.

The other pest is *caterpillars* which will eat the leaves unless a systemic insecticide such as Abol-X or Sevin is used.

Varieties

There is such a wide selection of rose varieties that it would be impertinent to make a list of the 'best'; instead I will give a few lists of varieties which I like and which are popular and easily obtainable.

Hybrid Tea

White	Virgo, McGredy's Ivory
Pink	Percy Thrower, Picture, Wendy Cussons, Caroline Testout, Eden Rose
Crimson/Scarlet	Fragrant Cloud, Superstar, Ena Harkness
Yellow	McGredy's Yellow, Peace, Spek's Yellow
Bicoloured	Dickson's Perfection, Tzigane, Mrs Sam McGredy

Floribunda

White	Iceberg
Pink	Jiminy Cricket, Ma Perkins, Vogue, Poulsen's Bedder, Queen Elizabeth.
Crimson/Scarlet	Orange Sensation, Red Favourite, Dorothy Wheatcroft, Frensham
Yellow	All Gold, Masquerade, Goldilocks

Climbers

White	Sanders' White
Pink	Mme Butterfly, Zepherine Drouhin
Crimson/Scarlet	Climbing Ena Harkness, Paul's Scarlet, Crimson Glory, Triumph
Yellow	Golden Shower, Christine

Ramblers

White	Snowflake, Seagull, Sanders' White
Pink	American Pillar, Dorothy Perkins, Dr Van Fleet, New Dawn
Scarlet	Bonfire, Crimson Shower, Romeo
Yellow	Gardenia, Goldfinch

Shrub roses

White	Damask Rose (white and red), Blanc Double de Coubert, Snowsprite, Blanche Moreau
Pink	Penelope, Stanwell Perpetual, Perle d'Or
Crimson/Scarlet	Cornelia, Wilhelm, Little Gem, *Rosa moyesii*
Yellow	Frühlingsgold, Chinatown, *Rosa hugonis*, Canary Bird.

BOOK LIST

Roses: Fairbrother, F. (Penguin Handbook)
Beginner's Guide to Rose Growing: Harris, Cyril C. (Pelham Books)
The Rose Garden: Brown, R. (Ward Lock)
Rose Growing for Everyone: le Grice, E. B. (Faber & Faber)
The ABC of Roses: Shewell-Cooper, W. E. (English Universities Press)
Roses for Enjoyment: Edwards, G. (Collingridge)
Plant Pruning in Pictures: Free, M. (London Museum Press)
Flowering Shrubs and Trees: Russell, L. R. (Studio Vista)
Shrubs for Amateurs: Bean, W. J. (Country Life)

Shrub Gardening for Flower Arrangement: Emberton, S. (Faber & Faber)
Multi-season Shrubs and Trees: Gorer, R. (Faber & Faber)
Success with Shrubs and Trees: Loads, F. (John Gifford)

9 *Fruit*

There are three types of fruit: tree fruits, such as apples and pears; stone fruits, such as plums or cherries; and bush fruits, such as gooseberries, blackcurrants and raspberries. There is obviously little uniformity in fruit-bearing plants, so fruit trees and the systems on which they are grown can be very complex. However, I propose to deal with the simplest fruits in the simplest ways and anyone wanting more complete instructions for unusual trees or circumstances should consult the books listed on p. 240.

SOIL

You must carefully consider the soil in which you intend to grow your fruit. An apple tree, for example, may cost a lot of money and take several years of waiting before it bears fruit, and to find after all this that you have planted the wrong variety in the wrong place is very saddening. In general terms, fruit needs a fairly rich soil with lots of humus. This does not mean that you can't grow fruit in a sandy soil, but simply that to do so is more difficult and demands more care in feeding and soil preparation. In fact, apart from heavy soil that is so badly drained as to be waterlogged, some fruit can be grown nearly anywhere.

Although you can't change your soil type much, you can always enrich it with lots of compost and farmyard manure if available. This not only helps to feed the plant but also improves the drainage. As with other trees and shrubs, I have to repeat that time spent preparing the ground before planting and making it more fertile will pay dividends many times over in later years.

POSITION

When you have decided that you'll grow fruit and are willing to enrich the soil, the next problem is where to grow it. It is well

216

known that the chief danger to fruit is *frost*. Vast sums of money are spent every year by fruit growers on precautions against frost but the home gardeners cannot afford either the time or the money to do this, and have to tackle the frost problem in other ways. First of all remember that cold air is heavy and will flow down a hill almost like water (in fact there is a distinct difference in temperature between the top and bottom of even a small slope on a frosty night). Take advantage of this by planting fruit trees at high spots in the garden and if you have rows, say, of strawberries, have them running up and down the hill and not across it, otherwise each row will act as a small dam for cold air; if the rows are well planned they will literally guide the frost down the hill away from the places where it can do damage. Following the same argument, have the smallest fruit at the top of the hill, for even in a frost pocket a tall apple tree may be high enough off the ground to miss the keenest frost, where a low bush may easily be frosted. Similarly a wall or a hedge will act as a dam to the flow of cold air, so be sure to have your fruit well clear if it is on the upper side of this kind of barrier. If on a slope, bush and tree fruit should be well spaced so as not to impede the free flow of air.

The most damaging frosts are those which come at blossom time, killing the young flowers. In many areas, especially in the North of England and Scotland, late frosts are inevitable and it is quite pointless to plant varieties of apple such as Laxton's Advance or Cox's Orange Pippin – for the first flowers early in spring and the Cox's only a little later so that in each case there is a fair chance that the whole crop will be destroyed by a May frost. It is far better to grow Worcester Pearmain and Edward VII, which are late-flowering apples and will normally escape all frosts. The same principles also apply to pears and plums – in frost pockets, or in a valley or in northern areas, much frost damage can be avoided by choosing the right varieties.

To ripen well, fruit needs sunshine so an orchard or garden on a gentle slope with a south or south-west exposure is an ideal position. You may not have much choice of aspect in a very small garden and it is therefore even more important to choose your variety carefully – pick those which flower and ripen their fruit later in the season.

In the very small garden full use should be made of the way in which almost any bush or tree can be trained to take the form the grower wants. A number of these forms are illustrated below (Fig. 29). Fruit can be grown against fences or walls, or trained along wires to separate a lawn from the vegetable garden, etc. Growing a cordon or espalier needs very careful attention to pruning detail; only if there is a real pressure for space should they be attempted; it is better to grow dwarf bushes which are easier to maintain although they are not necessarily so space-saving.

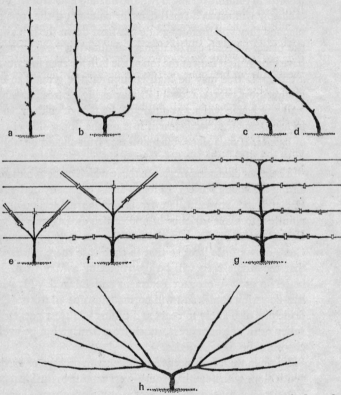

29. *Types of fruit tree: (a) single cordon (b) double vertical cordon (c) horizontal cordon (d) cordon (e, f, g) steps in training an espalier (h) fan-trained tree*

POLLINATION RULES

All garden fruit trees need pollination to form fruit. This means that the male reproductive cells (the pollen) must be transported by wind or insects to the female part of the flower (the stigma) where, if fertilization occurs, seeds and fruit will be produced. In most wild plants this is easily done – in fact many plants are able to fertilize themselves (self-fertile) – but many fruit trees cannot fertilize themselves, but must be fertilized by pollen from another fruit tree. An example will make this clear. Blenheim Orange apple sets little or no fruit with its own pollen, and requires a pollinator such as Grenadier. But Blenheim Orange cannot pollinate Grenadier, so if these two varieties are grown together there will be fruit on the Blenheim but none on the Grenadier. If, therefore, you want fruit on both trees you must plant a third variety, i.e. Cox's Orange. Cox's and Grenadier will pollinate each other *and* the Blenheim so that you get fruit on all three.

The reasons for this seemingly intricate system are connected with the structure of the reproductive cells and need not worry us here. The point to be made however is very important: if you plant one or even two trees of apple, pear or plum, make absolutely certain from the supplier that you get either self-fertile varieties, or compatible varieties which will cross-pollinate, or get a 'family tree' (see p. 73).

There are long lists of compatible varieties, and I will give suggestions when needed as we go through the fruit.

You also have to remember the season of flowering. Pollination and fertilization can only take place if both sets of flowers are in the right state at the same time. An *early*-flowering variety, even though it produces excellent pollen, cannot pollinate a *late*-flowering variety – the latter will still be in the bud stage when the pollen of the early variety is being carried about. Details of times of flowering will also be noted in the appropriate lists.

GRAFTED TREES

All tree fruits are grafted on a rootstock in very much the same way as rose bushes, though with fruits the rootstock is used to obtain better control of the way in which the tree will grow. This is easy to understand if you realize that all the water and mineral salts used by the tree are taken in by the roots. If the root system is small and inadequate the tree will be undernourished and so will not develop to its full extent. On the other hand, a partly starved tree will begin to bear fruit earlier than one which is growing very vigorously and making lots of wood. Thus an apple variety grafted on a dwarfing rootstock such as Malling IX will never grow to be a large tree, reaching only 10–12 ft in height as opposed to the 20 ft which the same apple variety might reach if grown on a vigorous stock such as Malling XVI. At the same time the dwarfing stock will induce fruiting in about seven years while the vigorous stock may take fifteen years. This means that in a small garden it is better to use dwarfing or at least non-vigorous stocks such as Malling IX, Malling 26 or Malling 106.

It is also possible to get apple rootstocks such as Malling Merton 106 which are resistant to a serious pest, woolly aphis. The advantages are enormous for growers – they now have a rootstock which will resist serious diseases on to which they can graft a top or scion producing fruit of a very high quality. This is really getting the best of both worlds.

Pears are usually grafted on to Quince stocks with Quince C as the dwarfing type, and it is the common wild plum stocks which induce dwarfing in domestic plum varieties.

PRUNING

Pruning is the great bugbear of all fruit growers, and beginners are understandably discouraged by the very elaborate accounts of how to do it. If you are growing one or two trees in a small garden choose bush trees or a dwarfing stock and you can avoid nearly all pruning. Remember also that the harder you prune the more the tree will grow and the more you will delay fruiting.

The first general rule is to get the framework and the shape of the tree established in the first two or three years by ruthless pruning and then only to prune lightly and when necessary.

But what is the framework and the best shape? The framework of a tree is best described as the trunk and the main branches (see Fig. 30). If you can imagine a bird's-eye view from the top of the

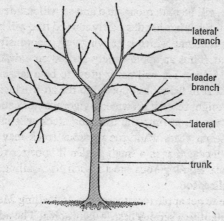

lateral branch

leader branch

lateral

trunk

30. *Fruit tree showing trunk, leaders and laterals. Note that the lateral branches bear still smaller secondary laterals.*

tree, the trunk should be central with the four or five main branches growing out like the spokes of an umbrella blown inside out. This stops the tree being one-sided so it will not be blown over in windy weather, allows easier spraying and fruit-picking. It is best to keep the number of main branches below six, otherwise the top or crown of the tree gets very crowded and branches rub against each other causing wounds which allow easy entry for disease.

The best shape for a fruit tree has been described as an open centre, an egg cup or a tulip shape, and these three names will clearly convey the general idea which is that the branches should be at the *outside* of the tree, not growing in towards the centre. Where this shape is not maintained and lots of small branches and even some big ones choke up the middle of the tree there will be a lack of air circulation through the crown, which will stay damp and so liable to attack by mildew or aphis. The fruit may also be very difficult to gather.

Pruning has two purposes other than that of shaping the tree. The first is the removal of dead, diseased, badly placed or thin

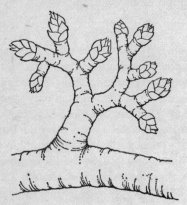

31. *A fruit spur of apple.*

spindly wood, and the second is to encourage and regulate the production of fruit buds. To the novice all buds are alike, but fruit buds are much fatter and rounder than the leaf buds and with a little practice can be spotted at a glance. Fruit buds are also often borne at the ends of very short branches called spurs, whereas leaf or growth buds are on the main stems, tend to be smaller, pointed, and lie flatter against the branch.

The art of pruning, therefore, is to produce the correct quantity of fruit buds without destroying the framework and shape of the tree. Generally speaking, nature will do this for you; everyone has experience or has heard of old trees which keep on yielding good crops year after year with no attention at all, so when you take your pruning knife or your sharp secateurs in hand don't let yourself be carried away in an orgy of destruction – remember *only prune if it is necessary*. If all the buds in Figure 31, for example, are allowed to develop into fruit they will produce overcrowded and distorted fruit, so reduce the number of spurs to five at the most by pruning off one of the bud branches. After the fruit is formed thin it further until the branch is carrying two or three apples at the most.

Detailed instructions for pruning different kinds of fruit trees and bushes are given under the different trees, p. 224ff.

FEEDING

Finally, feeding the trees is important. Once again there is such a store of fertility in most soils that the trees once established will carry on unfed for years, but remembering that the fruit you take away contains food that came from the soil, it is only sensible to replace it periodically. Small gardens generally have one or two trees rather than an orchard, and unless you use your fruit as a screen it is best to use the trees not only to supply fruit but also as specimen trees in the garden. This usually means allowing them plenty of room in a fairly conspicuous position, often in a lawn. A fine tree growing out of the lawn is very attractive but while the tree is young you should cut a circle of bare earth round its base. The little plot need not be absolutely bare and you can plant spring bulbs or a few simple annuals; however, if you allow the grass to develop right up to the tree, they will compete for food and anything you add will naturally reach the grass first. By feeding into the bare circle you can make sure that the fertilizer goes straight to the roots of the fruit tree. Another advantage of this cleared area is that it can be easily mulched and given an annual top dressing of compost or FYM.

APPLES

Apples are easily the most popular fruit. The trees should be planted in the dormant season between November and March. The ground must be well prepared and enriched with humus or FYM, the tree firmly staked, and all the rules given in Chapter 8 followed carefully.

Planting

Since apples are grafted, the point of union between the rootstock and the scion should be just above the soil surface. The junction is easily spotted by the bulge in the stem of the young tree. If you are planting a number of trees the distance between them will depend on the vigour and type of tree you intend to grow: trees on a dwarfing stock should be 8–10 ft apart; on a more vigorous stock you must allow 15 ft. Ordinary trees are very much more space-demanding, needing 30–40 ft between them.

Pruning

If the soil is in good condition and you manage to plant the tree before January, it can be pruned immediately, but if you do not plant until February or later leave it alone until the following year. If you can prune, all you need to do is to shorten each main shoot back by about one-third, ensuring that the cut is made above a bud pointing in the direction you want the future branch to grow.

By the following year a number of new shoots will have formed and you will then choose those branches which will be the 'leaders' and maintain the framework of the tree. The leaders will develop side branches known as 'laterals'. Annual winter pruning means shortening back the leaders by about half and the laterals to within three or four buds' distance from their junction with the leader.

In the first four or five years follow this pattern rigorously, departing from it only to remove badly placed or very weak spindly growth. Occasionally a lateral may be allowed to grow on as a leader in order to keep the tree in good shape. Fruit spurs will develop along the branches and if the tree is bearing too heavy a crop the spurs themselves can be thinned. As the tree gets older you will be able to relax on the pruning but make every effort to keep down the number of thin whippy branches.

This type of pruning is satisfactory for bush, standard or half-standard trees, but pyramids, cordons or espaliers demand a much more sophisticated form of pruning, the details of which can be found in *Basic Gardening* by S. B. Whitehead (see p. 24).

Feeding

One school of thought says that, provided you enrich the soil well at planting time, there will be no need to feed the tree at all in the future. 'A hungry tree goes in search of its own food and so produces a long and vigorous root system,' they say, and to a certain extent this is true. Certainly an overfed tree will produce any amount of foliage but little good fruit. Nevertheless keep an eye on the crop and if there are signs after some years of its falling off in quantity then a light dressing (2 oz. per square yard) of a balanced fertilizer such as Growmore given in spring in the area around the tree base will greatly improve growth and yield; mulching with well-rotted compost in May is also beneficial.

Picking

The fruit should never be picked until it is ripe. The test is to see how easily the apple comes away from the tree. You should not need much effort to pick it – take the fruit in the palm of your hand, lift it to the horizontal, and it should come away easily from its spur. Although most of the fruit will be ready at the same time, you may find that in order to ensure ripeness in each apple you have to make two or three pickings. Fruit should always be gathered dry and handled gently; every bump will produce a bruise.

Storing

Storing apples is tricky. Ideally you need a cool, dark, well-ventilated place such as a cellar, but as most modern houses don't have these you may have to improvise. The simplest method is to wrap each apple in a piece of newspaper and put them all on a tray in a dark cupboard. Only store good, healthy, unblemished fruit, otherwise you may find all the fruit rotting within a few weeks. If you do not wrap the fruit any disease will spread like wildfire, justifying the old saying that one rotten apple in a barrel ruins the lot. Finally remember that some apples store well and others should be eaten when picked, so don't expect long storage life from all the fruit – details given below.

All the varieties below, with the exception of those marked T,

225

The Penguin Book of Basic Gardening

set good pollen and can be used for pollinating each other, which means that apart from the self-fertile varieties they should be planted in a mixed group of two or three to ensure fruit production. The pollen of an eating variety will fertilize a cooker and vice-versa with no effects on the resulting fruit. Those marked T set very poor and inadequate pollen and *must* be planted with a good pollinator such as James Grieve, or else in a group along with two of the others.

EASY APPLE VARIETIES

EATING	COOKING
Early-flowering:	
Laxton's Advance (self-fertile)	Wagener (good keeper)
Lord Lambourne	
Sunset (good keeper)	
Ribstone Pippin (T)	
Mid-season-flowering:	
James Grieve (good pollinator)	Bramley's Seedling (keeps till
Laxton's Epicure	March) (T)
Cox's Orange Pippin (Not for North)	Grenadier
Blenheim Orange (T)	
Laxton's Superb (self-fertile but liable to miss fruiting on alternate years)	
Golden Delicious (needs pollinator)	
Late-flowering:	
Worcester Pearmain	Edward VII

BLACKCURRANTS

These are easy to grow in a small garden and can be used as a screen to hide one end of the vegetable garden. Blackcurrants should be grown as bushes and not trees, i.e. they should not be on a single stem or leg but have a number of shoots all emerging from the ground. They therefore grow rather densely and the fruit can be difficult to pick if it develops in the heart of the bush. They are best in direct sunlight but can stand light shade.

Planting

Blackcurrants are very gross feeders so the soil should be well dug and thoroughly enriched with farmyard manure or compost, and bone meal before planting. The planting hole should be deep enough to contain the roots, which should be well spread out. Planting can be done at any time between October and March, but the best results come from planting in November 6 ft apart. Firm well after planting.

Pruning

Immediately after planting, *each* shoot should be cut back to an outwardly pointing bud with the exception of a few strong shoots with dark bark which may be left to fruit in the first year. The reason is that blackcurrants bear their fruit on wood produced the previous year; therefore, pruning should be directed towards stimulating the growth of fresh shoots every year. If *all* the shoots are cut back after planting, the bush will certainly develop many branches but these will only fruit in the second year.

Irrespective of the treatment of the first-year bushes, future pruning is simple and only demands cutting back to near soil level roughly half the branches which have fruited. Do this immediately after fruiting and plenty of time will be left for new branches to bear fruit the following year to be produced. Remove weak and dead branches by pruning to soil level.

Feeding

Since they are heavy feeders, an annual dressing of a nitrogenous fertilizer or even a general fertilizer with a high percentage of nitrogen is required; this should be given at the rate of 2 oz. per square yard at the base of the bush in February/March. This should be followed in early May by a thick top dressing of farmyard manure or good compost enriched, say, with a little old poultry manure. The layer of compost not only improves the soil, but also helps feed the plant and acts as a weed smother, for weeds will grow luxuriantly in a soil which has been enriched for blackcurrants and constant weeding is necessary to stop the bushes being choked.

Pests and Diseases

The greatest problems of blackcurrant growing are a disease named big bud, and greenfly. The former is a very apt term and can be easily diagnosed by the swollen round terminal buds containing an insect pest which spreads a virus. To check the pest the big buds should be picked off and burned in winter and affected bushes sprayed with lime sulphur in spring just before the flowers open at the stage called the 'grape' stage (buds are slightly purple at this time). To prevent greenfly give a tar oil winter wash and in severe cases a spray with nicotine or derris, or some other aphicide, in the late spring.

Varieties

Boskoop Giant or Laxton's Giant (both earlies), Wellington XXX (mid season), Amos Black (late), Baldwin (late). (Wellington XXX is 'sulphur shy' and only a 2 per cent concentration of lime sulphur should be used.)

RED AND WHITE CURRANTS

Red and white currants are so alike that they can be discussed together. They are often grown as cordons, but in a small garden bushes on a very short single trunk (or leg) are preferable. They can be grown on any soil which is well drained and enriched annually with compost.

Planting

These currants may be planted between October and March, if possible towards the end of October. Since they grow into fairly large bushes and you will want to be able to pick the fruit from all round they should be given plenty of space, e.g. 5 ft, between the bushes, and if they are in rows 6 ft between the rows. The soil should be well firmed.

Pruning

Immediately after planting cut all the branches back to an outwardly point bud, removing about half their length. Red and white

228

currants fruit on old wood, i.e. wood made the previous year, so the aim of pruning is to encourage production of wood immediately after fruiting is over – this wood will ripen during the rest of the summer and will bear fruit the following year. However, unlike blackcurrants they are on a leg, so you cannot prune back to ground level; once fruiting is over you should shorten each lateral branch back to about 5 leaves (about half). The leaves remaining will carry on feeding the bush for the rest of the season and some new wood will be formed.

In winter complete the pruning by shortening each leading shoot by half and pruning back the laterals to an outward pointing bud about 2 in. from their attachment to the main branch. In all cases remove dead or spindly wood and try to keep the centre of the bush open.

Feeding

These are not such heavy feeders as blackcurrants and should be given an annual dressing of compost and an application of sulphate of potash at about 1 oz. per square yard each spring.

Pests

Aphids cause a red blistering and curling of the leaves which can be very damaging. A tar-oil wash in winter and a good spray with an aphicide, e.g. malathion or derris, as the leaves grow will minimize the damage, even if it does not produce a complete cure.

Varieties

Laxton's No 1 (early, red), Versailles (early, white), Red Lake (mid-season), White Dutch (mid-season), River's Late Red (late).

DAMSONS see Plums, p. 233.

GOOSEBERRIES

Gooseberries are a very popular bush fruit and can be easily accommodated in the smallest garden. They are often grown with red and white currants and used as a dessert fruit or made into jam. They can be grown as cordons or even as a gooseberry hedge but these require special pruning, so I will confine myself to the simplest form of gooseberry bush grown on a single leg. They do best in a moist but cool climate and many of the best gooseberries are grown in coastal areas.

Planting

Gooseberries should be planted in winter (October to March) in a well-drained, loamy soil. On clays liberal applications of organic materials such as farmyard manure or compost will improve the drainage, on sandy or gravelly soils it will allow the retention of water. The main fertilizer should be sulphate of potash at about 2 oz. per square yard when the ground is being prepared. The quickest results are obtained by planting two- or three-year-old trees.

Bushes should be stationed 5 ft apart in rows 6 ft apart. Spread the roots out in the planting hole and tread them in very firmly. The branches should then be shortened back to a suitable outwardly pointing bud removing about half the branch in the process. Gooseberries have very sharp thorns and a bush which is well shaped in its early years will make the gathering of fruit easier when it begins to bear. You should also take care to remove most of the inward-growing wood.

Pruning

Gooseberries bear their fruit on wood of the previous year and on older spur shoots. Once the bush is well established they can be treated like red currants by pruning laterals back to 5 leaves after fruiting in the summer and shortening back the main shoots by half and reducing the lateral shoots to 2 or 3 buds from the join with the main branch in winter.

Feeding

Top dress each spring with good organic material, compost or FYM. An application of sulphate of potash at 1 oz. per square yard in early spring will help fruit production.

Weeds and Mildew

The roots of gooseberries are just below the surface and so hoeing for weed control can be dangerous. Weeds should therefore be kept down by using mulches for smother in the summer, or by the application of paraquat around the base of the bush, taking care to prevent the substance splashing on to the leaves of the gooseberry.

Gooseberries often suffer from mildew which can be controlled by using a Karathane or Captan spray during the growing season at fourteen-day intervals. The post-fruiting pruning also helps to remove infected shoot tips.

Varieties

Early Sulphur (early, yellow), Lancashire Lad (mid-season, red), Traveller (mid-season, green), Leveller (mid-season, yellow), Lancer (late, green).

GREENGAGES see *Plums*, p. 233.

PEARS

Pears are much more difficult to grow than apples because they flower earlier in spring and are more frost-tender. They are therefore not very suitable for high or cold areas with frequent and late spring frosts, and even in good areas such as the South of England a sheltered spot free from north or north-east winds should be sought. As in the case of apples you should choose a south-facing slope where the air drainage will remove frosty air before it can do damage.

Pears are grafted on a rootstock of quince. For the smaller garden Quince C produces the best-shaped bush tree and will induce fruiting in about five years whereas a more vigorous stock may need eight to ten years before producing regular crops.

Planting

This should be done during the dormant period (November to March). Plant with the graft union just at or below soil level.

Bush trees should be about 15 ft from any other tree; standard trees on a vigorous stock will need 35 ft. Pears can of course be grown as cordons or espaliers.

Slightly acid loam and sandy soils need preparing with good farmyard manure or compost well mixed and dug in. Young trees should be staked and pruned rather like an apple tree (p. 224) by shortening back the main branches by half to an outwardly pointing bud and shaping the initial framework of the tree. Remove crossing and injured wood. Remember to have the graft union just at or above soil level.

Pruning

Bush trees should be pruned as for apples (p. 224), a little less severely in the first few years and then more severely as the plant ages and develops a fruit-bearing rhythm. Pears can be very prolific and it is always wise to reduce the number of fruiting spurs to avoid putting too great a strain on the tree. If the crop is very heavy it is advisable to thin the fruit so as to have large, well-shaped pears for eating. This is best done by cutting or twisting off the young fruit before it gets bigger than a small plum. If fruits are too close together and rub against each other rot will almost certainly set in and both pears will die or be misshapen.

Feeding

If the ground is well prepared no further feeding will be required during the first year, although a mulch with compost or some other organic material will prevent dryness at the roots. Thereafter a dressing of complete fertilizer at 2 oz. per square yard should be given each spring, followed by an annual mulch of well-rotted manure or compost in the summer.

Picking

Since a pear tree is quite large, the pears will obviously not all be ripe on the same day, so several pickings may be required with midseason or late varieties. It is easy to judge if the fruit is ready by resting the pear in the palm of your hand and lifting it to the horizontal. Ripe pears will separate from the tree cleanly, and unripe fruit will stay attached.

Store as for apples, p. 225.

Pests and Diseases

There are several of these affecting pears and the treatment is rather like that for apples, except for damage done by wasps and birds. This is very difficult to prevent and advice such as draping the tree in muslin or covering fruit with old nylon stockings is rather impracticable. Sprays to repel birds have been developed and also a kind of nylon cobwebbing which disintegrates after a few months, but the problems have not been solved satisfactorily so far.

Varieties

Here one runs into problems of pollination and time of flowering and care in selection should be taken if only a single tree is required.

EATING	COOKING
Mid-season flowering:	
Williams' Bon Chrétien (good fertility)	Pitmaston Duchess
Conference (self-fertile, but produces a better crop if mixed with other varieties).	
Doyenne de Comice (only in South)	
Late season (will keep in store):	
Josephine de Malines	Bellissime d'Hiver

The best *single* trees are Conference and Fertility Improved, both of which are self-fertile and of good quality.

PLUMS (including DAMSONS and GREENGAGES)

These stone fruits are at their best on chalk or limestone soil. Although hardy, they undoubtedly prefer sheltered warm spots, especially in the North. They all flower early, so care should be taken to avoid frost pockets and low-lying areas. As with apples and pears, pollination can be difficult, so if only one or two are to be planted great care should be taken to plant a self-fertile variety such as Victoria.

Planting

The area should be double dug and plenty of humus, and where necessary limestone, incorporated into the soil. Plant at intervals of about 15 ft at any time during the winter, but the earlier the better, and firmly stake young trees.

Pruning

Although plums can be grown as standard, cordons, espaliers, or fan-trained trees, the best form in small gardens is undoubtedly the bush. You should prune the trees when they are growing actively in *late spring*. Young bush trees should be left alone until they have settled down and are in their second year, when you should start to prepare a well-shaped tree by removing excess branches in early summer, leaving enough good strong branches to form a head all round the main trunk. These branches should be shortened back to about half length in April. When you have a good framework established, you need do no more pruning other than to remove dead and weak wood.

Feeding

The tree should be given a mulch of well-rotted compost or manure in May or June. When the tree is bearing, a winter dressing of a complete high nitrogen fertilizer at 1 oz. per square yard is also necessary. Some growers in lighter, more quickly draining areas prefer to use hoof and horn meal instead of sulphate of ammonia in their complete fertilizer because of its slow and steady release of nitrogen. Every third or fourth winter limestone at about 4 oz. per square yard around the root spread of the tree is very beneficial.

Thinning and Picking

Plums may bear very heavily indeed and the weight of the fruit can break branches so you should always thin out very heavy crops. This thinning can be done in two stages – early in June and then about three weeks later. Such treatment will reduce the strain on the tree and will ensure that those plums which are left are large and well shaped. The fruit should always be gathered dry and if possible the stalks cut with scissors – not simply torn off. Plums or greengages to be used for jam-making should always be picked before they are ripe – this gives the jam a much better flavour.

Pests and Diseases

One serious pest is plum aphis – this can be controlled by a winter wash with Malathion or Lindane. The other great problem is silver leaf disease. This fungus disease gives the leaves a metallic appearance and can fairly quickly kill a tree. The initial infection is through an open wound, particularly one left after pruning. You should therefore be very careful to prune only in late spring or even early summer and to cover any large pruning wound with a fungicidal paint. If you see any branches which seem to be attacked prune them off at once, ensuring that you have cut back to clear, healthy, light-coloured wood, and then paint over the cut surface. Prunings should be burned immediately.

Badly used secateurs or saws can actually spread disease instead of removing it, so if you are using a tool to cut out diseased wood give the blade a wash in a mild household disinfectant before moving on to healthy wood.

Varieties

DESSERT PLUMS
Victoria (self-fertile, mid season)
Denniston's superb (self-fertile, mid season)

COOKING PLUMS
Czar (self-fertile, stands a little frost, early August)
Pershore Yellow Egg (self-fertile, best quality, late August)

GAGES
Early Transparent (self-fertile, mid-August)
Cambridge Gage (self-fertile, late August)
Oullin's Golden Gage (self-fertile, mid-August)

DAMSONS (cooking only)
Merryweather (average flavour, very heavy crops)
Farleighs' Damson (makes good windbreak, heavy cropper)

RASPBERRIES

These are very easy to grow but they do require support during the growing season. The best way of doing this is to drive a stout pole into the ground at the end of each row and stretch wire (or a strong net) tightly between them. Two strands of wire are best at 3 and 5 ft respectively, although a third gives additional support.

Raspberries are easy to propagate; the stock can be increased simply by separating off excess canes with roots attached and planting them out in new rows.

Planting

Raspberries do best in a good, well-drained soil with a high humus content. The ground should therefore be well dug in late summer and the soil liberally mixed with compost. You can save trouble by

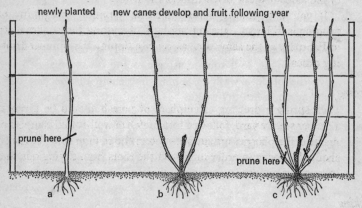

32. *Pruning raspberry canes.*

simply taking out a trench about 12 ins. deep and 18 ins. wide and enriching this soil with manure or compost as it is returned. On light sandy or gravel soils a dressing of bone meal at 3 oz. per square yard will pay dividends.

Planting should be done in winter and the earlier the better. You should have the canes 18 ins. and the rows 6 ft apart, running north–south if possible. Spread the roots out well about 6 ins. below the surface and tread the soil firmly as you plant. After planting cut all the canes back to a bud about 6 ins. from the ground. This encourages growth, and a number of new canes will develop during the following year, and bear fruit in the second year. Thus there will be no fruit in the first year of growth; this is unavoidable.

As new canes develop each year they should be tied to the wires with soft twine.

Pruning

This is done by cutting canes which have fruited back to soil level (see Fig. 32). A number of new canes will then develop – six of these should be kept and the rest removed. As the chosen canes develop they should be tied out fanwise on the wires and in February of the following year each cane should have its tip removed as far back as hard firm wood. This encourages the development of the side shoots which will bear the fruit.

If you are growing autumn-fruiting varieties, the timing of pruning is different – the cutting-back of fruiting canes takes place in February at the same time as you are tipping the summer-fruiting canes.

Feeding

Each spring a dressing of sulphate of potash should be given at 1 oz. per square yard, followed by a mulch of well-rotted compost or manure. Raspberries are surface-rooters and in light soils the mulch should be heavy in order to protect the roots from drying out, and to smother weeds.

Picking

Fruit should be gathered leaving the core or plug on the plant. Several pickings are necessary.

Pests and Diseases

The most serious pest is the raspberry beetle, which lays its eggs in the flower so that when the fruit is ripe you will find a small white grub inside. Since the infestation occurs at flowering time the canes must be treated about ten days after flowering begins, when

237

they should be sprayed with derris. This is usually in June and the spray should be repeated about two weeks later.

The other major difficulty with raspberries is their proneness to a virus which turns the leaves yellow and gradually reduces the yield until it is no longer worth growing the fruit. It is impossible to cure virus diseases; but they are usually spread by greenfly so you should always spray with derris or malathion regularly during the growing season to keep greenfly to a minimum, and make sure that the plants you buy are free of disease by buying so-called 'certified virus-free' stock.

Varieties

Malling Exploit (early), Malling Jewel (mid season), Norfolk Giant (late); Lloyd George can be either early or late depending on pruning time.

STRAWBERRIES

Strawberries do as well in Britain as in any other part of the world. They are not a permanent crop like apples or gooseberries, as they require renewal every two to five years, depending on yield. The reason is virus disease with which after a few years the plants are usually too heavily infected to be worth growing, despite the fact that you may (and should) start with virus-free 'certified' stock.

Because of this renewal, the strawberry bed is often included in the vegetable garden where it forms part of a rotation plan. In order to get the best coloured and flavoured fruit lots of sun is necessary and a south-facing position protected from cold winds is best.

Planting

Organic material is absolutely necessary – it is almost impossible to overdo the amount of farmyard manure or compost which can usefully be dug in and dressings of 1 cwt per 20 square yards are not uncommon. If the soil is enriched in this way there will be little need for additional feeding during the life-time of the bed.

To obtain fruit the year after planting the site should be prepared and virus-free stock planted out in August or early September. The plants should be about 18 ins. apart with 3 ft between the rows, and the roots should be well spaced out with the crown of the plant just above the soil surface after firming. If planting is delayed until the spring, you should remove the flowers in the first summer otherwise the plants may be weakened by bearing fruit before they are well established.

Pruning

No pruning in the ordinary sense is required, but strawberries produce 'runners', long shoots growing a small new plant at the tip, which should be cut off unless you want to propagate the plants, as they tend to use food which would otherwise go towards swelling the fruit.

Pests

The main problem with strawberries is to protect the fruit which is soft, easily damaged and liable to attack by slugs, mildew, birds and so on. Many techniques have been devised, of which the earliest was to put straw (hence the name) down between the rows and underneath the leaves soon after the flowering stage. This keeps the fruit clean and if you are so inclined can be burned off on a windy day later in the year. Various new techniques are beginning to supersede straw and the best of these is black polythene laid between the rows, weighted down with stones – this keeps the strawberry bed free of weeds and the fruit clean. Birds also are a problem and you can buy lengths of fish netting to protect the crop.

Once fruiting is over the rows should be cleaned up by weeding, taking away surplus runners and, on light soils, putting down a mulch of compost.

Varieties

Early:	Cambridge Favourite, Cambridge Rival, Royal Sovereign
Mid-Season:	Talisman, Paxton
Late:	Talisman

BOOK LIST

Fruit Grower's Encyclopaedia: Odhams
Establishing a Fruit Garden: Bell, G. (Stanley Paul)
Fruit Crops: Duggan, J. B. (Macdonald Horticultural Series)
Soft Fruit Growing: Gilbert, E. G. (Penguin Handbook)
A Concise Guide to Fruit Growing: Procter, R. (Muller)

10 House Plants

Part of the green revolution which is changing our lives is a consequence of flat and urban dwelling. People living in cities get tired of the noise and the dirt, of the glowing lights and of the grey dull colours. The continuing spread of central heating now assures a fairly constant temperature in the house (though too much dry heat can be damaging) and there is now scarcely a house or flat in the country which has not at least one pot plant growing – or slowly dying – in some window.

This chapter is intended to help the beginner in house plants. Accordingly we start at the beginning, which to most people is the gift or purchase of a plant at a local sale-of-work or market stall or multiple shop. Somehow or other it comes to the house and either lives or dies, depending on how it is treated.

It is a good idea to divide a potted plant mentally into its various parts, very crudely, and see what can be gained from the examination (Fig. 33). Firstly and most obviously there is the plant, and secondly there is the pot. Think a little more carefully and you will remember that there is also the soil or compost in which the plant is growing, and if the plant is tipped out it will be seen that at the bottom of the compost, over the hole in the base of the pot, are a number of pieces of broken pot usually called 'crocks'. In addition there is the label and maybe a small stake. All these have an important function and will be examined in turn.

THE POT

Very few beginners realize the importance of the pot and how vital it is to pay the right attention to it. Firstly, is it better to use plastic or clay pots? Until ten years ago plastic pots were viewed with considerable suspicion as it was thought they would keep air away from the roots and suffocate the plant, but this has been shown to be untrue. Plastic pots *are* non-porous and therefore do not allow air to pass in or water vapour to pass out. Old fashioned clay pots let water evaporate from the pot surface all the time and so tend to keep the root of the plant cool, but at the same time they let out a great deal of water. The lesson, therefore, is that plastic pots will heat up

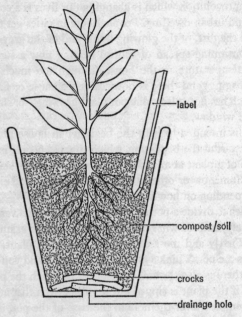

label

compost/soil

crocks

drainage hole

33.　*Cross-section of a plant pot showing contents.*

more than clay ones and so should always be shaded by being put in another container, but they need to be watered less frequently and great care should be taken not to overwater plants in them. Probably more house plants die of overwatering than of any other cause.

But plastic pots are cheap, hard to break, easily cleaned, and come in many colours and shapes, so that except for the larger sizes they will probably ultimately replace the old clay pots.

Secondly, what about the size of the pot? The size of pots is usually measured in terms of their diameter; thus they are called two-inch, five-inch and so on. Many amateurs read books with rather impressive instructions about 'repotting' and 'potting-on' and feel that all this is very difficult. The rules are in fact very simple.

A plant growing well in a pot should have its roots right at the edge of the pot. If they have reached the edge of the pot and are growing round then the plant is in danger of being pot-bound. This doesn't matter, for a plant grown 'tight' or pot-bound will usually bear more flowers and be sturdier than one grown in a pot which provides plenty of soil. The latter may produce more and maybe better leaves but will have fewer flowers.

How do you assess this situation? Hold the pot in your right hand and spread the fingers of your left hand over the top of the pot. The stem of the plant will probably be between the second and third finger of the left hand. Invert the pot and rap the rim smartly on a hard surface such as a ledge or wall. The action is rather like making sand-pies. The soil will separate from the pot and you will then be able to lift the pot away in the right hand and examine the plant and its roots which will be in your left hand (see p. 250). In a good, well-grown pot plant the roots should be to the side of the soil and may be growing round a little. If so, everything is all right, the pot can be replaced and the whole thing returned to its correct position for another year. If the roots are very much at the edge of the soil, winding round it and some turning brown, then repotting is needed in a slightly larger pot.

Why not start with a large pot and a small plant so that it will be years before repotting is necessary? The reason is that if plant roots are only occupying a small fraction of the soil in the pot, the unoccupied soil becomes waterlogged and acid. Thus as the roots grow out into this sour soil they are entering an inhospitable medium and the plant will suffer a check and may die.

There is also the fact that if you overpotted all plants you would not have room for a variety of smaller pots on your window ledge or verandah. You can be sure that when you buy a plant it is probably not overpotted (this would be expensive for the vendor) and it will be at least one or maybe more years before you need do anything about repotting.

For details of repotting and potting-on, see p. 249.

CROCKS

Most plants die if their roots are left in stagnant water. If you took a teacup, filled it with soil and then watered it, the water would sink to the bottom of the cup and collect there. Unless the watering was done very carefully the level of the water in the cup would rise and any plant growing in it would find its roots under water and would soon die.

To prevent this happening in a plant pot, drainage holes are punched in the bottom to allow excess water to drain away. But as the water drains away, it carries with it some of the compost, and over a year or so the pot could be emptied of soil. To check this loss pieces of broken pot or stones or any inert material are placed over the drainage holes – these are the 'crocks'. Their function is to slow drainage down so that the water does not rush out carrying soil with it, but rather trickles out and only a little compost is lost.

Crocks have another very useful function. Roots grow downwards and if there are no crocks present they block the drainage holes, causing water to collect. They may even grow out through the holes and into the material on which the pot is standing. Thus every time the pot is moved, the roots will be broken and killed. Even if the roots simply grow out and die in the air or against the window ledge, this is a constant drain on the life of the plant which can easily be avoided by crocking the pot.

A further danger can be produced by the entry of earth-worms through the drainage holes. If worms stick in the hole or block it the drainage is again impeded. Worms can easily get into pots sitting on a bench or even plunged in the soil in summer if there are no crocks.

SOIL OR COMPOST

When plants were first grown in pots and boxes the containers were filled simply with garden soil and, depending on the type of plant, condition of the garden, etc., very variable results were obtained. For this reason an intensive programme of research was set up in the John Innes Institute in Merton, Surrey, to test a number of different mixtures to find if there is a mixture which has universal value.

It soon became obvious that if seed is sown in a pot or box, then the seedlings require a set of environmental conditions different from those required by a mature plant. Different types of plant at different stages of growth require different composts, and so the simple goal was not reached. However, from this work the John Innes Institute developed a series of composts designated JI 1, 2 and 3, JI seed compost and JI cutting compost, all of which are almost ideal for their purposes.

All good potting composts are composed of a mixture of medium loam, sand and peat. The proportions of these three constituents vary as below:

PARTS BY VOLUME OF JOHN INNES COMPOSTS

	Seed Compost	Potting Compost			Cutting Compost
Sterilized medium loam	2	7			1
Horticultural peat	1	3			2
Coarse clean sand	1	2			3
FERTILIZER per bushel or FERTILIZER per cubic yd	1½oz. super-phosphates 2lb. super-phosphates	— —			— —
		No. 1	No. 2	No. 3	
John Innes Base Fert. per cu. yd of mixture		5lb.	10lb.	15lb.	
John Innes Base Fert. per bushel of mixture		4oz.	8oz.	12oz.	
Ground limestone per bushel of mixture		¾oz.	1½oz.	2¼oz.	

The original JI composts specified sterilized loam, e.g. from Kettering. This is virtually unobtainable now, but any good medium loam will be almost as satisfactory. Of course it is cheaper and much more satisfactory to mix one's own compost to the above formula, but for the first year or so it is probably easier to buy ready-mixed JI, although this is more expensive. The advantage of buying pre-packed JI compost is that you can obtain small quantities for a few pots or window boxes; if you are growing plants on a larger scale in a greenhouse, it is better to make your own.

If you examine the soil tipped out of a plant pot bought from a good nursery you can easily see the sand, loam, etc. and you can usually also see the small white spots of lime. (Note, however, if you are trying to grow rhododendrons, azaleas, ericas or camellias in pots use compost without limestone since these are lime-haters.)

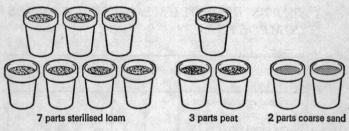

7 parts sterilised loam   3 parts peat   2 parts coarse sand

34. *Measuring compost formulae with flower pots.*

So if you are tempted just to dig up a spadeful of garden soil, put it in a pot and use that as your potting compost remember that conditions in pots are very different from those in the soil and do buy some ready-made JI or mix your own, using soil, compost from the compost heap, and coarse sand in the appropriate proportions. It is easy to measure quantities in 'flower-potfuls' (Fig. 34); thus for a seedling compost two flower-potfuls of soil, 1 of peat and 1 of sand, plus a little lime, will be adequate for most purposes and fertilizer can be added as a liquid feed later. (Other useful measures are given on p. 245.)

In the past few years composts much simpler than JI have been developed and have found wide acceptance. The most common is

Vermiculite which is made from crushed mica heated to a high temperature. The heat changes the water in the mica flakes to steam with enormous expansion powers, and the flake is 'exploded' to form a light-weight material which will hold lots of water and air. (The process resembles the puffing of popcorn.) Vermiculite is sterile and provided adequate liquid feed is applied plants will grow well in it. Once a month the vermiculite should be flooded and flushed with clear water to remove any toxic substances. It is particularly good for small light plants such as African violets.

The main virtues of vermiculite are lightness, complete sterility and cleanliness, neutrality and ease of purchase. The disadvantages are that it needs constant feeding, e.g. every two weeks, and it cannot support large plants without stakes.

Other media, sometimes called U.C. or soilless composts, have been developed in the University of California. These consist of a mixture of peat and coarse sand in varying proportions, and can be purchased as a sterile compost to which liquid feeds should be added. Soilless composts are rather like vermiculite in function, but are a little nearer to nature and are preferred by some growers. Vermiculite and soilless composts are very useful in high-rise flats as they are relatively light and very clean.

LABELS AND STAKES

There are so many different plants with new varieties coming out every year that it is impossible to keep track of them all even in a relatively small garden or flat if one relies on memory alone. You should therefore always check that there is a clear label on the pot, written in pencil for preference. Many people also enter the name of each plant and where it is planted (if outside) in a garden book much in the same way as they keep the addresses of friends in an address book. So don't discard the label. Remember too that general terms such as camellia are inadequate – you must also record the species and if available the name of the variety.

Not many pot plants require staking, but if a stake is provided or if there is a framework up which the plant scrambles then take care not to break it, or if you do replace it at once.

LIGHT AND WATER

The first thing most plants need is bright light and they should be positioned so as to get this. This does not mean that you stand them in direct sun all the time, but they should never be far from a window. Next, the plant requires watering. In a house, where there is no drying wind, plants do not require as much water as outside in the garden, and the first besetting sin is *overwatering*. It is very difficult to judge how much water to give a plant when you first buy it, for usually you don't know how long it has stood around before you made the purchase. The simplest thing to do then is to soak it until water runs through the drainage holes. This means the soil is saturated and it should then be ignored until there are signs of water shortage which may be shown by the leaves going limp or simply losing their healthy sheen. A little experience will rapidly teach you to anticipate this stage and the process can then be repeated. The weight of the pot is also a guide as dry soil is much lighter than wet and a little practice will make you fairly accurate in assessing whether water is needed or not.

How often you should water a plant will depend on the temperature, the sunshine, the season of the year and the type of plant, but it is always better to underwater than to overwater. It is also obvious, though often forgotten, that a plant which needs water every day in the summer may only need it every week or, if its leaves are shed, every month in winter. If there were hard and fast rules it would be easy, but the only guide is experience and that comes with time.

Another important point about watering: if the plant is watered from a little can with a spout, don't always water from the same side as the soil will be washed away. Always water from different sides in turn and ideally from a mini watering can with a fine spray.

FEEDING

If the compost is well made then the question of feeding need not arise for many months since there will be food in the soil. But there will come a time with long-lived plants such as azaleas or begonias when growth will be much improved by judicious feeding.

The simplest method is to add the appropriate quantity of a proprietary liquid feed to the watering can at each alternate watering – then you can both feed and water at the same time. The only drawback here is that a lot of food may be lost in the drainage water, and this may prove quite costly.

Another common method is to sprinkle a little mild feed such as dried blood on the surface of the soil in the pot and let it wash in as the plant is watered. Again this is easy, but you may overfeed the plant this way and unless mild fertilizers are used you may scorch the foliage and even the roots if a concentrated solution of fertilizer is washed down to the roots by the watering. It is never wise to use strong chemical fertilizers such as sulphate of ammonia in this way – they can be very damaging in strong solutions.

Some growers don't feed the plant as such, but remove part of the compost from the top of the pot each year and replace it with fresh compost containing its own food materials. This is a very reliable way for some years, but eventually the soil below the surface becomes exhausted and re-potting is necessary.

Finally, when should a plant be fed? The experienced grower can tell by the lack-lustre appearance of the plant and by the slowing-down of growth, but the beginner needs rules to follow. These are common sense; for example, it is pointless to feed a pot plant when it is not growing. Thus the ordinary geranium (pelargonium) should be dormant and nearly dry all winter, but should be gently watered as the days lengthen and spring comes on. Spring therefore is the time to feed it and then taper the feed off as autumn or winter approaches again. Other plants may have differing annual cycles and many such as cyclamen may flower in winter. They should therefore be fed in autumn and winter; as the leaves begin to die down in spring, both food and water can be withheld until the soil is nearly dry.

RE-POTTING AND POTTING-ON

These are two jobs which need to be done when the plant shows signs of being pot-bound. Plants which are simply transferre from one pot to another are said to be 're-potted', the term 'potting-on' is used for the transfer of such plants as chrysanthemums to successively larger pots as the plant grows older and larger.

If growth in spring is sluggish then re-potting may be necessary. The golden rule is to re-pot into a *slightly* larger pot, *not* into a very big one. Chrysanthemum growers may pot-on three or four times in one season before they have the plant in its final pot. The operation should be carried out as follows:

(1) Have the fresh compost ready for use.
(2) If you are re-potting into a clay pot soak the pot, preferably overnight, before use; this is not necessary with plastic pots.
(3) Put enough crocks over the drainage holes to allow drainage, but not soil loss.
(4) Cover the crocks with a layer of fresh compost.
(5) Water the plant thoroughly and then remove it from its pot by inverting the pot and knocking the rim on a hard surface. The whole contents of the pot should come out as a single mass (Figs. 35a and b).
(6) Take away old crocks, tease out tangled roots, but avoid root damage.

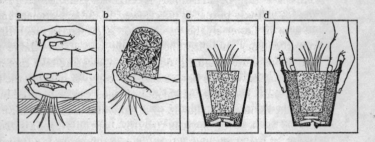

35. *Potting-on.*

(7) Rest the plant on top of the compost layer in the new pot (Fig. 35c) and gradually fill the space around the plant with fresh compost. This compost should be firmed down with the thumbs or a ramming stick (Fig. 35d).
(8) Continue adding compost and firming down until the new pot is

filled to about one inch from the top. The original pot-full of soil should now be completely buried and the new pot tapped several times smartly on the table to settle the contents.

(9) The plant should then be watered thoroughly and placed in a shady place for a few days until there are signs of growth. Then place the pot in its permanent site.

PROPAGATION, see pp. 179–185.

HANGING BASKETS AND WINDOW-BOXES

There are special problems involved in these, but the general principles of 'container growing' are outlined above, and answers to special problems should be sought in specialist books, see Book List, p. 259.

EASY HOUSE PLANTS

African Violet (Saintpaulia)

This is a very popular small greenhouse plant which produces masses of lovely purple or pink flowers in the late summer and can be kept in flower all the year round. It prefers as much light as possible, though not direct hot sunshine, and will not thrive unless the temperature is around 60°F. When watering take care not to splash the leaves; it is best to keep the compost moist to the touch all the time. In winter the amount of water can be reduced but the pots should never be allowed to dry out and the temperature must not fall below 50°F. One important tip about Saintpaulia is that they like to be underpotted and they can easily be grown in vermiculite or one of the soilless composts almost as well as in JI No. 3. Any reputable liquid feed given regularly each week in the growing season will improve the plants and increase the size of the flowers.

Azalea

Azaleas are grown indoors because in appropriate conditions they will flower from October until early February. These are expensive but long-lived plants and therefore deserve careful treatment. They should be grown in a fairly quick-draining soil, and care must be taken to avoid lime since they are lime-hating plants. A suitable compost is 3 parts peat, 1 part loam and 1 part silver sand.

The plants are usually bought in flower in winter, and after flowering all the old flowers should be removed by hand and the plants allowed to become much drier by less frequent watering. With the onset of spring in March or April watering should be increased again and new growth will appear. When the chance of frost has gone, the pot with the azalea should be taken out of doors and plunged in the ground up to its neck. This should be done in an area free of lime and exposed to bright sun. Over periods of drought the pot may be watered, although in our climate this is usually unnecessary. By late September the flower buds will have been set and the pot can be lifted and brought indoors. It should then be watered and given a liquid feed every week, and will come into bloom about December.

Begonia

There are many different kinds of begonia and it is impossible to give a short account satisfactory for all. Nevertheless, most varieties prefer a light, rich, open compost. They are primarily greenhouse plants and the temperature should never fall below 50°F for good growth. Begonias also prefer a moist, humid air and from what has been said it will be appreciated that although very often grown in porches and sun lounges they will not be at their best under these conditions.

Although they prefer high temperatures they also like shade and they should never be exposed to direct sunlight if possible. The watering of begonias should be done with care and the plants should always be allowed to get to the point of wilting before additional water is added. Water should never be allowed to splash on the leaves as this very often starts off a rot which can easily kill the plant. Anyone who wants to cultivate begonias should consult one of the specialized books on the subject, see Book List, p. 259.

Bulbs

There are very many different kinds of bulb and treatment differs, but in general there are a few useful tips which can be used for daffodils, hyacinths, etc., grown in the house. Bulbs should be planted during September and October in bowls, with the nose of the bulb just clear of the soil. The fibre should be watered in around them and the bowls then put in a cool, dark place. They should then be left strictly alone until the flower buds are actually out of the necks of the bulbs, when they can be moved to a warm, but if possible still dark, position. Once the buds are about 2–4 ins. high they can be brought into full light and rewatered; they should flower in a relatively short time.

Busy Lizzie (Impatiens)

This is a very quick-growing, free-flowering plant which will do well under almost any situation. They do however prefer a light airy sunny position with plenty of water in the summer, and a warm, light position with very little water in the winter. *Impatiens* grows so quickly that it is quite often necessary to re-pot it twice in the year, usually in March and July. Any shoot cut off and put in JI No. 3 will almost certainly take root and produce a new plant.

CACTI & SUCCULENTS

Many plants which grow in dry conditions have the ability to store water in fleshy leaves or stems. Such a plant is called a succulent. There are many types of succulent ranging from the spiny cacti of the desert to the thick, fleshy-leaved Sedums which we grow on rockeries. Most gardeners simply apply the name Cactus to all of them, although botanically speaking this term should only be applied to members of a specific family. The range of form and structure in cacti is very wide and many only flower rarely, though the most unlikely-looking cactus plants have large beautiful flowers.

Most cacti (and succulents) need lots of light and air and although ideally suited to a greenhouse will survive and even flourish in a well-lit, airy, sunny room. In fact they are very hard to kill, and to this must be attributed their popularity as house plants. Their main enemy is water and the surest way to kill both cacti and succulents is to grow them in waterlogged soil or in a still, damp, humid atmosphere. Nevertheless they *do* need water and the routine treatment is: reduce water progressively during October–March until the soil is well-nigh dry. In April add a little water, and as growth continues increase the water supply until in the heat of summer (May, June, July) they may need water twice a week. Then as the days get shorter and colder reduce water supply to the winter schedule. They may shrivel a bit in winter but generally they will come to no permanent harm. Most desert cacti can stand cold and even frost provided the soil is dry, and it is partly for this reason that we withhold water during cold winter months. This not only gives the plant a necessary rest but also makes it more resistant to frost.

Some succulents such as Epiphyllum and Schlumbergera (the Easter and Christmas Cacti) enjoy a damp atmosphere, but this is unusual and most plants are not so fussy. If it is possible most cacti should be baked in summer and certainly do not require shading from direct sun provided ventilation is good.

A great many different soil mixtures have been recommended for cacti but they have two characteristics in common: (1) they are quickly draining and gritty; (2) they are not rich in fertilizer or plant foods. A good mixture, then, is John Innes No. 1, with about one quarter of the total volume of coarse sand, grit, broken brick or pots added to increase the porosity and the drainage. Some succulents such as Epiphyllum or Echeveria like loam or leaf mould in the compost, but remember that in all cases quick drainage is essential.

Cacti and succulents can grow quickly and may need re-potting every second or third year. Always put plenty of crocks in the pot and never put a small cactus in a large pot, for if there is unused soil it will go sour in the pot and damage the plant. When re-potting prickly or spiny cacti it is wise to use thick gloves or to hold the plants by means of a piece of cloth or newspaper looped around them.

Many cacti produce lots of new side growths, often called off-sets or colloquially 'pups'. These can easily be broken or cut off at re-potting time and put into a new small pot where they will grow. An increase in number can easily be achieved by taking cuttings. Wherever a stem is jointed or has leaves, parts can be detached which will usually root quite easily, especially if taken in late spring or early summer. Always allow the cuttings to dry out on the cut surface so as to form a callus or skin, and root the pieces in coarse sand and peat mixture.

Simple succulents and cacti include Agave, Aloe, Bryophyllum, Cereus, Crassula, Echeveria, Echinocactus, Epiphyllum, Euphorbia, Kalanchoe, Kleinia, Mammilaria, Lithops, Mesembryanthemum, Opuntia, Rhipsalis, Schlumbergera, Sedum, Sempervivum, Stapelia, etc.

Cyclamen

This is a very popular pot plant whose delicate flowers like butterflies are very much admired. If you look at a cyclamen you will see that the leaves and the flowers grow from a bulb-like corm, the surface of which is above soil level. Great care must be taken in watering cyclamen to be sure that water does not lie in the hollow of the corm as this can very easily start a rot from which the plant will die. It is therefore usually best to water from the bottom up. Once again, these plants are usually bought when in flower and as each flower dies it should be picked off. Once flowering has finished water should be withheld for some time until all the leaves have died. The corm can then be plunged in a border during the summer or taken out of its present pot and repotted. In August watering can start again and the plant should come into flower around Christmas.

Cyclamen is ideal for a cool, light, airy room and it is best at a temperature of about 55°F. It flowers over a long period of time and can give a great deal of satisfaction, though it is a difficult plant to keep year after year.

Geranium (Pelargonium)

Most of the plants grown as geraniums are, in fact, pelargoniums and can be grown very simply in an ordinary JI compost. They flower brightly in the summer both inside and outside the house, and can be kept in bloom until the autumn. As the flowers die the dead heads should be removed, and before frost occurs the plants should be brought inside and allowed to dry off. The plant will spend the winter in this state but should be kept in the lightest possible window away from frost. As the days lengthen, watering should begin again and new growths will appear.

The production of new growths can be greatly encouraged by cutting back the original plant to 3–4 ins. from the pot surface before you start watering in the spring. This will produce a number of side shoots, some of which can be taken as cuttings in August. The ideal plant should be bushy and this is best achieved by continually cutting back each year.

Hydrangea

Hydrangeas are usually grown as house plants and their name is derived from the fact that they like plenty of water. This should be obvious from their large green leaves which are always cool and lose water to the atmosphere. They grow best in a rich mixture of 2 parts loam to 1 part sand with, if possible, some rich compost. At the end of the summer hydrangeas should have their flowering heads cut off as soon as they have faded and the plant should be kept outside to enable the wood to ripen up for flowering the following year. In September it can be brought into the house and water gradually withheld so that the leaves die and drop off leaving a round bud at the tip. The plant will overwinter in this state. Watering should begin again in spring and the plant will come into flower and produce leaves by June or early July.

Hydrangeas dislike hot dry conditions such as are normally found in centrally heated buildings, but will stay in flower over a long period of time in a light, cool room out of draughts.

Indiarubber Plant (Ficus)

These are really trees but if grown as pot plants will stay relatively small for a number of years. The most common is *Ficus elastica*, which is grown for its large dark green glossy leaves. This plant grows best in centrally heated rooms at 65–75°F, but will survive at lower temperatures provided there is not a great fluctuation.

Ficus is not very light-demanding and will do well in any light but not sunlit room.

Watering is very important – if the plants are overwatered, they are liable to rot and die. In winter the soil should be allowed to become quite dry between waterings, but in spring and summer when the light is good and the plant is growing well they should be watered and fed each week. The leaves should also be washed with cold water occasionally. Ficus should be grown in a rich peat compost, such as JI No. 3, with a little added peat or leaf mould.

Ivies (Hedera species)

This well-known plant has many highly decorative varieties with variegated leaves and is very useful as a climber or trailer. Ivies are very undemanding both as regards light and temperature and will do surprisingly well in a relatively shaded room. However, they do prefer good strong light but not direct sunlight and the coloured varieties will do best under these conditions. During winter, ivy species rest, so the pots should be kept fairly dry – simply wash the leaves every month with a fine spray. With the onset of spring the plants can be re-watered and they will grow freely right through the summer. They should be fed with a liquid soluble food every week and will grow well in JI No. 3. When re-potting is necessary this should be done in spring.

Kangaroo Vine (Cissus and Rhoicissus)

These are among the hardiest and most satisfactory house plants. They are grown for their light green foliage, which is produced in profusion even under very unfavourable conditions. They will climb or trail and since they prefer cool temperatures and dullish light they are ideal for houses which are not centrally heated. Being very quick-growing they need to be fed and watered weekly in the summer, but in the winter they should be kept on the dry side and only watered when they seem to be wilting.

If they lose their vigour they can be pruned or cut hard back and will usually start all over again. They should be grown in a John Innes compost, preferably JI No. 3.

Poinsettia

Poinsettia have become very popular in recent years because of the bright red leaf-like bracts which surround the rather insipid flowers. This is a tropical tree which is kept in a dwarfed condition in pots in Britain. It should therefore be treated as a tropical plant, as it grows best at high temperatures and dislikes sudden changes of temperature. The soil in which it grows should be rich, consisting of good loam and if possible some animal manure well rotted and decayed. They demand plenty of light and water when growing, but after they have flowered and the coloured bracts drop off they should be cut back and gradually allowed to dry out. After the resting period the watering can start again and fresh shoots will appear which, if fed and watered each week, will produce new bracts at their crown. You may find it is easy to grow the plant but very difficult to get the bracts to colour properly; this is almost certainly the result of low temperatures during the night and a lack of sufficient bright sunshine, although a daily dark period of about 12 hours is also essential.

Tradescantia (Wandering Jew)

These are well-known plants generally grown for their foliage, although the flowers are also very attractive. They are useful in hanging baskets as they are trailers, and almost any part of the plant, if cut off and put into soil, will throw roots and form a new plant. They are rather light-demanding and look their best in containers on wall brackets or on hanging baskets. They will grow in almost any kind of compost so long as the drainage is reasonably good. They should be watered every week during the growing season and fed on alternate weeks. They thrive at moderate temperatures of about 50°F.

BOOK LIST

The Rochford Book of House Plants: Rochford, T. & Gorer, R.
(Faber & Faber)
The Effective Use of House Plants: Alphen, C. Van (Blandford
Press)
Indoor Plants: Field, X. (Hamlyn)
Indoor Plants in Colour: Gorer, R. (Blandford)
The Rochford Book of Flowering Pot Plants: Rochford, T. &
Gorer, R. (Faber & Faber)
Rochford Plants for Everyone: Rochford, T. & Gorer, R. (Faber &
Faber)
Indoor Gardening: Stevenson, V. (Arthur Barker)
House Plants, Cacti, and Succulents: Huxley, A. (Hamlyn)

Gardening Calendar

It is obvious that the timing of work in the garden cannot be the same for all parts of the country. For example, in Devon and Cornwall it may be perfectly safe to put tender plants outside in late March whereas it would be sheer folly in Durham or Aberdeen. You have therefore to use your common sense in interpreting dates. A *rough* guide is to add a week to the following dates for each 100 miles north of the South Coast. Again, such a rule of thumb does not work exactly, for even in the North of Ireland or Scotland there are very mild areas, especially by the sea, where early planting is quite possible. At the risk of repetition use your common sense and ask experienced growers in your area if you have doubts.

JANUARY

Lawn

Very little work can be done on the lawn this month so it is a good time to overhaul equipment, service mowers, etc. Avoid walking on the lawn when it is very wet and during heavy frosts.

Vegetables

Plan the garden and order seeds. Start to sprout early potatoes, 2 per tuber.
Prepare trenches for peas and beans.
Divide rhubarb crowns and cover some with boxes or buckets for early forcing.
Protect anything under cloches in frosty weather.

Fruit

Check greasebands on fruit trees.
Protect buds of gooseberry and red currants against birds by stringing cotton.

Spray with winter wash all established fruit trees.
Prune apple, pear.

Shrubs

Prune climbing roses and late-flowering shrubs such as *Buddleia davidii*.
Prepare shrub borders or rose beds for spring planting.

Flowers

Plan flower beds and order seeds.
Dig ground for planting in February or March.
Pot sweet peas singly if sown in October.
Plant begonia tubers and pot lily bulbs – both indoors.
Where necessary protect plants, e.g. hydrangea, against extreme frost by covering them with straw or matting.

Indoor

If possible give a temperature of about 50°F, i.e. 10°C. Seeds of half-hardy annuals may be sown in greenhouse or frames for later planting out.

General

Digging of heavy soils should be finished by end of month.

FEBRUARY

Lawn

Towards the end of month, lawn may be top dressed with sand or finely riddled compost.
Cultivation of new area to be sown should be begun by raking and weeding.

Vegetables

Sow early peas, broad beans, cabbage, leeks.
Plant shallots and onion sets.
In mild coastal areas plant early potatoes.
If you have a cold frame, sow stump carrots, lettuce, half-hardy annuals, and tomatoes for later planting out.

Fruit

Cut down newly planted raspberries to 6 ins. from ground.
Remove tips of established autumn fruiting canes.
FYM on currant and gooseberry bushes, and sulphate of potash at
1 oz. per square yard.
Start a strawberry bed.
All kinds of trees can still be planted.

Flowers

Plant standard, climbing and rambling roses and cut back hybrid
tea and floribunda roses.
Sow plants for bedding inside a warm frame or house.
Prune *Clematis jackmanii* and other similar varieties to 10 ins. of
previous year's growth.
Prune summer jasmine by thinning, and cut back side shoots of
winter jasmine as soon as flowers die.
Many house plants, e.g. cineraria, should be repotted if necessary.

Indoors

Bulbs which have flowered indoors, daffodil, snowdrop, etc.,
should be planted outdoors in a sheltered spot to ripen off before
being used for naturalization.

General

Finish applying lime to those areas of the garden where it is needed.

MARCH

Lawn

If mild a first high cut can be taken.
Continue breaking down any new areas for seeding.
At the end of the month give the first dressing of fertilizer. (In the
north this should be delayed until there are signs of growth.)

Vegetables

Sow broad beans, cauliflower, Brussels sprouts, cabbage, leeks, lettuce, onions, parsley, peas, radish and turnips.

Very early cauliflowers may be planted out; also early sown leeks.

Fruit

Finish planting fruit trees and pruning newly established trees.

Spray blackcurrants with lime sulphur against big bud.

Fertilize trees with sulphate of potash at 3 oz. per square yard, or a general fertilizer – sulphate of potash 3 parts, superphosphates 5 parts, sulphate of ammonia 2 parts – at 2 oz. per square yard below the canopy of the trees.

Plant strawberries.

Shrubs

Give roses early spray of Captan to control black spot and BHC against greenfly.

Plant forsythia, weigela, deutzia.

Flowers

Plant summer-flowering bulbs such as gladiolus, lilies, montbretia.

Hardy border perennials can be planted, e.g. phlox, delphinium, lupin, geum, potentilla, Michaelmas daisy, pinks.

Transplant Christmas rose and iris.

Put autumn-sown sweet peas out in the open garden.

Indoors

Half-hardy annuals such as aster, nemesia, phlox and zinnia can be sown.

Put dahlia tubers and chrysanthemum shoots in moist warmed soil and you will soon be able to take cuttings.

Cuttings can also be taken of coleus, begonias, fuchsias, zonal pelargoniums.

General

Protect seedlings with slugbait where necessary.

Make sure the soil is in good condition before you work with it.

The Penguin Book of Basic Gardening

You will know the soil is right when it has a dry crumbly texture and breaks up easily when turned over.

APRIL

Lawn

Increase frequency of mowing. The grass can now be cut shorter until it is at a minimum in June.

If patches are dying or if birds are pecking the lawn you have worms or leather jackets so put on BHC immediately. At the end of month, if weather is fine, a new lawn should be seeded.

Vegetables

Plant all potatoes before end of month. Start successively sowing main-crop peas, carrots. Sow salad lettuce every 10 days.

Sow seeds of Brussels sprouts, winter cabbage.

Early cabbage and cauliflower – remember to apply calomel dust around cauliflowers.

Fruit

Before buds open spray apple and pear trees with a good fungicide, e.g. Captan (against apple scab), and again at pink bud stage, towards the end of the month.

In later areas spray blackcurrants at grape stage with lime sulphur.

Mulch and hoe among fruit trees.

Remove half the flowers on maiden strawberries, if planted later than September.

Shrubs

Plant evergreen shrubs and conifers.

Plant clematis.

Prune early-flowering shrubs such as ribes, forsythia, and trim winter-flowering heathers.

Light dressing of fertilizer to encourage growth on all shrubs.

Flowers

Plant out early chrysanthemums.
Sow hardy annuals.
Tidy away spring-flowering bulbs to a reserve bed.

Frames & Indoors

Sow winter-flowering primulas in sifted soil.
Plant up hanging baskets and put in position.
Prick out half-hardy annuals.

General

Persistent weed-killers containing simazine should be applied to drives and paths.

MAY

Lawn

Lower blades of mower and cut lawn more frequently and more closely.
Weed-killers can be used to remove daisies, etc.
Seeding weed grasses such as ryegrass should have tall spikes cut off.

Vegetables

Pinch out tops of broad beans.
Plant out cauliflowers, sprouts.
Continue successional sowing of all vegetables and thin the early crops.
Earth up early potatoes.
Sow French beans.
Remove side shoots of tomato plants.

Fruit

Remove surplus raspberry suckers.
Hoe strawberry bed to keep down weeds before strawing; if frost seems likely, cover strawberry tops with lightly shaken straw.

Shrubs

Mulch most trees and shrubs.
Continue spraying roses.
Prune *Clematis montana*.

Flowers

Plant dahlia tubers outside.
Pinch out tops of early chrysanthemums.
Divide and re-plant perennial spring-flowering plants such as poly-anthus.
Plant out half-hardy annuals, e.g. antirrhinum, zinnia.
Sow annuals in their final station.
Thin and stake herbaceous plants.

Frames & Indoors

Begin feeding tomatoes and pinch out the side shoots.
Sow seeds of calceolaria, primula and rock plants.

General

Frequent hoeing will keep down weeds.
Staking and tying of all tall plants are important.

JUNE

Lawn

Full-scale mowing.
If there is a drought raise blade slightly and leave the clippings on the lawn. Continue removing and killing weeds. Clover can be very noticeable in June and can be selectively killed by special clover weed-killer (Clovotox).
A light dressing of a good lawn fertilizer should be given in either June or July.
New lawns may also be lightly fed now.

Vegetables

Plant out celery, marrows, cucumbers, cauliflowers for summer use, and leeks, cabbages and Brussels sprouts for winter use.

Sow winter swedes.

Final earthing-up of late potatoes.

Top dress vegetables with weak nitrogenous food to stimulate growth.

Look out for carrot fly and cabbage root fly and dust with BHC or Calomel Dust.

Fruit

Net strawberries and raspberries.

Spray raspberries with derris against raspberry beetle and repeat in 10 days.

Mulch tree fruits and straw strawberry beds. Separate strawberry runners if necessary.

Watch plums for silver leaf and cut it out if it appears.

Prune gooseberries and red currants.

Shrubs

Prune lilac, weigela, philadelphus, spiraea and deutzia as soon as flowers fade.

Remove faded flowers from rhododendron and azaleas.

Trim heathers to remove old flower heads.

Spray roses with Captan in clean-air areas to protect them against black spot.

Flowers

Put out all half-hardy or tender plants.

Pot-on chrysanthemums and watch those planted outside in order to stop them at the appropriate time.

Divide overgrown clumps of May-flowering perennials.

Frames & Indoors

Bury azaleas and other winter-flowering indoor plants up to the rim of the pot outside in a sunny spot.

Provide adequate ventilation in sun lounges, porches, etc.

Winter-flowering bulbs, e.g. arum, freesia, amaryllis, should be dried off a little and rested.

Sow winter-flowering primulas, calceolarias, cinerarias.

General

If dead flowers are removed from plants as soon as the petals fall, the flowering season will be prolonged.

Keep weeds down by hoeing.

Water if necessary and mulch if you have the material.

JULY

Lawn

As for JUNE.

Vegetables

Final sowing of stump-rooted carrots and peas, and plant autumn cauliflowers.

Where early crops are cleared plant leeks, onions, Brussels sprouts and winter greens generally.

At the end of month bend over tops of onions to help bulb ripening.

Remove tomato side shoots.

Lift shallots to dry.

Fruit

Early pears begin to ripen and if necessary a very restricted pruning can be done (see p. 232).

Prune blackcurrants and summer-fruiting raspberries immediately after fruiting.

Mulch trees growing against a wall.

Immediately all strawberries are gathered remove straw and weeds.

Shrubs

Clip evergreen hedges.

Layer suitable shrubs, e.g. clematis.

Cut roses with long stems – this amounts to summer pruning.

Half-ripe wood cuttings can be taken from most shrubs and also cuttings of shrub and rambler roses.

Flowers

Take cuttings of pinks and helianthemums.
Disbud chrysanthemums.
Continue spraying against greenfly and mildew.

Indoor

Prick out seedlings sown last month. Start cyclamen into growth again by watering.
Pot freesia corms.

General

Weeding, watering and hoeing continue to be principal tasks.

AUGUST

Lawn

Continue cutting as for June and July.
Areas for seeding in September/October should be cleared and very carefully prepared. Seeding can begin at the beginning of September.

Vegetables

Sow spring cabbage.
Sow lettuce and spring onions for early salad.
Lift onions to dry.
Earth up celery and leeks.
Lift second early potatoes.

Fruit

Plant strawberry runners in their fruiting position.
Shorten young side shoots of cordon apples and pears to one third.
Cut out much two-year old wood in blackcurrants.
Tie in new raspberry canes after thinning to 5–6 per plant.

Shrubs

Continue taking cuttings of hardy shrubs, e.g. *Berberis darwinii*.
Continue to mulch round shrubs.

Flowers

Sow hardy annuals, calendula, nigella, larkspur for next season in favourable site.

Plant bulbs of Madonna lily, autumn crocus, hardy cyclamen, etc.

Take cuttings of geraniums.

Plant prepared bulbs for Christmas flowering.

Indoors

Sow lettuce in frame for winter use.

Sow cyclamen and greenhouse annuals.

Take cuttings of hydrangea.

Place indoor plants in a cool shady situation.

General

Sow rape on bare soil to be dug in as green manure.

If you go on holiday, encourage a neighbour to harvest and use ripe vegetables.

SEPTEMBER

Lawn

Watch April-seeded lawns for disease and treat with lawn fungicide if necessary.

A top dressing of coarse sand should be given and the lawn cut less frequently.

Towards the end of the month forking and spiking can begin. De-worming is possible.

Vegetables

Plant out cabbages for spring cutting.

Continue to earth up celery.

Lift and store carrot and beetroot.

Break up and double dig new land for vegetables.

Fruit

Clear fruit store before putting in the new crop.

Thin out weak raspberry canes.

Grease-band fruit trees to prevent insects crawling up.
Remove tips of gooseberry shoots if mildewed and burn them.
Can re-plant strawberry beds with virus-free stock.

Shrubs

Cut old wood from rambler roses to encourage new growth.
Plant evergreen trees and shrubs.

Flowers

Chrysanthemums for indoor flowering should be brought inside.
Plant hardy lilies outside.
Plant bulbs outside for spring flowering.
Continue to take cuttings of geranium and other bedding plants.
Sow hardy annuals.
Bring in bedding plants for over-wintering.

Frame & Indoors

Bring in pot plants before frosts come.
Sow sweet peas for planting outside in spring.
Prick out August-sown annuals for indoor display.
Pot bulbs for winter flowers.

General

Start new compost heap.
Dig in green manure.

OCTOBER

Lawn

Brown patch may appear this month, so if dead or dying brown
areas are seen treat with fungicide.
Cut and tidy up edges for winter.
Remove fallen leaves.
Continue spiking and sanding.
If lawns are being made from turf, turves can be laid in any mild
spell of weather between September and March.

Vegetables

Final earthing of celery before frost gets severe.
Double dig for peas, beans, onions.
Harvest all maincrop beet, potatoes, turnips before severe frosts.
Continue planting spring cabbage.

Fruit

Take cuttings of gooseberries and all currants.
Basic slag can be applied to acid soil at 6 oz. per square yard.

Shrubs

Hardwood cuttings of most shrubs can be taken.
Plant deciduous trees and shrubs, including roses.

Flowers

Plant biennials and perennials to flower next season.
Sow sweet peas in boxes in cold frame.
After first frost lift dahlia tubers, dry and store in cool dry place;
same with gladioli and montbretia.
Lift summer bedding plants and either put on compost heap if
annuals or into cold frames or greenhouse if perennials and prepare
soil for planting out wallflower, polyanthus and spring-flowering
plants.
Divide perennials, using strong outer shoots for re-planting.

Frame & Indoors

Plant indoor bulbs, keep cool and dark.
Bring in primulas, cyclamen and calceolarias.
Early chrysanthemums should be cut back and over-wintered in a
cold frame.

General

Gather leaves and stack for leaf mould.
Keep putting dead plants on compost heap.
Dig when possible.

NOVEMBER

Lawn

Cut if necessary, but not too close.
Hollow tine if drainage bad and cover with coarse sand.

Vegetables

Lift some rhubarb roots and allow to get frosted before re-planting in order to get early stalks.
Remove decaying leaves from winter greens such as Brussels sprouts, curly kale, etc.
Sow broad beans in sheltered southern area.
Begin digging over the vegetable garden.

Fruit

Prune established apple and pear trees, collect and burn prunings.
Inspect fruit in store regularly.
Plant blackcurrants and raspberries.
Plant fruit trees in well-prepared and enriched soil.

Shrubs

Provide shelter of straw or sacking for newly planted shrubs.
Prune climbing plants, e.g. honeysuckle, rose, abutilon.
Take hard-wood cuttings.
Prepare soil for planting shrubs.

Flowers

Plant tulips and other bulbs outside.
Lift chrysanthemums and put in cold frame to over-winter.
Remove fallen leaves from rockeries.
Cut down dead tops of perennials and fork over the beds.
Plant hardy herbaceous annuals and perennials.

Frames & Indoors

Spring clean and re-paint cold frames.
Have mats or protective materials available to cover frames in severe frosts.

Keep glass clean to ensure good light.
Reduce water to plants in houses not centrally heated.
Fill and replant window-boxes, using JI or other good compost.

General

Apply lime.
Begin general garden construction work.

DECEMBER

Lawn

As for NOVEMBER.

Vegetables

Cover celery with straw or sacking to protect against frost.
Lift and use parsnips.
Check clamps, and throw out any diseased or rotting vegetables.
Dig where necessary and check drainage.

Fruit

Continue checking stored fruit.
Tar oil winter wash or DNOC wash fruit trees not done in November.
Spray with winter wash all established fruit trees.
Finish pruning and new plantings.
Thin spurs of old apple and pears.

Shrubs

Plant trees and shrubs whenever the weather is mild and dry.
Winter pruning and removal of dead or badly placed wood should be completed.

Flowers

Protect delphinium, lupin etc., against slugs using bait or well-weathered cinders.

274

Indoors

Reduce watering and keep most plants away from frost but in as much light as possible.

Make up loam and compost for spring use.

General

Have maintenance done on garden tools and machinery.

Consult catalogues and make plans for next year.

Clean out stores and toolshed.

Index

Abol-X, 213
Acer, 185
Acer japonicum, 78
Amitrole, 60
Annual Meadow Grass (*Poa annua*), 83
Annuals, 133, 137, 138, 144, 148, 169
Aphids, 222, 229
  plum, 235
  root, 120
  woolly, 220
Apples, picking, 225
  pollination, 219
  shortage of potash in, 41
  storing, 225–6
  varieties, 217, 219, 226
Apple trees, dwarf, 72
  feeding, 219, 225
  planting, 224
  pollination, 226
  pruning, 174, 224
Arbutus unedo, 186
Aruncus, 61
Asters, 137
Astilbe, 61
Astilbe biternata, 61
Aucuba japonica, 186
Azaleas, 33, 52, 187, 248, 251–2.
  See also Rhododendron

Bamboo canes, 138–9, 150
Basic slag, 54
BDH soil indicator, 51
Bed, feeding a, 137
  planning a, 135–7
  shape, 136–7

Beech, 136
Begonias, 249, 252
Benlate, 213
Bents (Agrostis), 83, 87
Berberis, 170, 177–8, 187
Biennials, 133, 143
Big bud, 228
Bindweed, 144
Birds, peas and, 123
  strawberries and, 239
Blackcurrants, 72
  feeding, 227
  pests and diseases, 228
  planting, 227
  pruning, 227
  varieties, 228
Blackflies, 112
Black spot, 212
Blenheim Orange apple, 219
Bolters, 121–2
Bone meal, 42, 54
  for the cultivation of bulbs, 150
  for the cultivation of ground-cover plants, 60
  for the cultivation of leeks, 119
  for the planting of blackcurrants and raspberries, 227, 238
Borders, feeding of, 137
  planning of, 135–7
  shape, 136–7
Botrytis, 110
Branched pea sticks, 150
Branched twigs, 139
Brassicas, 115. *See also* Cabbage, Brussels sprouts, Cauliflower, Broccoli
'Break bud', 155, 158

Concrete slabs, making, 68–71
Conifers, 168, 177
Construction work, 74, 77
Cordons, **218**, 232
Corms, **134**, 150
Cornus, 192
Cornus alba, 174, 192
Cotoneasters, 170, 176–7, 192–3
Cotyledons, 141–2. *See also* Seed
    leaves
Couch grass, 108, 144
Cox's Orange Pippin apple, 217
    and pollination, 219
Crabs, flowering. *See* Malus
Crataegus, 193
Crocks, 241, 244, 250
Crocus, 138, 151
Crop rotation, **96–7**
Crown bud, **158**
Currants, flowering. *See* Ribes
Cuttings, half-ripe, 183
    ripe and hardwood, 183
    soft, 183
    from a tree or shrub, 182–5
Cyclamen, 151, 249, 255
Cytisus, 183

Daffodils, 134, 151, 253. *See also*
    Bulbs
Dahlias, 134, 154, 159–60
    cactus-flowered, 159
Dalapon, 108
Damsons. *See* Plums
Daphne, 194
Deciduous plants, 170–71
Derris, 112, 120, 127, 228, 229,
    238
Deutzia, 194
Die-back, 210
Dibber, **11–12**, 105
Digging, 99
    double, 100
    single, 100
Dinocap, 213

Disabled Living Foundation, 13
Division, shrubs, 179
Dogwood, 61
Drainage, 21–4
    on clay soil, 99
Dried blood, 41, 48, 54
Dust Bowl of America, 44
Dutch Hoe, **10**, 107
Dwarf beans, 112–13
    varieties, 112

Early cabbage, 115
Echeveria, 254
Edward VII apple, 217
Epiphyllum, 254
Erica carnea var. Springwood
    White, 59
Ericas, 33, 52, 194–5. *See also*
    Heather
Espaliers, **218**, 232
Euonymus, 195
Evergreen plants, 170, 177

'Family' tree, **73**
Farm Yard Manure (FYM), 43,
    44–5, 46, 47, 54, 121, 145,
    155, 223, 227
    in planting strawberries, 238–9
Feltham First, 122
Fertilizers, artificial, 38–9, 106
    natural organic, 38–9
    table of main, 54
Fertilizer dressings, 43
Fescues (Festuca), 83, 87
Ficus elastica. *See* Indiarubber
    plant
Flea beetle, 127
Floribunda roses, 207–8, 209, 213
    pruning, 211
Flowers, calendar, 261–74
    in clumps, 134
    cut, 133
    planting out, 143
    pricking and transplanting, 141–3
    sowing seeds for, 139–41

Index

Index

division, 150
feeding, 150
as ground-cover plants, 59
hoeing, 150
list of twenty, 152–3
staking, 150
thinning, 150
Petunias, 138
Philadelphus, 200
Photosynthesis, 32
Pieris, 200–201
Pine tree, 136
Plums, 233–5. *See also* Prunus
feeding, 234
frost danger, 233
pests and diseases, 235
planting, 234
pollination, 233
pruning, 234
thinning and picking, 234–5
varieties, 235
Poinsettia, 258
Polyanthus roses, 207–8
Pots, clay, 241–2, 250
cross-section of, 242
plastic, 241–2
size of, 242
Potatoes, on clay soil, 30
crop rotation for, 96
cultivation, 124
early crops of, 27
fertilizers for, 41, 52, 106
soil for, 123–4
storage in clamps, 110–11
varieties, 124–5
weed control, 108
Potato scab, 124
Potting-on, 249–50
'Pre-emergence' weed-killing, 108
Primula, 61
Privet, 170
cuttings, 184
Prunus, 201
Prunus cerasifera pissartii, 170

Pyracantha, on clay soil, 30
Pyrethrum, 150

Quince, for grafting pears, 220, 231. See also *Chaenomeles*

Radish, 110
cultivation, 125
as intercropping plant, 97
soil for, 125
varieties, 125
Ramblers, 208, 210, 214
pruning, 212
Raspberries, 236–8
feeding, 237
pests and diseases, 237
planting, 236
pruning, 236, 237
varieties, 238
Raspberry beetle, 237
Red and White Currants, feeding, 228–9
pests, 229
planting, 228
pruning, 228
varieties, 229
Re-potting, 249–50
Rhizomes, 134, 150
Rhododendrons, 33, 52, 201–2
on chalky soil, 167
Rhoicissus. *See* Kangaroo vine
Rhubarb, cultivation, 126
soil for, 126
varieties, 126
Rhus, 202
Ribes, 202
Ridging, 124
Rock rose, see Cistus
Rose mildew, 213
Roses, 207–14
artificial fertilizers for, 106
canker, 208
container-grown, 208
feeding, 210

Index

preparation and planting, 208
problems, 212–13
pruning, 174, 209, 210–12
types of, 207–8
varieties, 213–14
Rowan tree, 165. *See also* Sorbus
Runner beans, 113
varieties, 113–14
Rushes, 21
'Ryegrass-free' mixtures, 83

Saintpaulia. *See* African violets
Salix x grahamii, 61
Salvia, 143
Schlumbergera, 254
Scilla, 151
'Scorch', 41
Seaweed, 49, 54
Sedums, 253
Seed compost, 140
Seed leaves, 141. *See also* Cotyledons
Seeds, sowing, 139–41
treated, 15
Secateurs, 11
care and storage of, 13–14
Sevin, 213
Sewage sludge, 48–9, 54
Shallots, 110
Shears, 12
care and storage of, 13–14
Shrub roses, 208, 214
pruning, 210
Shrubs, 137, 138, 144, 145, 164
autumn, 206
calendar, 261, 263, 264, 266–9, 271–4
for chalky soils, 207
container-grown, 168, 169
evergreen, 168
expansion factor in, 56, 166
feeding, 172
as ground-cover plants, 59
labelling, 172

mulching, 173
planting, 166–70
for planting in shade, 207
propagation, 179–85
pruning, 174–8
spring-flowering, 205
staking, 169–72
for town gardens, 206
winter-flowering, 206
Silver leaf disease, 235
Silver sand, 252
Silver weed, 21
Simazin, 67
Slug pellets, 144
Slugs, 47, 108, 110, 144, 239
Snowdrops, 138, 151
Soakaway, 24
Soil conditioners, 29
Soils, suitable plants for, 35–7
types and their treatment, 26–37
table of, 36, 37
Sorbus, 203
Sorbus aucuparia, 165, 203
Sowing, successional, 97–9
Sphagnum moss, 181
Spent hops, 49, 54. *See also* Hop manure
Spiraeas, 176, 179, 203
Spring cabbage. *See* Early cabbage
Spring onion, 97
varieties, 115
Staking, 113, 123, 138–9, 169
Standard roses, 207, 208, 210, 211–12
Strawberries, 217, 238–9
pests, 239
planting, 238–9
pruning, 239
varieties, 239
virus disease of, 239
Succulents, 253–5
Sugar beet, early crops of, 27
Sulphate of ammonia, 40, 45, 46, 87, 154

More about Penguins
and Pelicans